Creating Hitler's Germany

Creating Hitler's Germany
The Rise of Extremism

Tim Heath

PEN & SWORD
HISTORY

AN IMPRINT OF PEN & SWORD BOOKS LTD.
YORKSHIRE – PHILADELPHIA

First published in Great Britain in 2019 by
PEN AND SWORD HISTORY
An imprint of
Pen & Sword Books Ltd
Yorkshire - Philadelphia

ISBN 9781526732972

Typeset in India By IMPEC eSolutions
Printed and bound in the UK by TJ International Ltd.

Pen & Sword Books Ltd incorporates the Imprints of Pen & Sword Books
Archaeology, Atlas, Aviation, Battleground, Discovery, Family History, History,
Maritime, Military, Naval, Politics, Railways, Select, Transport, True Crime,
Fiction, Frontline Books, Leo Cooper, Praetorian Press, Seaforth Publishing,
Wharncliffe and White Owl.

For a complete list of Pen & Sword titles please contact

PEN & SWORD BOOKS LIMITED
47 Church Street, Barnsley, South Yorkshire, S70 2AS, England
E-mail: enquiries@pen-and-sword.co.uk
Website: www.pen-and-sword.co.uk

or

PEN AND SWORD BOOKS
1950 Lawrence Rd, Havertown, PA 19083, USA
E-mail: Uspen-and-sword@casematepublishers.com
Website: www.penandswordbooks.com

Contents

In Memory of 4919046 Fusilier, Alfred Heath, 2nd Battalion Lancashire Fusiliers, killed in action, aged 23, on 17 August 1943, Italy, and Siegfried Strelow, killed in action, aged 18, on 1 March 1945, Silesia.

At the going down of the sun and in the morning, we will remember them.

Introduction

*C*reating Hitler's Germany* was not written with the intention of producing a chronological analysis of Germany throughout its most troubled, if not darkest, period in its history but to try and understand what social and political factors influenced its aggression through the earlier part of the twentieth century. From testimonies in the form of personal letters, notes and diary entries, plus first-hand accounts, *Creating Hitler's Germany* not only attempts to understand Germany's pursuit of world domination but also its journey to genocide. It also examines Germany's eventual destruction and the reciprocal genocide that was visited upon the country itself at the close of the Second World War in 1945. This work is unequalled in its mix of life, love and tragedy, all intertwined with the horrors of war, as witnessed by those who were there and who lived to tell the tale. The previously unpublished story of Werner, Hilde and Alexander Kohlman provides a unique introduction to the work and, along with the private diaries and letters of young Jewish socialite Melitta Jorg, contributions from the private family archives of Albert and Emira Friest, Ingrid and Andreas Hoess, Paulina Rischner and Ursula and Rudi Metschuldt, plus many other first-hand accounts, makes *Creating Hitler's Germany* essential reading if one is to understand the very embryo of Adolf Hitler's Third Reich.

These unheard voices, reminiscences and collective experiences of a generation effectively conceived upon a bed of bayonets are still very much the source of fascination and, sometimes, revulsion. In many cases, the natural curiosity that we historians possess to document and preserve what are merely segments of Third Reich history means that we are often ignorant as to their importance in the modern world. Germany was a nation with the deep resentment that resulted from Versailles woven into its social fabric. After 1918 the country found itself caught in a trap and, like a desperate wild animal in the same predicament, was ready to chew through a snared limb in order to free itself. The foundations for the rise of a dictatorship, such as that of Adolf Hitler's Nazi Party, were in a sense set by those nations who had emerged victorious from the First World War. It is easy, after the passing of so many years, to discuss alternative scenarios. Solutions that may have prevented a Second World War involving Germany matter no longer within our modern hindsight. There are many essential lessons to be learned in order to prevent such catastrophes occurring again. *Creating Hitler's Germany* represents a nation's journey not only through everyday life and the war but also through its own conscience, pain and inevitable search for some form of absolution from its past. For thousands of Germans, the birth of Hitler's Third Reich represented hope and salvation from the despair of Versailles. However, it soon came to represent abuse, suffering, discrimination, fear, intimidation and mass murder. Why did so many follow such a fratricidal regime so willingly to their own destruction? Why did many otherwise good men become murderers in the heat of battle? And why have so few spoken out on the reciprocal genocide visited upon the Germans themselves at the closing stages of the Second World War? I feel that the answers, or at least some of them, will be discovered within the pages of this unique book as they are given by those who were there.

The devil whispered to the soldier, 'A storm is coming'.
The soldier replied, 'I am the storm.'

Chapter One

Love Before War

Werner Kohlman and Hilde Schramm had been born and raised in the city of Hamburg. They had known each other for a great many years. They had both attended the same school, sharing the same group of friends. They both loved books, particularly those on ancient fairy tales. Neither owned many books, but the few that they possessed between them had great sentimental value. As children they talked of how they wanted to travel the world when they were old enough to leave home. They had the same dreams and aspirations as any other children. They both came from what can only best be described as working-class backgrounds. Their upbringing was harsh at times and they and their parents often had very little. It was, in many respects, a subsistence existence based upon the hopes and dreams of adulthood. Their homes were small terraced houses built mainly for the shipping and railway workers. In these cramped houses families shared bedrooms and it was not uncommon for several boys and girls to have to share a single bedroom. In wintertime the houses were cold and damp, and water leaked in through ceilings and walls whenever it rained. In the summer conditions were a little better, as the children played on the streets outside their homes or basked in the sunshine.

Werner and Hilde would often walk the short distance to their local school together. They would chat about all manner of things as they did. Hilde often stopped to pick a few flowers from the gardens of houses along the way. On one occasion, an angry old lady charged out of her home to confront Hilde about stealing her flowers. Werner grabbed her by the hand and they ran away laughing. Later at school their escapade of earlier in the day was reported. Hilde was called to the front of their small class to receive a verbal rebuke from the headmaster. For his part in the crime, Werner was made to lie across the headmaster's heavy oak desk and given a thrashing with the cane across his backside. Hilde tried to explain that the deed was all her fault, but this did not save poor Werner's buttocks from the stick. As they walked back home that day, Hilde was very concerned for her friend's predicament. Werner tried to reassure her with the words, 'It didn't hurt that much', to which Hilde replied, 'Well, why were you crying then?' Instead of becoming angry with Hilde, Werner just laughed. They parted at the end of their street, each going their separate ways, saying they would see each other tomorrow. As they grew older, the routine continued. They spent much time in each other's company, reading and discussing stories they had heard from grown-ups.

By their teens, it was obvious that they had developed affection for each other. Back then it was frowned upon for a young man to be alone unsupervised with a young girl outside of marriage. Kissing and holding hands was not allowed. It was often impossible to escape the eyes of the chaperone that would be allocated the task of keeping an eye on the couple. There were dances, usually organised by the local church, and young courting couples could attend providing they were chaperoned. Werner and Hilde attended their first local dance when Werner was eighteen and Hilde seventeen. Hilde's aunt would be their constant companion throughout the evening, including the walk home afterwards. Werner would ensure the two ladies were walked home safely. There was no goodnight kiss for Hilde, just a fond wave with the promise of seeing her the next day. Werner knew that he would need to find suitable employment before he could even think of asking for Hilde's hand in marriage. Werner met with Hilde's father to discuss the prospect of him proposing to his daughter. As expected, Hilde's father was stern with Werner, despite having known the young man for many years. Hilde's father questioned Werner on how he would support his daughter and where they proposed to live. Hilde's father explained he did not want his daughter marrying a drunkard or layabout and, though Werner was visibly shocked at this response, it made him all the more determined to prove himself worthy. Werner went along to the local railway company and managed to find a job keeping the station platforms tidy and free of litter. This also involved cleaning the toilets, which was an unpleasant task. As he often complained to Hilde, 'Some dirty beast has shit all over the floor again!' Feeling proud at having secured at least one of the prerequisites of marriage to Hilde, Werner's thoughts then turned to seeking accommodation. It seems luck smiled upon the young man again. After discussing his plans with his employer he was told he could have one of the railway workers' homes if he wished. The rent was competitive, but he could afford it. His boss promised promotion and a wage rise if he worked hard and proved himself reliable. With all this in place, Werner again asked to speak to Hilde's father about marrying his daughter. Werner explained to him all he had done and, after a tense silence, Hilde's father suggested a meeting with Werner's family to discuss things further. If it all worked out, Werner would be granted permission to propose marriage to Hilde.

The two families were not strangers to one another, but they had invested much pride in their respective children, particularly the daughters. Werner's family was invited for tea to the Schramm household so that the prospective marriage could be discussed. Werner's father wore his one and only suit that he wore to church every week and the women wore every piece of finery they owned. After the family conference, Hilde's father and mother finally gave their blessing and the young lovers took a stroll along the banks of the River Elbe in the warm afternoon sunshine of that beautiful August day in 1912. For the first time since their schooldays they walked alone arm in arm before Werner, picking his moment carefully, proposed to the young girl he had fallen in love with some years before. He stopped momentarily and, going down on one knee, took Hilde's hand in his and asked her to marry him. The young girl smiled and, with no hesitation, replied, 'Yes, of course I will marry you.' Werner did not have enough money for an engagement ring. His mother, mindful of this, gave him one that had belonged to her in the hope that the simple gold band would fit Hilde's slender fingers. Werner slid the ring on Hilde's wedding ring finger effortlessly, as if it had been made for her hand. Then they embraced, Werner gently kissing the beautiful young woman on the lips for the first time. As the shadows of late afternoon began to grow they walked back to their homes arm in arm, a proud young couple.

A date was arranged for the wedding. In the months leading up to it, Werner worked very hard in his daytime job. After work, before heading home for his evening meal with his parents, he went to the small terraced cottage where he and Hilde would live as man and wife and spent time cleaning and decorating it in readiness. The cottage was only partially furnished, but friends and family helped out with the things they couldn't afford for their new house.

In May 1913 Werner and Hilde were married; a very simple ceremony in a small Catholic chapel. To their surprise their parents had pooled funds so that the couple could have a short honeymoon on Sylt, a popular German holiday island in the North Sea. Its long sandy beaches would be like a paradise compared to the banks of the Elbe in Hamburg. The couple spent three nights there staying in a small guesthouse. Most of their time was spent on romantic walks along the beautiful beaches, drinking coffee and sharing cakes on the seafront, and discussing their future together. During their evening walks they would often meet other couples along the way. They would stop to talk for a few minutes, sharing the exhilaration of the moment. Werner even admitted, within the privacy of his journal, that the couple had found a quiet spot where they had made love for the very first time. He wrote:

> Unrestrained, we are free from all eyes in this German paradise of the North. Even our parents have never been here yet; here we are married and alone. As we walked the sands in the evenings, on more than one occasion, the sounds of couples in the throes of passion could be heard from nearby sand dunes. Why are we not to do the same? We are full of youthful exuberance; maybe a son will come from our unions on Sylt. I do not want this to end, but know that soon we will be travelling back home to Hamburg to begin a new chapter in our lives. I hope we come here again as this place is intoxicating. The fresh sea air and being here with the girl I love is everything and anything a man could want. It all makes me angry and sad that I do not have the wealth, as do some, to live in places like these. Are we all not the creatures of one universe entitled to the same things?

It is clear at this point that the honeymoon at Sylt had instilled some inner rebellion within Werner's soul. Questioning the ethics of the haves and have nots were not the normal thought processes of this humble working-class young man. Sylt was very much like the apple in the Garden of Eden. Werner wanted to reach out to it and take a big bite.

Upon the couple's return to Hamburg, Werner was determined to do everything possible to better things for himself and his new wife. He understood that hard work was the only way out of poverty and he would work day and night if he had to. Hilde worked briefly as a housekeeper for a local business owner. It was laborious work and she did not enjoy it, describing the lady of the house as a 'bully'. Her duties included washing clothes, cleaning furniture and personal effects, as well as scrubbing floors and sometimes helping to prepare food in the kitchen. The skin on her hands soon became dry and chapped with her daily routine. She would return home tired after a long day and then begin her own chores, trying to get everything done before Werner's return home in the evening. She would clean the cottage, scrub the floors, prepare any washing then cook a meal. By the time everything was cleared away after their evening meal Hilde and Werner were exhausted. They would kiss one another goodnight, fall into bed and immediately fall asleep, to be woken the next morning at 6 am. Werner would wearily rise from the comfort of their bed and wash in a small basin that sat on an old table in their room. He would put on his work clothes, make tea or coffee and sit smoking a cigarette outside in the small backyard where other men would be carrying out the same early-morning ritual. The men rarely engaged in any small talk, other than the courteous 'Guten morgen' [Good morning], as they prepared themselves mentally for the long day ahead. Sometimes the sound of someone hawking phlegm from deep within their lungs could be heard followed by the sound of it being spat forth. Werner would listen intently to these noises as he sat smoking, and drinking his tea or coffee. He would then disappear back inside to wake Hilde ready for her day's work. He would kiss her on the cheek then take his cloth-wrapped lunch bundle out of the pantry before setting off down the road to work.

Werner's journey to work was a pleasant one. On his way, he met acquaintances who worked in the shipyards and ports and they stopped briefly to chat. Werner always arrived at the station ten minutes early to start his day. His menial tasks were interrupted by the conversation of the public going about their business and occasionally a pretty girl would walk by catching his eye. Taking out his pocket watch that his mother and father bought for him as part of his wedding gift, he would look at the small photograph of Hilde that he had placed inside the cover and smile before placing the watch back in his pocket. His boss reminded him that the toilets were to be his first job of the day, 'They must be clean and fresh to start the day, as customers don't like using dirty toilets and it looks bad on us if they are not clean!' Werner muttered obscenities under his breath as he removed the streaks of excrement from the sides of the porcelain bowls. A mop and bucket were used to clean the floors. He mopped up the puddles of urine that had already begun to form on the beautifully ornate tiled flooring. He swept the platform, emptying the bins as he went.

By the time these first tasks of the day were completed it was time for the morning break. Tea and coffee was brewed and the workers congregated to have a drink and a smoke. Some sat reading newspapers while others chatted. The young men were amusing to Werner. He listened to them talk about the pretty women they had spotted getting on and off the trains. They dreamed of taking them out as girlfriends while the older men teased them, saying they would never have enough money for the likes of those young ladies. Werner again took out his watch, flipping up the silver lid to admire the photograph of his young wife. The others asked if they could have a look and he obliged by passing the pocket watch around. They all agreed that Hilde was a beautiful girl and they congratulated Werner on a fine catch. A disgruntled loud cough from the boss reminds the men that break time is over and they rose from their chairs and headed back to their posts to continue their work. Werner has to go back to the toilets to check they have not been fouled.

The highlight of Werner's day was his hour-long lunch break. He ate his bread rolls, washed down with a cup of coffee, and then put his feet up and lies back in his chair for a nap. Within minutes he was sound asleep, oblivious to the conversation of the other men or the arguments of those playing cards. One of them roused Werner at the end of their lunch break. He stretched wearily as he rose from his chair, then watered the hanging flower baskets before checking that the station clock was keeping good time. He cheerfully assisted passengers with their heavy cases as they boarded their trains. He voluntarily worked until 7 pm for some extra pay. Werner worked at the station six days a week, with Sunday being his only day off. As it was Friday – payday – he stopped on his way home to buy himself a beer, one of the few luxuries that he allowed himself each week. He also bought some flowers for Hilde, another weekly ritual. He presented the flowers to Hilde when he got home and kissed her lovingly on the lips. These were halcyon days and, though Werner and Hilde worked hard, they enjoyed life and were happy.

The assassination of Archduke Franz Ferdinand of Austria-Hungary on 28 June 1914 was the beginning of a nightmare for Germany. The ramifications of this single act carried out by nineteen-year-old Serbian nationalist terrorist Gavrilo Princip would reach far into the country's future. It is difficult to comprehend how the actions of just one man could lead to the outbreak of a war which would cost the lives of over thirty-eight million people. Princip's actions set in motion a chain of events that ended the complex defensive strategy of European nations at the time. As a result of the assassination Austria-Hungary declared war on Serbia. Russia then became involved to defend Serbia, and Germany, seeing Russia mobilize its forces, declared war on Russia. France was then brought into the conflict against Germany and Austria-Hungary, leading Germany to attack France through Belgium, thus pulling Britain into the escalating conflict. Japan became involved, followed later by Italy and the USA, which entered the war on the side of the Allies.

Prior to the outbreak of the First World War in 1914 many countries had imperialist desires and this increasing competition for territory helped push the world towards global conflict. Other factors included the arms race that had begun to develop between Britain, Germany and Russia at the beginning of the twentieth century. Furthermore, the desire of the Slavic peoples in Bosnia and Herzegovina to no longer be a part of Austria-Hungary and instead ally themselves with Serbia was also a factor in the outbreak of the First World War. The assassination of Archduke Ferdinand was carried out in protest at Austria-Hungary having control over Serbia. The assassin, Gavrilo Princip, had been a member of the Black Hand, a Serbian nationalist terrorist group. The Black Hand's first assassination attempt had failed when, earlier the same day, a grenade was thrown at the Archduke's car. Thanks to the skill and vigilance of the driver, tragedy was averted. Later in the day, Princip was dispatched to Sarajevo, where he would carry out his successful attempt on the life of the Archduke. In the wake of the events in Sarajevo, the foundations for one of the bloodiest wars in human history were laid.

The feelings of the German people at that time showed little in the way of concern. Germany was, at the time, one of the most powerful military forces in the world. Many were of the opinion that any war would be short lived and that Germany would emerge victorious. In fact, most of the nations involved in the fighting were convinced that it would be over by Christmas. But this would prove hopelessly optimistic and, as Germany began its attack on the Western Front, the reality slowly began to dawn, on Germans, as well as the people of other nations, that this was not going to be a short war.

Hilde and Werner's lives, as those of many Germans, were not affected by the outbreak of war. Initially there was little threat to the country's economic infrastructure, but the British naval blockade of the country, in November 1914, prevented many essential imported foodstuffs, goods and other supplies from arriving in Germany, forcing the country to rely entirely on its own agricultural resources to feed its people. Germany had made no economic plans for a protracted war in Europe. In 1914, she relied on the importation of goods for around a third of her foodstuffs, fodder and fertilizers. A lack of equipment, supplies and fertilizers saw crop yields diminish alarmingly. The lack of fodder for farm animals in particular meant that valuable livestock slowly starved beyond use. As a consequence, supplies of meat and milk products, vital for Germany to sustain its war effort on the battlefield and the home front, were greatly reduced. The army was, of course, given priority for food supplies. On the home front, the increasing shortages of even the most basic of foods was becoming a serious problem and local authorities were shouldered with the burden of dealing with the angry populace. The effects of famine in German society began to take effect, particularly from the years 1915-1916. Although many German citizens could find work the vast majority of workers did not earn enough to provide for their families. As a result the infant mortality rate in Germany among poor and working-class families began to rise. The wealthy, meanwhile, were largely unaffected by the country's economic situation, seemingly detached from the problems faced by the lower classes.

Werner Kohlman became increasingly despondent on the Hamburg railway. Many of his friends had volunteered to join the German army and gone off to fight in the war and, for this reason, he felt a lesser man. He made his feelings known to his young wife who became increasingly concerned. She did not want her beloved Werner to go to war and the couple argued over the issue. Hilde wrote in her diary, 'I cannot understand why he wants to go out there and fight. It's not as if he has to, he has a choice to stay here with me. I am terrified he will have his own way and end up being killed or crippled. What do I do if he goes and never comes back?'

The Battle of the Marne, which took place on 7-12 of September 1914, destroyed any illusions of a quick and easy war. The battle ended with an Allied victory over the German army, which had suffered 67,700 casualties in the battle, and set the stage for four years of stalemate in the form of trench warfare. As news of the heavy casualties reached the German populace back home, more and more young men began to volunteer for the army. Werner and Hilde argued more than ever over the rights and wrongs of the war. After one particularly fierce altercation, Werner insisted he was going to volunteer to go and fight for his country and that such an action was his moral duty. Hilde wrote again:

> I know I can do little to dissuade my love from making his decision. It is becoming policy now and men are being called up to fight all over Germany. I am afraid as we have spent so little time together and I am afraid of becoming a widow. This war is beginning to make me feel fear. I am frightened that this is all going to go the wrong way. The omens are not good for us at this time. Less and less goods are in the shops and we have to make sacrifices more and more to cope with this. It can only get much worse.

By January 1915 Werner Kohlman had volunteered for military service. He passed his medical before undergoing intensive training. In most respects he was a satisfactory recruit. His basic marksmanship was not brilliant but was good enough and he soon adapted to the military way of life. In fact, he found it all quite exciting upon joining the Hamburg 76 Regiment. After completing his training he was granted some leave to be with his young wife. Hilde broke down in tears as she saw Werner in his military uniform for the first time. The painfully brief period of leave was spent visiting family. Werner wanted to ensure that, if the worst happened and he did not return, Hilde would be looked after. He wrote numerous letters, instructing his family that they should only be opened if he failed to return home from the war. Werner also went to a local photographer to have a portrait photograph taken of him in uniform. The photographer was a family friend who even waived his fee, telling Werner, 'Be careful out there, boy, there are dreadful things happening!' Like thousands of other volunteers, Werner had little understanding of what he was going into. He was young, headstrong and patriotic, and believed he may not even get to fire a shot in anger. The reality would be very different.

Chapter Two

Mud, Blood and Machine Guns

Werner Kohlman revealed many of the reminiscences contained within this chapter upon his return from fighting in the First World War. Werner wrote many letters to Hilde during their long period of separation, most of them typical of any soldier on the frontline with a sweetheart back home. The letters were filled with messages of undying love, as well as enquiries and regards to everyone at home. Werner's letters revealed little of the horrors he witnessed in the trenches of the Western Front. All personal mail to and from soldiers on the frontline was subject to strict censorship rules. Any letter containing even the slightest hint of operational details could be stopped and returned to its sender, often with the offending text redacted. Censorship was harsh, but it was imperative that morale be maintained. It also lessened the risk of the enemy discovering vital information through careless talk.

Werner and his comrades were transported to the battlefront by train. The journey was not an unpleasant one. The only thing to shatter the relative peace of the rhythmic rocking of the train was the Sergeant frequently reminding the men to check their kit to ensure their weapons were serviceable. He walked up and down barking orders and scolding any recruit who was not quick enough to answer his demands. Nothing escaped his attention; buttons had to be gleaming and boots had to shine. As he passed by, some young men would pull funny faces behind his back. But they soon learned that this was not a good idea as the Sergeant seemingly had eyes in the back of his head. As he walked down the narrow carriage, one young man pulled a funny face, confident that the Sergeant was oblivious to his prank. The Sergeant, however, swung round, eyes bulging, and shouted in the young private's face, 'Don't you ever dare to attempt to ridicule me!' He then unsheathed his bayonet, placing the gleaming steel blade across the young soldier's forehead, and said menacingly. 'I hope you are ready for what is about to come. I am. I have been there. But you? No, you haven't yet, have you? You have no fucking idea. Pull yourself together or I will insert this in your arse next time!' The young private is visibly shocked and Werner notes his reaction. He decides there and then that playing the game by the rules will be the easiest way to get through this.

These young men were all going to hell, one way or another. Many would never see home again. The First World War brought many military innovations to the fore. The combined use of machine guns and heavy artillery brought death on an industrial scale. As Werner and his comrades disembarked from their train into the dim light of a late afternoon, they heard the sound of the guns in the distance. As night fell they were billeted in a Belgian village. The boom of artillery could still be heard but now, with darkness falling, they could see the flashes of exploding shells light up the skies around them. It reminded Werner of the thunderstorms he had witnessed as a child back in Hamburg. The men settled down in the remains of an old house to try and get some sleep. Werner found the conditions most uncomfortable and this, combined with the excitement of the day, meant that sleep would be impossible. Werner began to think that he would probably never be able to sleep again properly until back home with Hilde. Alone with his thoughts, his predicament became all too apparent during the long hours of darkness. He closed his eyes yet all he could see was Hilde's smiling face. The arguments they had before he left Hamburg reverberated through his mind, making him feel sad for the first time. Tears began to form in his eyes as it slowly began to dawn on him that this was no game; this war was real. It was a very long wait until the light of dawn rescued Werner from his melancholy, and the indignity of frequent urinating brought on by nerves. Every time he needed to piss he had to clear a guard or sentry. A password was issued to avoid anyone being accidentally shot. If you forgot the password you were in serious trouble, so Werner etched it into the lid of his tobacco box with the point of his bayonet. The men were roused and soon hot drinks were being prepared along with a breakfast of bread and eggs.

The ruined building where they had spent the night would soon appear luxurious compared to the conditions they would have to endure over the coming months. Werner wrote to Hilde at every opportunity, sending her letters and, where possible, a postcard. His unit was pushing towards France and the British lines and as they marched forwards the scenery became ever more depressing. Columns of refugees fleeing the fighting were a constant sight along their route. Werner noted their wretched state, particularly the children. Compassion rose inside him at the sight of these people dressed in rags, many walking barefoot, carrying what few possessions they had in small carts. On the one occasion, a group of children came up to them, looking for sweets or any other items the soldiers might spare them from their rations. Werner wrote of these little children:

> They look like street urchins. The girls wear tatty, dirty and torn dresses with nothing on their feet. They have dirty faces yet they smile at us and talk with us. The boys are much the same and they like to look at our rifles and bayonets. We share some of the food we have with them, as not all children here are friendly like these. They are pleased even with just the smallest of morsels. We even have our photographs taken with them.

Mostly though the children eyed the passing German soldiers with cold, blank stares. Werner wondered what thoughts were going through their minds. Few young men were evident among the long train of refugees, maybe because they had been killed or taken prisoner. The only men were those in old age and Werner watched them as they shuffled along awkwardly, some aided by sticks. No one spoke; both soldiers and refugees eyed one another cautiously with that curiosity that only prevails in situations such as these. Werner later wrote in his journal:

> I wanted to know about these people. Where they had come from, where they were going. Did they hate us Germans? That was probably a stupid thing to think. Of course they hate us; I could sense it and I saw it in the eyes of those children. One child in particular fixed me with a steely glare, a little girl who could have been no more than six years of age. Her dark eyes pierced through the dirty lank hair of her head that fell over her face. I saw hate in the eyes of a child that day. Had she been

an adult, would I have challenged her? Would I have expressed
any hatred back towards her? I don't know and I still don't.

The shell-blighted landscape was like a scene from hell: smashed buildings
and piles of rubble, devoid of all traces of humankind. The sounds of the
guns grew louder as Werner and his unit neared the battlefront. They
marched throughout the days, spending the nights in any ruin which
could offer shelter. At night, it was nothing out of the ordinary to be
approached by local women offering sexual services for a small fee or
some unobtainable luxury such as a piece of soap. The officers made no
attempt to deter their men from pursuing sexual favours with these ladies.
It was not until men began to contract various sexual diseases that these
activities were curtailed. The men were then allocated French brothels,
which were controlled so that precautions could be supplied to counter
the risk of sexual diseases. Werner noted that many of the new friends
he had made in his unit frequented brothels at every given opportunity.
Afterwards, the young men would delight in sharing the details of their
sexual exploits. One young soldier complained that he had been cheated;
the woman, he said, 'was huge, with ankles resembling tree trunks!'
Another remarked that he had the most wonderful time with a beautiful
young Belgian-born maiden, adding that, 'I climbed upon her and grunted
merrily like a boar pig!' Another remarked that the woman he had was a
big, blonde girl who was horribly morose and incapable of conversation,
appearing to have a rape fetish. She had diseased toenails on the one foot
and told him her 'working name' was Tiana or something, adding that
'she squawked rather like a chicken' when they had intercourse. The men
laughed about their antics, asking why Werner did not seek these women
as they did. He did his best to explain that he had a beautiful wife waiting
for him back in Germany and that he could never betray her by having
sex with French whores. He would show his friends the small photograph
of Hilde, which he kept inside his pocket watch. He felt that some of the
men of his unit were convinced that he was a homosexual.

The proximity to the front line meant that now the men were seeing
the horrific results of the war at first hand. Wounded men were brought
to the rear where Werner's unit was instructed to help them board trucks
and troop trains. Some of the wounded had bandages around their heads

that were oozing blood, or lay on stretchers moaning incoherently, while others had arms or legs missing. The range of injuries was frightening to those who had yet to see the horrors of war up close. Werner wrote:

I saw one poor fellow who had been caught in the blast of a phosphorus shell. It would have been kinder to have just shot him rather than see him suffer what must have been a world of agony. Artillery is the greatest fear of all. The thought of losing an arm, a leg or both is something that weighs heavily upon the mind of a soldier. To be killed outright is a mercy. To suffer mutilation, a slow lingering death, in the mud of the battlefield or in a hospital bed many miles from home is incomprehensible. I have heard stories of this war from the wounded soldiers. They are frightful to hear.

Just a short distance further would bring Werner and his unit into range of the British and French artillery and soon they were digging holes in the ground to shelter in or sleep in at night. Artillery fire became more intense and Werner began to see the first casualties amongst his own unit. He learned, like many, to greatly fear the anti-personnel shells known as shrapnel. These were high-explosive artillery shells packed with lead antimony balls. At a given point, a pre-set time fuse would detonate the shell, spraying the target area with these high velocity projectiles. Werner recalled several men being caught out in the open by a British 18-pounder shrapnel bombardment:

These poor souls had no way of escape, the shrapnel balls tore through their bodies as if they were paper. The bodies were unrecognizable afterwards. They looked just like raw meat. Some were cut to pieces like beef steaks. The bodies were hastily buried and marked with simple wooden crosses. Some of the bodies were in that many pieces you had to just collect what you could find. I recall finding a piece of one man's face. It was part of his jaw as you could see the pearly white teeth. Sometimes it was a hand, foot or a leg. These blasts were capable of severing a man's head from off his shoulders, hurling it like a football through the air for yards. I recall one young man telling me he had a head sail down and splosh beside him in his water-filled hole. The head bobbed up and down for a moment then sank into the putrid water.

Werner also witnessed the power of the German artillery as they advanced upon the rearmost positions. He recalled:

The big artillery guns were fascinating things. We had small-calibre field pieces of 7.7cm up to these truly massive 42cm behemoths. The 42cm weapons were ideal against heavily fortified enemy targets. We had used these big guns in Belgium to crush the forts there. Just the sight of these monsters should be enough to instill fear into an enemy. Witnessing one of these big guns discharge its ammunition was some spectacle to watch. The British had big guns of their own too. These left craters deep enough to bury a horse inside. If one of these big shells landed on you there would be nothing left of you to even send home in a letter!

After the First Battle of the Aisne, which took place 12-15 September 1914, the whole pattern of the war on the Western Front changed. Neither side was capable of taking any ground so began to dig in. The fighting that ensued consisted of skirmishes in no man's land. This was a stretch of barren land that lay between the German and British trenches. It was strewn with barbed wire entanglements designed to snare any attacking infantry. The landscape was heavily cratered by the near constant artillery bombardments. In no man's land two things were king: the machine gun and artillery. When either side attempted to take ground they were mown down by machine guns and shrapnel shells day and night.

The German trench systems were a complete contrast to those of the opposing British. The Germans dug very deep, constructing living quarters, and first aid and command posts well below the ground. These were almost impervious to all but the very heaviest of bombardments. The British trenches were mainly shallow, miserable, water-filled hell holes. These trenches themselves created casualties as men fell ill from the damp, cold, disease and trench foot. The German trench networks offered a higher degree of protection from the elements which boosted morale and helped prevent men from falling ill from the sometimes extreme conditions. Werner wrote of the German trenches:

> They are more like mines than trenches where men should fight from. Light is created with small fuel-filled lanterns and there is that dank, earthy smell deep below the ground. It is not always warm, but it is a lot warmer than it is above the ground. When the shells land we hear the 'crump' sound of the explosion, sometimes a little dust falls from the ceilings. Some men are claustrophobic; you can see they are fighting the will to not run in panic for the surface. The thought of being buried alive down here is a reality, but it is far more dangerous above ground than down here. Sometimes, there is an alarm and the watch will shout 'The British are coming!' We will scramble up the labyrinth of tunnels up to the firing steps, our weapons pointing into the inky blackness of night. Often the alarm call is false. At night, those on watch through fatigue or fear see things that are not really there. The mind plays tricks on you; flares are fired into the night sky to illuminate any coming attack on us. Often there is nothing; the light from the flares revealing water-filled shell craters and the rotting corpse of a horse or something. There aren't even any rats out there; nothing moves, only death lives out there. Only death is safe from death if that makes any sense. This is not a time or place for philosophy but my thoughts constantly question my own mortality.

Werner also wrote of the many misconceptions of the dangers of trench warfare:

> It all seems peaceful somewhat quiet sometimes in the day. One can forget that we are deep in war. Yesterday, a young man strolled up and down our trench then he climbed up the firing step peering over the crest. He had just remarked, 'It is so peaceful out there, it's not like we are at war at all is it?' In a

split second that followed his last word, his head exploded much like a fruit struck a heavy blow with a club. The headless body stood rigid for some seconds before falling slowly backwards. It fell with a sickening thump to the bottom of the trench. We found fragments of the man's skull on the floor of the trench and the remains of cerebral tissue were everywhere. This was not shrapnel or any grenade; this was the bullet from the rifle of an enemy sniper. Orders were soon given that no man is to look over the crest of our trenches. We have to use periscope equipment if we are to avoid having our heads blown off. These periscope things are quite marvellous as one can look over the crest of a trench at the British lines. If shot, the worst that will happen is that the periscope will be smashed, rather than your skull and brains. These things are constructed from wood with angled mirrors inside. We all have these periscopes now. Any man caught looking out over enemy positions without a periscope will be subjected to a severe reprimand, if his head is not shot off first!

Back home in Hamburg, Hilde continued to write letters to Werner. She was not having a very happy time; she was missing her husband and had little money or food. Her job as a housekeeper to a wealthy family was depressing her greatly. She accidentally broke an ornament whilst dusting the family's drawing room. She knew she would be severely scolded by the lady of the house but felt honesty was the best policy. She explained to her employer what happened and that she was sorry, that she was just very tired and melancholic due to her husband being away at war. The lady of the house, showing no understanding, shouted at Hilde, 'You stupid, useless young woman! Do you know how much this thing cost?' Hilde tried to remain calm, replying, 'Sorry, Frau Boersch.' The lady of the house then screamed, 'Get out of here! Go home! You will receive no pay for today's work as recompense.'

Hilde made her way home in the pouring rain that afternoon. She wept virtually all the way, until she met a friend who stopped to ask her what was wrong. The friend took Hilde into her home for some tea. Hilde sat shaking from the chill while the friend wrapped a blanket around her and poured her a cup of steaming hot tea. The friend asked what Hilde had been crying for. Hilde explained what had happened earlier that day. The friend was sympathetic saying, 'I don't know how you can work for that ogre Boersch, as she is an old witch!' She then passed Hilde a leaflet, saying, 'Why don't you try for work here? The money will be better and you won't have anyone on your back all day long.' The leaflet showed an advert asking for women to volunteer for war work in the munitions factories. Hilde looked at the leaflet, deciding she would go there the next day to seek employment. She never returned to the Boerschs. ignoring several letters from them.

The next letter Werner received from his beloved Hilde explained that she was no longer working for the Boersch family and that she had found alternative employment. Censorship would have prevented her from explaining more about the work she was doing. She would tell Werner all about it when he returned home. Like many wives, Hilde was hoping that the war would be over by Christmas 1915. Many thought it would have been over by Christmas 1914, but the reality was, of course, that the war would drag on for four more miserable years, with a death toll far greater than that of any previous war. The mood for Werner and his colleagues in the trenches soon became subdued after the initial excitement of the approach of Christmas 1915. Germany's Christmas traditions run deep and German High Command understood that, at this time of year especially, it was vital to maintain the morale of the men. Many would be missing loved ones back home and it would be easy for the men to slip into depression. Those back home were encouraged to make gifts for their menfolk on the battlefront and the German people set about the task with a commendable zeal. Soon, Werner and his friends were deluged with all manner of gifts, mainly in the form of hand-knitted gloves and jumpers to help keep them warm. Snow had already begun to fall, carpeting the landscape, and the air was bitterly cold, particularly on moonlit nights. Werner and his colleagues probably fared better than their British counterparts. The Germans were issued with thick, heavy greatcoats, which they could wrap around themselves like a blanket. These coats made movement somewhat restrictive, but they were great when on sentry duty or for sleeping. On the run up to Christmas Day 1915, Werner received cards from his parents-in-law and, of course, Hilde. The cards were traditionally handmade with great detail and adorned with messages of love. Werner vividly recalled Christmas Eve 1915:

> We are in reasonably good cheer, but, strangely, a group of fellows begin to sing our Christmas hymn 'Silent Night'. All goes quiet and throughout we are deep in thought. We think of our families back home and, as the hymn is sung, our eyes are full of tears. I think of my beautiful Hilde and what she will be doing back home and I hold my head in my hands and cry like a child. I miss her so much and just want to be back home with her, so as we can get on with our lives. Maybe this war will soon be over, I don't know. I can only hope and pray that this will be the last Christmas that we will have to spend apart.

As dawn broke on Christmas morning 1915, Werner wrote:

> Our senior officers rouse us with a bottle of brandy and cigars. We wish each other a Merry Christmas, shake hands and distribute gifts amongst ourselves. I am given a cigarette lighter that is made from an empty bullet casing. Packages brought in from home are torn open. We go through them like excited children. My beloved Hilde has sent me a small silver cigarette box and this is inscribed 'To my love, Werner, from Hilde, Happy Christmas 1915.' There are some hand-knitted woollen gloves, a green coloured scarf and three letters also in the package. The letters are from Hilde, my parents and my in-laws. I read through them over and over again. The love and warmth I feel from this is intoxicating and already I am feeling better; the sadness lifts a little. Along the lines, there are rumours of the British throwing packages of small gifts across to us and our boys are doing the same. There are shouts of 'Happy Christmas!' rather than the crack of rifle fire from the direction of the enemy positions, which in some places are just yards apart. How can we possibly kill one another on Christmas Day; yet our orders are to stand firm, be prepared for attack and to stay down away from the crest of our trenches.

We spend the day reading our letters, smoking cigarettes and cigars, enjoying the few treats sent by our people back home. We even have fruitcake and stollen, which we eat with abandon. We sing carols and try our best to cheer one another up, as soon this day will be over and the fighting will undoubtedly begin again.

At this point Werner's writings appeared to temporarily cease for some reason. Hilde continued to write and he wrote back, the content of his letters giving little away as to his whereabouts and general activities. His journal begins again in June 1916, though it has never been ascertained as to why he stopped writing. It is possible he only wished to note down worthwhile events which he felt were of more importance. Either way, his granddaughter and great-granddaughter have never discovered the reason. Werner's next writing refers to a British and French attack on the German lines. There was a sustained preliminary bombardment that forced the Germans to remain below ground. When the bombardment ceased, the Germans came out to take up their positions along the parapets. Werner described what happened next:

It was night time, maybe the early hours, I don't know, as the days and nights seemed to blur into one. When they attacked, everything just erupted; there was rifle, machine gun and artillery fire. Flares were fired to provide light and in this light we could see the enemy advancing upon us. Their long bayonets on the end of their rifles glinted momentarily in the flickering light of flares. We poured round after round through our weapons at them. I could see men fall as I shot them. Trench bombs were hurled toward the enemy and their detonations flashed in the darkness, bodies and body parts sent airborne. Our machine guns seemed to stop the attack after just a few minutes. These weapons took a heavy toll with men falling dead into the mud whilst others were called to retreat. Tracers zipped past and overhead and I heard enemy bullets thud into the ground nearby. This, it seemed, was a probing attack of some sort and the enemy fell back to their lines.

I recall one of the enemy becoming tangled up in barbed wire. He fought desperately to escape its grasp until an enfilade of rifle bullets stopped him. He slumped into the wire that was now embracing his corpse, the head tilted forward as if in deep thought. The body remained there, slowly decaying on the wire like some form of hideous sculpture. The enemy artillery continued to shell our position for some time afterwards. The noise is indescribable and it is foolhardy to even consider going above ground during bombardments. If you place an ear at the entrance to our little bunker, down in our trench, you can hear the curious whine that shrapnel makes. You can even decipher the size of the artillery being used, not only by the depth of the blast but the shrapnel. Sleep is fitful at these times, but it is surprising how you adjust to this hellish environment. Some are driven mad by the constant rumble of artillery above ground, convinced they will be buried alive at any second. Some of these men become so demented and irrational they have to be removed and sometimes restrained with bindings. The reality is we could, of course, become entombed here, but our trenches and bunkers are dug well and are deep. We would have to be pretty unlucky and to be hit with the biggest of shells for this to happen. By first light, the bombardment has stopped. Shell fragments litter the trenches and these are picked up and examined. I find a shard of copper from a British shell embedded in the wall of our trench. It weighs around half a pound and such an evil missile could remove a man's head with ease. I place the lump of copper into my pocket. We clear up and shore the defences as it starts to rain. The rain seems incessant here at times. It soaks you through, chilling you to the bone. Sometimes it's that cold that you yearn for some action. We light cigarettes, as the smoke is soothing. There are few comforts in this place apart from cigarettes, letters from home and rations.

Werner's last action of the First World War came in December 1916. It is believed he was involved in the battle for the fortified French town of

Verdun. His granddaughter recalled him talking of a major battle for a French town. In his private journal he wrote:

> We head into a storm of artillery, rifle and machine-gun fire. Our artillery hit back and how could anyone possibly survive a battering like that. Hundreds of guns firing back and forth as each side desperately attempts to gain the tactical advantage. At the end of it all, it is us the infantry who have to get up, go forward and take ground off the enemy, killing him along the way if necessary. We attach our bayonets to the ends of our rifles as we prepare to move out of our positions. The bayonets make a characteristic click as they are fixed. The order to advance is given and we are up and going forwards. Our artillery, combined with the machine gunners, covers our advance as best as they can. Even so, I see some men fall to our own fire. I cannot go to the aid of these fellow Germans, even though a voice within me is screaming to go and help them. We keep moving forward, as this is our only hope now. We reach some piles of rubble and exchange rifle fire with the enemy. When I look back at the route we have come across there are many bodies on the ground. Some are moving while others lie still. We are shouted at to keep firing and move forward as we do so. As we enter the town, I surprise a Frenchman. Of the two of us, I am the quicker and shoot him and watch as he slumps to the ground. We exchange more shots and are kept at bay for some time. To try and move out of here at this point would be suicide.

This is the point where Werner Kohlman's war ended. It is not known at what point in the attack it came, but Werner was caught with a group of his comrades in a shell blast. The shell was probably fired by a heavy Howitzer, as Werner recalled that he did not hear the 'whooshing' noise of an approaching shell. He believes the round that badly wounded him, and killed seven other Germans, came directly from above at a very steep angle. It may have been a trench mortar, but either way it remains a mystery. Werner recalled:

I heard not a thing. One moment, I was crouched down just moving forward through the remains of a large building, which had collapsed under the shelling, when there was this tremendous explosion. It blew my ears out, picked me up and threw me for several yards. I fell heavily to the ground with my ears ringing loudly. I lay still for some minutes with the ringing noise still in my ears. I tried to get up but couldn't. It felt as if my right leg was just not responding to what I wanted it to do. I sat up, propping myself against the remains of a wall. I looked down at my right leg; I could see a lot of blood yet felt no pain at that point. The first discomfort I felt was from my hip area. When I put my hand down there to feel what damage had been done, all I could feel was warm, wet flesh. I pulled my jacket up to see what had happened and I could see that shrapnel had sliced through my hip into the bone. I had a small cut just above my left eye but other than that nothing. I was soon taken from the scene where a medic looked at my wounded hip and began to make his assessment. The wound was cleaned, as it had bits of dirt and masonry embedded within it. It was later explained to me that the wound was going to need surgery as there had been some bone damage, and damage to the surrounding tissues. The wound was cleaned and packed as best as possible and I was evacuated to the rear. The journey starting on a stretcher, then an old lorry; it was not pleasant at all. I was sharing the back of the lorry with men who had legs and arms, or both, blown off. These poor souls were injected with morphine and were in a delirium, crying out randomly.

We eventually arrived at what was described as a hospital. One by one we were carried off the lorry into the building. It looked like an abandoned chateau that our Red Cross was using as a hospital. The nurses were among the first women I had seen since the whores who came around touting their services at what now seemed an age ago. They were a beautiful sight and I felt safe now. We were taken inside, our wounds were then assessed and cleaned again and the worst cases were dealt with first. Men went off to have surgery rapidly as the doctors and nurses worked non-stop to clear the queue of wounded. For the first time, I began to feel pain. The pain grew in intensity to the point where I had to cry out 'Nurse!' To my aid came this young dark-haired German girl. She checked and noted I had a slight fever and then proceeded to stick something sharp up my arse. She rolled me back over on to my back and gave me another injection into my arm. I don't recall much after that as I drifted into a hazy sleep. When I woke I was told I'd been put out for three days and that surgery had been carried out on my damaged hip. A doctor came and explained the damage was not as extensive as he had first feared. I would walk again, but not without the aid of a stick, probably for life. There may come a time when a further operation may be necessary, but this would be discussed once back home. As soon as home was mentioned I panicked that I would need to let Hilde know that I would be okay. I was assured that Hilde would be notified and not to worry about anything.

I remained at the chateau for two weeks before I could be transported back home to Hamburg. When I finally arrived back in the city, I was taken to the main hospital to undergo further assessment to my injury. Hilde was already waiting there for me and she was hysterical, but obviously happy I was alive. It took some time to calm her down before she could speak properly. She held my hands and just kept telling me, 'I'm so glad to have you back as so many have been killed.' It slowly dawned on me just how lucky I was to have survived. It appeared people back home knew more about the horrors of what was going on than we had thought. We only heard what we were supposed to hear. Back home the rumours of the mass casualties could not be quelled amongst the population. Public opinion in Germany was slowly turning against the war. I was still convinced we were right to go to war and that we would prevail. I knew that I would never be able to fight again and that my right leg was now partially crippled. I would always be a patriot, believing that Germany would conquer its enemies.

Of course, the reality was very different for Germany. With the entry of the United States into the First World War, a German surrender was more or less inevitable. Germany was just not strong enough to repel the combined military efforts of Britain, France and the USA. The First World War ended at 11 am on 11 November 1918. The total number of casualties is estimated to have been around thirty-eight million. For Germany, the loss of the First World War was a disaster in many ways. Many German soldiers returned home as angry, embittered and deeply disillusioned men. Even though they were back home with their families their problems were just beginning.

Chapter Three

Versailles - The Catalyst for Hate

Germany's participation in the First World War had proved an extremely costly endeavour, but her losses in men and material were just the tip of the iceberg. After the end of the war, a new democratic government was formed in Germany. This became known unofficially as the Weimar Republic, after the city of Weimar, where its first constitutional assembly took place, in February 1919, one month after the Paris Peace Conference had been convened to establish the terms of peace at the end of the war. This was followed, in June 1919, by the implementation of the infamous Treaty of Versailles, which was announced without the consultation of German politicians. The problems that were to haunt the Weimar Republic in the years following the First World War – hyperinflation combined with political extremism – meant the Weimar government was as loathed as the Treaty of Versailles itself. Many German people blamed the new democratic government rather than their wartime leaders for the country's defeat and the humiliating terms of the Treaty of Versailles. Despite the general opposition of German society at the time, the Weimar government successfully reformed the currency, unified tax policies and organized the railway system.

First World War veteran Theobald Ebner was typical of many of the German soldiers who returned home after defeat in 1918:

Our political leaders were reduced to the status of mice. They failed to challenge what many of us felt were extremely unfavourable terms for Germany and its people. They allowed Germany to be cowed by the victors without so much as an argument or dialogue. Those of us who returned home felt totally betrayed by these people who now represented us. From the minute that the Treaty of Versailles was signed, we as a nation were doomed. The greatest problem of all with Versailles was that it was beyond the capability of our generation to challenge or suppress. I had never cared for politics, but I understood the implications of us losing the First World War very clearly. I felt great fear for the future of Germany, for my family and myself. My family were far from wealthy. We could not just pack up and leave Germany like some of the rich families did. I felt it would have been far fairer had there been more negotiation on the terms of Versailles. Germany had been beaten, even though we as soldiers fought as hard as we could on the battlefields. We left thousands of our comrades behind lying in the mud of France and returned home to be governed as a defeated people who were, it seemed, going to be punished for this for what would seem an eternity. Did I feel personally that there would be another war? The answer is, yes I did and the cause would be Versailles. That Treaty, as it has since been proved, was instrumental in the events leading to the Second World War. That is a fact that cannot be denied. After 1918, there was no investment in Germany. Instead, political parties, especially the communists, set out to exploit German society. The Jews in Germany prospered and flourished. The path to resentment against the Jews and upper classes was not that rapid. It was just a question of time and I feared there would be a civil war in Germany. Most of us returned home to work in factories, shops, offices or farms. We were paid wages that soon amounted to nothing. Money became worthless in Germany. Whole families starved or died of the cold in the winter, unable to afford fuel to heat their homes. It was terrible in Germany after 1918. Many of us existed on stale bread and watery broth. Poor nutrition meant those who became sick often died. As a soldier who had fought, I was a patriot. I wanted vengeance upon the idiots who had allowed Germany to sink into this depression.

The seeds of vengeance Theobald Ebner had yearned for were planted during the years following the Treaty of Versailles, nourished by the suffering of the German people. The treaty requested that the new German Government surrender approximately ten per cent of its pre-war territory in Europe plus all of its overseas concerns. The German Army and Navy were also subject to strict limitations. Kaiser Wilhelm II, along with a number of other high ranking German officials, were to be indicted as war criminals. The Treaty of Versailles, combined with the 1921 London Schedule of Payments, required Germany to pay 132 billion gold marks in reparations. This figure was divided into three categories of bonds: A, B and C. Of the three categories, Germany was only obliged to contribute towards A and B; a figure totalling some 50 billion marks. The remaining C bonds were merely a deception fabricated to deceive the Anglo-French public into believing that Germany was being heavily fined and punished for the First World War. Such deception had not gone unnoticed by the French who, in 1923, occupied the Ruhr Valley, the industrial heartland of Germany, to enforce the policy of reparations. The arrival of French and Belgian soldiers in the Ruhr was not welcomed and the treatment of the German population during the occupation was particularly harsh. On 10 March 1923, a French army officer was assassinated and tensions in the region increased as a result. Many Germans reported that they had suffered beatings or other abuse from French soldiers in retaliation. On the day of the French officer's funeral, any German, regardless of their age, who did not remove their hat as the funeral procession passed through the streets, was beaten by French soldiers. German women were also jostled in the streets and subjected to abuse. The French soldiers were particularly fond of harassing young German women and sexual assaults, including rape, also took place under the French occupation. The Germans soon came to loathe the French, vowing that vengeance would be theirs someday.

The French occupation of the Ruhr caused an international crisis that resulted in the Dawes Plan of 1924. It suggested a new payment plan and the raising of international loans to help Germany meet her reparation commitments. It was hoped that implementation of the plan would end hyperinflation and restore some form of stability to the Weimar economy. Despite the good intentions of the Dawes Plan, by 1928 Germany was insisting on a new payment method. This resulted in the Young Plan; basically the second renegotiation of Germany's First

World War reparation payments. The Young Plan was chaired by a new committee under direction of the American Owen D. Young. It calculated German war reparation requirements at a figure of 112 billion marks. A payment schedule was set out and, if adhered to, Germany would have until 1988 to complete her payments.

Former German soldier Gunther Priestl wrote in his journal at the time:

> There are all these plans, yet none of them are working. It is only a matter of time before it all collapses and where will we be then? We are angry, as we have returned home to a Germany which does not feel like Germany anymore. Many are restless as they have no work, yet the rich seem to be doing very well out of all of this. Chaos is impending; many are concerned about this journey. The French are in the Ruhr Valley dictating to us, beating our people and even assaulting our women. We, who fought for our beloved Germany, are of the opinion that there are forces acting in this world who wish to ruin Germany. Many of us are becoming political, as we have no choice. Germany faces civil war as everyone is angry.

In 1931 the German economy collapsed, forcing all reparation payments to be suspended for one year. In 1932, during the Lausanne Conference, Germany's reparation payments were cancelled altogether. Upon examination of Germany's war reparation payments, we can see that between 1919 and 1932 Germany had contributed less than 21 billion marks. German society viewed the reparations as unjust and many other countries were of the view that the reparation figures were a deliberate attempt to destroy Germany's economy. However, many also believed at the time that the reparations Germany had been obliged to pay were not unduly severe. Germany could have met her obligations, had the political will been in place to do so. One British diplomat of the time remarked:

> Germany had to be punished for her actions. What were we, the victors, supposed to do? There was no alternative to a heavy financial penalty that might deter future German leaders

having any expansionist aspirations within Europe. German aggression in Europe had to be deterred. Yet, with hindsight, the financial penalties imposed upon Germany after 1918 very likely set the stage for a second war of even greater and far more disastrous proportions than the first. We should have insisted on having more control and influence over Germany's social and political infrastructure. Our lack of foresight was our grave folly.

Either way, the reparations imposed on Germany were viewed as a humiliation by politicians and society alike. Werner Kohlman wrote of the situation:

> I feel betrayed by our politicians. What kind of Germany have we now? We have become a grovelling pariah state crippled by years of conflict; a society as divided as ever. I am partially crippled due to the shrapnel injury, yet I have been trying to find work, as I need to help support my wife and myself. The wealthy have food, but we lower classes live like dogs. We are hungry, cold and thoroughly disillusioned with it all. I was a soldier and I went to fight a war for my country where many I knew did not return. It makes me feel sick that I fought for these wealthy parasites who have seemingly suffered little from the effects of war. My sister's children have no shoes on their feet when they visit us. They are cold, dirty and hungry; our home is a reek of sadness and vermin. If this is Germany's future, then we have no future. We can only pray for salvation or a miracle. Only time will tell if we are worthy of either of these.

The words of Werner Kohlman, spoken privately within the pages of his journal, serve as a stark warning of things to come. The implementation of infrastructural penalties placed upon Germany by her conquerors added further fuel to the growing resentment and hatred. After 1918 Germany's armed forces were limited to 100,000 men. Military conscription was outlawed, meaning that only volunteers could be accepted for military service. Germany was prohibited from manufacturing armoured vehicles, submarines or aircraft. The German navy was only permitted to build six battleships and these vessels were subject to specific weight restrictions. The Rhineland was declared a demilitarized zone where no armed forces were permitted to enter. German territories were also carved up: Alsace-Lorraine was returned to France; Eupen, Moresnet and Malmedy went to Belgium; North Schleswig went to Denmark; West Prussia and Posen went to Poland; Memel went to Lithuania; Danzig became a free city under the auspices of the League of Nations, giving Poland a seaport; and the Saar region came under the control of the League of Nations for fifteen years, after which time a vote would be held regarding its future status. German colonies were also subject to control under the League of Nations. Convened on 10 January 1920 in the wake of the Paris Peace Conference, the League of Nations was an intergovernmental organisation based in Geneva, Switzerland, whose principal mission was to provide resolutions for any international dispute and promote world peace through collective security and disarmament.

Despite its good intentions, however, the League of Nations was universally despised by the German people, who viewed it as an extension of the Treaty of Versailles. Class conflict soon began to spread in post-war Germany as resentment grew towards the wealthy shopkeepers and factory owners. Industrial action was taken and as factories closed men became unemployed. The transport infrastructure began to break down, leading to shortages of fuel, which in turn led to industrial production grinding to a halt. By November 1918 Germany's descent into political chaos, verging on anarchy, was being felt not only by those in power in Germany but around the world. The omens were not good, but the world failed to act. The November revolution was just one of many mass demonstrations arising from extreme social unrest and would result in the replacement of Germany's Imperial Government with that of the victorious Weimar Republic.

Kristien Traumann, who had served as a Staff Officer in the German Imperial Army during the First World War, recalled:

> I was never happy with that bastard that was the Weimar government. It was a weak government with only short-term

solutions to Germany's long-term problems. It did not reflect my views whatsoever. We needed change, but there was so much political and economic turmoil that change could not evolve in the way that it should. I came home to my family and was forced to beg for work to try and support them. Humans cannot live off bread, soup and a few rotten potatoes for long. The rich were throwing better food to their pigs and chickens. I was angry; in fact I was beside myself with anger. In the winter of 1920, I lost my youngest daughter. She became ill, but even the hospital could not reverse her illness. It was just a severe cold at first, but she died. Had we all had proper food we may have fared better. The situation made me very resentful of the rich in our society. Had I been able to, I think, I could have shot them all without remorse. I hated the French and a thirst for vengeance burned deep within me. I prayed for the day where I would see the French suffer and beg for food or a piece of coal like we are having to do.

Things were no better for Werner and Hilde Kohlman who were trying, with great difficulty, to return to relative normality. Hilde had been in the employment of the munitions effort throughout the First World War, but this was terminated with the cessation of hostilities. She would have to seek work again with her hated former employer as Werner could not work in the same capacity as he had before. Werner wrote:

Today I went back to where I worked on the railway to talk with the director. I told him I can still do my job, but he disagreed with me. 'How can you possibly do your job having to get around with a stick Werner?' I almost broke my stick when I hit the desk he was sitting behind. It was no use; all the begging in the world would have made no difference to this imbecile. Worse still, we will lose the cottage, as we can no longer live there if I do not work for the railway anymore. I am beyond anger, as I fought for this country and have been wounded. We lose the war and we lose everything. Well the working class and the poor do. The rich seem to be doing okay and this damn Versailles thing. I damn it to hell and I despise it. It will kill Germany to the point where the Communists will take power. Maybe that is what Britain and France wants? I don't know. Maybe it's what the world wants? I had to return home and break the bad news to Hilde about the cottage. She sat and wept at the kitchen table. Later on, we had to talk about what we were going to do. My father visited and I told him of these events and he was as disgusted as I was. He stormed down to the railway director's office and was gone for nearly an hour. When he came back he had a contract in his hands. It stated that, due to my honourable war service, we can reside at the cottage for a period of one year. This is a goodwill gesture, but I still have no work and will have to seek out a desk job or something. I don't want to be some bloody clerk sat at a desk in some stuffy office, I really don't.

Things became steadily worse for the Kohlmans. Hilde had to return to her former employers, the Boersch family, and beg for her job back. They agreed, but paid her less money than before. The Boerschs were a wealthy family yet complained that the political situation in Germany meant that they would have to be very careful with all financial outgoings. This did not prevent the family from continuing to eat well and dress in their finery. In fact, they seemed to do well despite the defeat of Germany in the war. Hilde described them as rude, selfish and unpleasant people. She hated the work, but, like many young women, was left with little option so long as Werner was unemployed. Only as joint earners could they work towards a better life. It seemed even hope was a commodity far beyond the reach of many Germans during this critical period in their country's history. A despairing teacher wrote of the problems faced by many Germans at the time:

Children come to school and they appear as vagrants. Their bodies dirty, clothes are dirty and in rags, they have no shoes on their feet and their heads are thick with lice. The winter has exacerbated the problems particularly with health. Small children would not attend due to sickness. You would not see them again, just hear the news that they had died.

Chapter Four

The Wrong Side of Nowhere

By 1923 the fortunes of the wealthy German families such as the Boerschs had begun to decline. Hilde Kohlman arrived early one morning at the Boerschs' house to carry out her housekeeping duties as normal and was alarmed to be greeted by the sight of packing cases stacked up in the hallway. The family had taken down all of their paintings and photographs, leaving the walls bare. Ornaments and china had also vanished from their usual places. Frau Boersch asked Hilde if she could talk with her for a few minutes on a matter of grave importance. Hilde followed her into the library, now totally devoid of the literary works which had previously adorned the many bookshelves. She asked Hilde to take a seat and then sat opposite her by the large ornate fireplace. Hilde recalled the conversation in her journal:

> Frau Boersch appeared slightly flustered, as if all of this was some huge inconvenience in her itinerary. She began by saying, 'Germany has changed, politics have changed and we as a family have decided to leave for Switzerland. Things are not good for us here anymore. I hope you will understand. I will write you references, but will have to hereby terminate your employment as of today. I will of course see that all of your financial settlements are met satisfactorily. I can only offer apologies.' The news came as a hammer blow to the young Hilde.

Werner had managed to secure work at a factory in Hamburg assembling door fittings. It was a job that he could sit down and do, where his disability would not be an issue. However, his wage was by no means adequate in the economic climate of the time. To make matters worse Hilde had been sick for several mornings in a row. Her concerned father took her to the doctor who, after a brief examination, declared that Hilde was pregnant. The news was not met with jubilation, as Hilde and Werner were struggling to buy basic foodstuffs on their meagre earnings without having a child to feed as well. Hilde broke down in her father's arms. He suggested they move in with him and her mother so that they could help with the baby and pool their resources to help get through these tough economic times. When Werner arrived home from work later that day, Hilde had to break the news that she was pregnant. Werner was elated. He hugged Hilde, kissing her several times in excitement. She said they needed to discuss how they were going to survive with a baby to care for and mentioned the offer of living with her parents. But Werner dismissed this idea out of hand, refusing to discuss it any further: 'I will have no wife or child of mine being brought up or financed by my in-laws. What kind of a man would I be if I allowed that to happen?' Werner assured Hilde they would be alright and that the in-laws were welcome to come to help Hilde if they wished. Hilde let it go, but brought it up again a few days later after a particularly hard day. Werner's reaction was far more aggressive on this occasion. He shouted, 'I will have none of this!' and slammed his fist hard upon the kitchen table. 'Now shut up! I will hear no more on this. Do you understand?'

Hilde had noticed that Werner was not the happy-go-lucky young man he once was. His experiences in the war, combined with his injury, had seemingly changed his attitude. He was angry and resentful of those who were better off than they were. He constantly argued that the Weimar government was treacherously incompetent, calling them, 'Dogs who were not fit to shit on German streets.' Werner had never sworn in Hilde's presence before and the steady deterioration in his behaviour concerned her greatly. She raised her concerns to Werner's mother, suggesting she try to persuade him to see a doctor. Werner's mother would hear none of it, saying, 'My son is not a mad man. He fought in a war. Is it no wonder he is angry and upset? You should concern yourself with your duty as my son's wife, not his doctor!' The only people Hilde could turn to in times of stress were her parents. They had begun to doubt the future of their daughter's marriage, but understood that divorce or even leaving Werner temporarily was out of the question. Women had little choice in those days but to carry on and earn what little money they could. Hilde took on two jobs: the first as a cook at a local school, the other as a laundry assistant. Neither was particularly helpful from a financial point of view. Hyperinflation had rendered the German currency worthless; in November 1923 a loaf of bread had risen in price to 200,000 million marks. Banknotes were best used for fuel for lighting fires in the harsh winters that followed.

By December of 1923 Hilde Kohlman had given birth to a baby boy. He was as healthy as could be expected under the circumstances, but weighed only 6lb and doctors doubted he would survive the winter. Werner decided that the boy be named Alexander. 'He will be a great man one day,' he declared to his in-laws after their first visit to their house to see their new grandchild. During that winter the couple slept in the tiny living room of their cottage with their new son as it was the only room with a fireplace. Werner would hobble around outside for hours looking for anything he could use for fuel to keep the fire going so his wife and child would stay warm. If Alexander caught a chill, there was every chance he would not survive. Hunger was also an ever-present misery as there was no welfare system for poor families. Such depravation drove some to commit suicide rather than slowly starving to death, and there were even cases of husbands killing their wives and children before taking their own lives.

For Hilde and Werner, the birth of their son provided some distraction from the problems that surrounded them and, with the help of their parents, they were able to get by. Werner's working day was long and monotonous, and the pay was very poor, but it was a means to an end. During their breaks at the factory, Werner and the other men would discuss politics. Then they started to meet after work to discuss politics while drinking cheap, locally distilled moonshine. This was made with anything that could be commandeered, traded or stolen. For example, a consignment of potatoes was stolen from a French barracks and then distributed amongst the families of several men. Some of the potatoes were used for food, but most went towards the making of strong liquor. Most of the resulting home brews were lethal to men whose stomachs had shrunk from lack of food. Werner was one of the men who began to drink very heavily. He would work a full day's shift at the factory then, rather than go straight home, began drinking with his work colleagues. He would arrive home hours later, barely able to even stand or talk. He would fall over and break things and often vomited on the floor. Hilde would follow him around, cursing him, not only for being late home and drunk, but also for neglecting his role as a father to their baby son.

As Werner's drinking habit worsened, he became violent. What started off as a few broken ornaments thrown against the wall in anger steadily progressed to the physical abuse of his young wife. Hilde wrote of her torment, 'I have never in my life ever been struck a blow by a man until this day. It hurt and it had left a mark on my face, the humiliation being worse than the blows. I have to carry on for all our sakes.' Hilde was not alone in her suffering, as other wives she spoke with were experiencing similar problems. In Hilde's case, the abrasion on her right cheek did not go unnoticed by her parents or in-laws. They questioned her as to how she got the mark on her face. Eventually she broke down and confided in her parents. Her father insisted she and the baby move in with them until Werner's drinking stopped. Only then would he be invited to join them. Hilde's father believed that with patience and family intervention the problem could be solved. He suspected that Werner's wartime experiences and resulting disability could have made him mentally unstable, though this was no excuse for striking his daughter. After some persuasion, Hilde agreed to her father's plan as a short-term solution. Besides, she had baby Alexander to think about; putting his safety first became Hilde's priority.

When Werner left for work one morning, Hilde packed some things for herself and her baby and left the railway cottage for her parent's home a short distance away. She left Werner a short note on the kitchen table. Hilde knew her husband would return home drunk and would probably be incapable of reading the note. Either way, it would come as a heavy blow to a man broken, not only by the years of war, but also social circumstances. Early the next morning, Werner arrived at Hilde's parents' home begging to see his wife. He appeared beside himself with grief at the prospect of losing Hilde and his baby son. Hilde's father shouted angrily at Werner, 'For God's sake, man, pull yourself together!' The two men exchanged angry words for some minutes until things calmed down. Hilde watched from the upstairs window as Werner wiped his eyes before being allowed into the house by her father, who called her down into the kitchen so they could sit down to discuss the situation. Werner asked of his son, to which Hilde's mother snapped, 'Your son is sleeping upstairs!' Hilde's parents were rightfully angry, but, after warning their troubled son-in-law of the consequences of not changing his ways, let their daughter and the baby return home with him.

For a time things seemed to improve. Werner stayed off the drink and even cut down on his cigarette habit. He would come straight home from his work at the factory after volunteering to work extra hours. 'Werner had friends living in the Ruhr who wrote him letters telling him they would often go out at night to steal coal, usually from the French forces garrisoned there'. Nobody asked any questions about where the coal came from; it had great value, becoming a form of currency on a thriving black-market. Coal could be either sold or traded for food and other goods, and soon became nicknamed 'Black Gold' by many Germans. A few lumps of coal could mean the difference between life and death. But stealing coal soon became a risky undertaking. After one coal merchant was beaten quite severely after disturbing intruders, new measures were introduced to deal with the problem. The coal yards were soon being patrolled by armed men who would shoot at anyone attempting to break in. Ironically, most of the men guarding the coal yards were paid with coal.

The years that followed were very hard for Werner and Hilde, but they, like many Germans, were united in their situation. They worked as hard as they could to provide for themselves and their baby son, and many families helped each other to survive during these hard times. By 1928 Werner and Hilde were celebrating Alexander's fifth birthday. Despite being a rather sickly infant, Alexander had survived the privations of his infancy. Werner and Hilde were now living at a different address, nearer to the little factory where Werner worked as a hinge fitter. Hilde also worked, as a cook at a local children's orphanage. This was also the year that the federal elections took place in Germany. The political chaos that had dogged the country since the end of the First World War was still very much in existence. There had been ripples of social discontent throughout the previous years and a new political force had been making its presence felt since February 1920, fuelled by the undercurrent of resentment. This fledgling political force became known as the NSDAP – National Socialist German Workers Party – or Nazi Party. Initially branded as a band of thugs, it would be some years before this fledgling political movement would gather sufficient support in Germany. In the meantime things only improved slowly for the likes of Hilde and Werner Kohlman.

The couple's move to a new address for a time seemed to breathe new life into Werner though there were still issues in their private life. Hilde confided to her sister that they had not made love for months. Hilde had tried everything to invigorate the couple's sex life, but to no avail. Hilde's sister suggested several things for her to try, but advised that if they failed she should get Werner to seek medical help. The next evening the couple retired to bed as normal. Hilde made a concerted effort to rouse her husband's passions, but was unsuccessful. As her sister had advised, she then performed oral sex upon the partially comatose Werner. This time she did get a response, but seconds later she was at the sink spitting out semen and gagging while she rinsed her mouth with water. The next morning Werner rose early, leaving the house before Hilde. He did not kiss his wife or tell her he loved her, as he always used to. Hilde was woken by the sound of the door closing as Werner headed off for work. She laid and cried in frustration and despair. Later that day Hilde finished her work at the orphanage and headed to her parents' house to collect Alexander.

Due to several pages missing from the Kohlman family journals it is not easy for Werner and Hilde's grandchildren to ascertain clearly what happened next. They had been told that Werner, for whatever reason, drank himself to death. His lifeless body was discovered beside a city canal next to an empty spirits bottle. A policeman arrived with the local Catholic priest to break the news to Hilde and her parents were summoned to support their heartbroken daughter. Hilde's mother tried to explain to Alexander that his father would not be coming home. When the child repeatedly asked, 'Where is daddy?' he was told that his father had simply been called to heaven. Werner had doted on his young son and Alexander's subsequent behaviour was understandable under the circumstances. He had begun to wet the bed, became difficult and rarely slept through the night. Hilde and Werner's parents both helped all they could so that Hilde could continue working to support herself and Alexander, but it was far from easy. Even with her job at the orphanage, she did not have enough money. Many of the young girls Hilde worked with were in the same situation. One girl confided that when she could not pay her bills, she would sell her body to make enough money. Hilde was horrified at such a proposal, but when the girl mentioned the kind of money she could make from what she described as 'fucking the rich Jews' it began to make sense why so many sold their bodies. Hilde dismissed the idea without further discussion. The other girls laughed at her in disgust and said to her, 'You have a child, you are on your own; how do you suppose you are going to survive?' Hilde ignored this comment, hiding her growing concern.

The family came together for Werner's funeral, which was a very basic affair with few formalities. In the months following Werner's death, Hilde tried to come to terms with the loss and supported Alexander as best as she could. She frequently broke down in tears at work, becoming so stressed that she had to be sent home. Hilde was a proud woman who did not wish her parents to have to support her and Alexander. Things were hard enough for the family as it was. Employment for women in Germany during the years of depression was never really a problem. There were more jobs for women than there were for men. Female labour was always cheaper and therefore a greater percentage of men were turned away from jobs than women. Things were still very difficult; wages were not nearly high enough to live on comfortably. It was a subsistence existence, yet the rich continued to prosper in Germany while the poor and working classes suffered most from the effects of the depression.

Hilde did the best she could to provide for herself and her young son. On weekends, she and Alexander would go to stay with her parents, who frequently asked her to live with them so that they could help more. Hilde was adamant she would be alright. Furthermore, she did not feel ready to leave what was, in effect, the last part of Werner she had left; the home that they had shared. On weekdays she would rise early, getting Alexander out of bed and ready to go to his grandparents while she went to work. Both sets of grandparents took it in turns to have Alexander who, despite the tragedy of losing his father, was now settling down at his first school. He was described as a likeable child who was bright and inquiring. It was only when Alexander reached the age of ten that his personality began to change, reflecting the circumstances that surrounded him. Hilde would insist he be in bed by 8 pm and he would argue that he was not a baby and wanted to stay up later.

There was good reason why Hilde wanted her young son in bed early during the week. Like so many young women finding themselves in difficult circumstances, and through sheer desperation, she had begun to sell her body for money and other goods. She despised herself for doing it, but had little choice in the end. Encouraged by the girls she worked with, she was introduced to a number of wealthy businessmen in Hamburg. Hilde hated each and every one of them, as she knew they were just exploiting her situation. Some of her clients were what she described as, 'Old, balding, fat men with foul, stinking beards, old enough to be my grandfather. Some were the opposite; just teenagers of the wealthy set. Either way, it was humiliating.' One thing all of her clients had in common was that they were all wealthy businessmen from the Hamburg Jewish community. They lived an opulent lifestyle and could afford the best food and wine. They enjoyed frequenting brothels, procuring young women to satisfy their needs, and they would pay good money. Often the girls they wanted most were barely out of their teens.

Hilde continued writing in her journal and said of one encounter, 'It hurt and it was rough. Afterwards, I felt I had been given a bouquet of thorns by this man. He put on his shiny, black leather shoes, silk shirt, and waistcoat with its gold watch. I felt physically sick. My son was just yards away, sleeping. No doubt he left me to return to his wife and family.' Unbeknown to Hilde, Alexander often lay awake in his bed at night. He heard his mother open the door to these strange men from the city. He also heard the strange noises coming from downstairs. The noises frightened him to the point that he dared not go to see what it was. He would often question his mother next morning, but would always be told, 'It's nothing for you to worry about. You should have been sleeping!' It was only a matter of time before Alexander would discover what was really happening. He crept downstairs one evening, several minutes after hearing the front door open. Following the source of the strange noises, he discovered his mother on the kitchen table with one of her clients. Both were startled at being discovered. The man quickly dressed, cursing as he left the house without paying.

It was also around this time that local children attempted to assert their dominance over Alexander at school. They taunted him regularly, calling him a 'bastard'. Alexander soon learned that to fight fire with fire was the only way to survive. He was a strong boy and recalled in his first fight with another boy, 'I threw the hardest punch I could and struck him flush on the jaw. He fell back onto the ground; blood seeped from his lips. He went home crying and complained to his mother and father that I had knocked out two of his teeth!' As a result of this incident, the boy's parents called at Hilde's house, threatening her with the police if it happened again. They also complained to the school. This did not deter Alexander. He became involved in more and more fights with the other boys, usually outside school. Most of the boys he fought were much older than he was, yet they always came off worse, with black eyes, split lips and bloody noses. Things came to a head when a boy at his school taunted him about his father's death. The boy goaded him, saying, 'Your father was a drunkard, a rascal!' Alexander felled the boy with his trademark left hook then dragged him into the toilets where he proceeded to force the boy's head into a lavatory bowl whilst pulling the chain. This incident caused even more trouble for Alexander. He was summoned to the headmaster's office and verbally scolded, then brought before the school to receive a thrashing. But when the headmaster tried to administer the punishment he ended up on the receiving end of Alexander's left hook.

The incident caused great distress amongst the family. Hilde and Werner's parents both spoke to the angry young lad to try to find what was bothering him. Even the local Burgermeister [mayor] was called in to talk to the boy. Alexander eventually confided in his grandparents that strange men were coming to the house and that he had seen his mother with one of them on top of her. The constant goading by other children about his dead father had also caused him to explode in rage. Having been raised in the squalor of the post-war years and losing his father at a young age, it is perhaps no surprise that Alexander's character became defined by his surroundings and upbringing, but his family were unaware of the poison fermenting within him.

With the cat out of the bag, Hilde had to explain her actions to her horrified family. Her mother wept, while her father said he would find the men who had been paying his daughter, give them a hiding and tell their families. This did not happen of course, but it was clear something had to be done. In the event, Hilde and Alexander went to live with her mother and father. Alexander's uncle Frank took charge of the boy, teaching him the rudiments of discipline and exercise. He taught the young Alexander that controlled violence was to be used only when absolutely necessary. He used to tell the boy, 'Don't you go looking for trouble. But should it come to you, let them have it!' They could often be seen in the backyard, sparring or doing press-ups. Uncle Frank became a kind of father figure to the young Alexander, who was now coming of age in an era where strength, not weakness, was seen as a prerequisite. It was the nucleus of a new German society, the leader of which would be a man named Adolf Hitler.

Chapter Five

Our Friend Hitler

The economic depression of 1929 was just one of the factors which facilitated Adolf Hitler's ascent to power in Germany. Hitler was well known to the German public prior to his political campaign of 1933. He was also well known to the authorities, who viewed him, along with the fledgling Nazi Party, as nothing more than thugs. In his youth, prior to the outbreak of the First World War, Hitler had spent most of his time idle. He had a passion for art and architecture, dreaming of becoming an artist. Many who knew him at this time described him as a highly-strung fantasist. Hitler was rejected by the Vienna Academy of Fine Arts in October of 1907, whereupon he returned home to his mother who was dying from breast cancer. Hitler's mother succumbed to the disease in 1908. There can be no doubt that his 'miserable time' in Vienna, coupled with the loss of his mother, was a contributing factor in shaping his character.

At the outbreak of the First World War, Hitler enlisted in the German Army and rose to the rank of corporal. His military service, albeit brief, undoubtedly restored much self-confidence in the young man. His bravery, combined with his devotion to duty, was reflected in the award of the Iron Cross 1st Class. His comrades in the trenches described him as a loner. He never joined them when they went off to court the favours of prostitutes while on leave. In fact, his only real companion was a dog that had deserted from the British lines. As the First World War came to an end, Hitler found himself recovering in hospital from the effects of a gas shell attack. When the news was broken to him that Germany had lost the war, he was beside himself with rage and grief. Similar to Werner Kohlman, Hitler felt the government had betrayed him and his comrades. After his release from hospital, he was employed by the German Army to investigate the many small political parties that had sprung up amidst the chaos at the end of the war. An attempted revolution by the Communists had been suppressed, but Germany was becoming a breeding ground of resentment. It was in this atmosphere of social and political unrest that Hitler grew as a political force. He was a skilled orator, and knew how to control the emotions of those who came to listen to him talk. He preyed upon the fears of his audiences and exploited their hatred of the Weimar government and Treaty of Versailles.

Munich was to become the spiritual home of the Nazis. It was in Munich, on 16 October 1919, that Hitler gave his first pre-arranged public speech. Hitler had joined the Deutsche Arbeiterpartei [German Workers Party] the previous month. Otto Rische lived in Munich with his wife and three children. He was another disgruntled soldier who had fought in the First World War and had witnessed the decline in Germany's fortunes in the preceding years:

> It was several friends of mine, who I had served with in the army, that persuaded me to go with them to listen to this new speaker. It was at the Hofbraukeller, a restaurant in Haidhausen owned by the Hofbrau brewery. I believe this was Hitler's first official public speech and there were a hundred or so people in attendance. When we arrived, we bought ourselves beer and settled down to listen to what the man had to say. My initial thoughts when I first saw Hitler was that he didn't look much. I was going to drink my glass of beer and go home, but my friends told me I must wait. I sat back down and as Hitler came in I waited to listen. There was some raucous applause and cheering from the crowd as he entered the room. When he began to talk, it was like being hit on the head. This unassuming man with his small, black, well-trimmed moustache instantly grabbed your attention. He was very outspoken about the Weimar government. In a most skilled rhetoric, he poured scorn on Weimar, the Treaty of Versailles and the Communists. Everything he said appealed to us, but here, in this place, were barely one hundred people. I can remember thinking to myself, what possible difference could he and this small workers party make in the current political

state? It was a whirlpool of clashing ideologies rather than one defined one. We were like sheep running in all directions from a wolf. I thought, what he was saying was right and he was certainly passionate about what he was saying. My friends just said we have to support Hitler, as the more of us who join him, the louder a voice and greater political influence we will have. I would say that's how many joined in the political group that would become the Nazi Party. Just a hundred or so people, but then the hundreds grew to thousands.

Otto Rische was just the kind of German that Hitler had hoped to influence. He had been a shopkeeper before going to war in 1914, after which his parents took over the business. After 1918, the business began to struggle in the poor economic climate. The Rische family had to adapt in order for their business to survive the depression that followed and Hitler seemed like a light at the end of a dark tunnel. He offered hope and promised prosperity for all Germans. Otto wrote of the situation, 'I hate nothing as much as I hate our government right at this moment!'

Another Munich resident, Albert Friest, who worked at a Munich bank, also succumbed to Hitler's charisma:

After Hitler had spoken, people were left almost star struck by the man. He was surrounded by his supporters, some of whom would become familiar faces in the future Third Reich. At these early meetings, it was quite easy to approach Hitler, shake his hand and congratulate him. Naturally, he wanted to court every piece of support from society as he could. He had a firm yet courteous nature, smiled and was happy to engage in conversation. Even in these early meetings, anti-Semitic language was prevalent. He had to find political scapegoats and Jews and Communists fitted this perfectly. He made no effort to hide his dislike of Jewry and Communists. I felt that this was a man that hated a lot of things about Germany at that time. He hated the fact we lost the war, he hated the fact that Jews had thrived and prospered over what he termed indigenous Germans and he hated seeing the German people suffering from the consequences of Versailles. Yes, I would say he was a man full of hatred, yet I had to admire his tenacity in getting up in public and speaking out for Germans and Germany. It's no surprise his popularity soared over the years. Once you heard him speak, that was it, you were captivated.

Ingrid Altmann worked as a secretary for a legal firm in Munich. She recalled accompanying her then boyfriend, Andreas Hoess, to hear Hitler speak, on 24 February 1920. This was one of his larger meetings, with around two thousand people in attendance. The venue was the Hofbrauhaus in Munich and this was also the date that the new National Socialist German Workers Party [NSDAP or Nazi Party] was officially founded. The Sturmabteilung, or SA, were there. These men were often referred to as Braunhemden, or 'Brownshirts', due to the colour of their uniform shirts. The SA became the paramilitary wing of the fledgling Nazi Party. Their role was to provide protection for Hitler, his staff and his supporters at the rallies. They were also employed to disrupt meetings of the opposing political parties. The SA soon became adept at using violence and intimidation, not just against political opponents, but also Germany's Jewish population. The SA would later be dissolved after a bloody purge that saw many of its founding members murdered or imprisoned during the 'Night of the Long Knives'. Ingrid wrote of the event on 24 February 1920:

> I was angry with Andreas. All men appear to have this political preoccupation. They read politics and discuss politics, even in the cinema. I would have rather been taken out to dinner than witness some war veteran tell us all the things we Germans already know. I could not have been more wrong. Contrary to being boring, this Adolf was quite some show! He whispered softly, like a man would do in his lover's ear, then he would explode into fury, deriding the old German attitude, cowardice and betrayal of 1918. Shaking his fist in the air he grasped his audience and held them all by the throat before calming down and letting them gather their breath. I was hypnotized by this man and somewhat intrigued. His enemies called him the

failed artist, the bastard, but he was actually very charming. Andreas had associates who were friends of this Adolf and they introduced us after his speech. As I explained, he came across as the perfect gentleman. He took my hand and bowed his head and kissed my knuckles. At the end of the evening, I removed the white gloves I was wearing and never washed or wore them again. Why I did that, I'm not sure. It was strange; this Adolf was not exactly an attractive man, yet I felt an attraction of sorts towards him, which was quite inexplicable. Andreas sensed this and I'm sure he was jealous. I was not the only woman to be granted an audience, but he made you feel like you were the only woman in the room. When he greeted you it was unconditional sincerity.

Ingrid Altmann would be among the first of thousands of German women and girls to fall under the Hitler spell. Not everyone was spellbound, however, as Melitta Jorg wrote in a letter to her friend in Norway:

There is a thuggish air about the National Socialists. Their leader is a man named Adolf Hitler. He is not a German but Austrian, yet he is telling us that my father's generation are traitors. He wants Germany to be great again and says he will rebuild her to her former glory. How will he accomplish this task? War? It makes me squirm when you see these high society darlings grovelling to him and how he stares them in the eyes. It would appear that he is making love to them with his eyes as he clasps their hands and kisses them graciously, as if a kind of statesman. The man is quite repulsive, supports racial theories, hates anything Jewish and incites violence in my opinion. My old friend Bernd loves the man and she goes to listen to him talk. She will have nothing said against the man. We argue, I say he is ugly inside and out and she protests to the contrary. Poor deluded darling, sigh!

Melitta Jorg, described by her great-granddaughter as a charming socialite, would later flee Germany after Hitler and the Nazis came to power. Her family was of Jewish ancestry and under no illusion as to what was going to happen to them. They packed up their belongings and left their home for France, only to move again as Hitler's army spread across Europe. Melitta and her family were among the lucky ones, finally arriving in England sometime in the late 1930s. The word 'war' in Melitta's letter was strangely prophetic.

Hitler continued to speak publicly and his efforts attracted much support, but the fledgling NSDAP had nowhere near the level of support required to have any serious political influence on German society at the time. Hitler must have grown frustrated as he was a man with huge political ambition. Matters came to a head on 8-9 November 1923, when the Nazi Party made its attempt to seize power in Munich. Before the putsch began, Hitler proclaimed, 'You can see what motivates us is neither self-conceit or self-interest, but only a burning desire to join the battle in this grave hour for our German fatherland. One last thing I can tell you. Either the German revolution begins tonight or we will all be dead by dawn.' The Nazis marched to the centre of Munich where they confronted the police. A pitched battle ensued and shots were fired. Sixteen Nazi Party members were subsequently killed, along with four police officers. Hitler himself was not wounded in any of the clashes. He had locked arms with Max Erwin Von Scheubner-Richter who was shot and fell dead to the pavement, dragging Hitler with him. The leader was spirited away, escaping immediate arrest.

Melitta Jorg was in America when she heard news of the Munich Putsch. She wrote to her friend in Norway:

> I see there have been deaths, yet the ringleader cordially referred to as 'our friend Hitler' has escaped death himself. Hopefully, he will languish in prison for a very long time and when he finally emerges from the gates, he will be a forgotten entity and drift quietly into obscurity. Let's hope common sense prevails within that blighted land. Its people are great, but they lack self-determination. The racists cannot be allowed to gain power. This would be Germany's ultimate failing.

Far from fading into obscurity, Hitler's failed attempt to seize power only served to elevate his profile. The story was emblazoned across the front pages of newspapers all over the world. Upon Hitler's arrest, a twenty-four day trial followed. Hitler dominated proceedings at his trial with his powerful personality and oratorical skills. He was unrepentant, reiterating his nationalist sentiments to his audience, and was found guilty of treason and sentenced to five years imprisonment at Landsberg Prison in Bavaria, in south-west Germany.

Hitler spent much of his time in prison talking politics to anyone who would listen, though those around him had little choice. When some inmates became annoyed at his constant rhetoric he decided to write it all down in a book, which would be titled *Mein Kampf* [My Struggle]. The writing of *Mein Kampf* kept Hitler focussed during his time in prison. It was an exploration of his political ideology, describing his path to anti-semitism and also encompassing his plans for Germany's future. Fellow prisoner and future Deputy Führer Rudolf Hess edited the book and it was published in 1925.

Hitler served only nine months of his five year sentence and was released from Landsberg Prison on 20 December 1924. He now understood that, instead of violence or force, he would have to adopt legitimate means in order to achieve power. Propaganda would become the favoured weapon of the Nazis during their gradual ascent to power. The Nazi Party became masters of propaganda and how it could be utilized to influence a society. In *Mein Kampf*, Hitler devoted a substantial portion of his writings to the subject. He wrote in one passage:

> One must find the appropriate psychological form that will arrest the attention and appeal to the hearts of the national masses. The broad masses of the people are not made up of diplomats or professors of public jurisprudence, nor simply of persons who are able to form reasoned judgement in given cases, but a vacillating crowd of human children who are constantly wavering between one idea and another. The great majority of a nation is so feminine in its character and outlook that its thought and conduct are ruled by sentiment rather than by sober reasoning. This sentiment, however, is not complex but simple and consistent. It is not highly differentiated, but has only the negative and positive notions of love and hatred, right and wrong, truth and falsehood.

From February 1925, the *Volkischer Beobachter* ['Peoples Observer'] newspaper was reinstituted and published by the Nazi Party. The publication had a circulation of 26,175 by 1929 and it was used to transmit some of the most virulently anti-Semitic material ever used by the Nazis. The hatred of Jewry featured prominently in many of its issues, but other racial groups in Germany would also come under attack. Melitta Jorg received a copy of *Mein Kampf* on her nineteenth birthday, in 1926, along with a copy of the *Volkischer Beobachter*. She had been sent these as a gift from a friend living in Germany. No offense had ever been intended, but Melitta sat down to pen a letter to her friend. Several drafts were thrown in the waste bin as she struggled to find the right words. As the chiming clock on the mantle in the library struck quarter past eleven in the evening she finally wrote:

> I am sending gratitude in much abundance for the birthday wishes and gifts. I have read the edition of *Mein Kampf*, absorbed much of the venom within its pages and I'm feeling rather sick now. Such a waste of trees and I confess to not be quivering about the knees with excitement upon what I have read. The text is written by the most cunning of monsters yet quite juvenile, vague and somewhat dull. It's his political perspective, it is not representative of the Germany I once knew and loved. I once sat by the stream in Gerda's [do you remember her?] garden; occasionally I saw fish in beautiful clear water. Will that same water one day run red with the blood of the very Germans who embraced this rubbish? I can see we are never going to agree, we are worshippers with polar faiths in one sense. The Beobachter is shocking, but only in the sense of those risqué Parisian gentlemen's shows that take place within dark basements in streets frequented by those of ill repute. I shall not retain it you understand? I hope you are keeping well and over your cold. Mit Liebe, Mel.

Melitta Jorg's friend back in Germany never wrote to her again. The birthday copy of Hitler's *Mein Kampf*, along with the issue of the *Volkischer Beobachter*, was consigned to the log fire in Melitta's father's library. It seemed that many of the friends she left behind in Germany were now avoiding contact with the Jorgs. Even Melitta's father and mother were receiving far fewer letters from people who were once good friends. Melitta's father did receive one letter that set the record straight: 'I am sorry, but myself and my family can no longer correspond or have any associations with Jews!' Germany was still eight years from the persecution of the Jews becoming Nazi policy, but even during these early years, racial prejudice was becoming commonplace. Violence against Jews did occur, but was usually perpetrated in private, out of sight of any witnesses.

The great-granddaughter of a Munich Jew named Albert Cohen recalled how her great-grandfather had been subjected to a brutal beating one night as he walked home along a dark city street:

He had just left the Rabbi's home and was walking what was a relatively short distance to his home. He was aware of footsteps behind him, but was unconcerned as he'd never had reason to fear any attack as he was a popular man within his community. From the sounds behind there were three or four individuals following him. They closed the distance rapidly and, without any warning or provocation, he was struck a blow on the head from behind. As he fell to the ground, he was set upon; one attacker sat on top of him, reigning blows on his face, while the others were kicking him from either side. They dragged him a few yards along the ground and removed his silver watch. They again kicked him and, satisfied they had inflicted enough injury, there they left him, covered in blood. The attackers ran off. All through the attack they never uttered a word. He was found some twenty minutes later and the alarm was raised. He was taken to hospital, where it was discovered he had two broken ribs, and cuts and bruises to his head and body. After this incident he was terrified to go out, even in daylight. He was also fearful for the safety of his family. In the event, he and his family moved in with relatives. The idea was safety in numbers and we started to go out as a group; never on our own. The attackers' identities were never ascertained and it remains a mystery to this day. My great-grandfather believed they were Nazi members who carried out the attack. As support for Hitler increased over the following years, Nazi thugs would come into our communities, usually at night, looking for Jews. If they found any, they were attacked and beaten up. They wanted us gone and this was one way to achieve that objective. A few months after the attack, we moved to the USA, as we had some family there and could support ourselves. Even in the USA, we felt like aliens on a separate planet, as if the whole world was turning against us. Maybe that was just paranoia, but that's how it felt. Germany was becoming a very dangerous place for Jews and their families.

Paulina Grier recalls her father talking of the situation in Germany in the years after Hitler's release from prison. Paulina explained:

My father became a 'Brownshirt' or 'Stormtrooper', as the SA were often known. He never made any attempt to hide his contempt for Jews. He openly talked about it in front of my three brothers and me. He would say to me, 'If I ever catch you talking to a Jew I will throw you out of this house!' He hated them and his explanations as to why were varied. I'd ask him 'why, father?' He would reply, 'Because they are to blame for us not having enough to eat, for controlling all of our finance and business and the influence they have upon these things. This Weimar government will fall one day, you will see.' I know very well from my earliest memories that my father would come home, men would call and they would be out until late. He would say he was on SA business or to discuss politics, but one morning I noticed my father had skinned knuckles, as if he had hit something or someone. When I asked how he had done it he laughed, saying something like, 'Well, if you see an old Jew without his teeth you will know!' To me, at the time, it was hard to understand. Did I sit and think about the rights and wrongs? Yes, of course I did. It did not make me feel good. In fact, I felt uneasy about it all, as many young children would. When you are young, violence is something difficult to understand. My father brought my three brothers up quite differently to me. Don't get me wrong, if they put a foot wrong as they say, he'd beat them savagely for it, usually with his leather belt. He talked to them about the National Socialists, made them read *Mein Kampf*, filling their bodies with hate. As a girl, things were a little different for me. I would be sent into the kitchen to help my mother and we generally stayed in the kitchen until our work was done. I still had to read *Mein Kampf*; once my brothers had read it, I was made to read it. Father would make us read out passages of the book from memory. If we couldn't do it, he would hit us. He was not a nice man in many ways, not like a good father is in today's society. When the Brownshirts were effectively demobilized there was a kind of change of allegiance. My father liked Rohm [Ernst Rohm, leader of the SA from 1930 to 1934] and when the SA leadership was purged and its ranks considerably reduced, my father was very angry about it. He couldn't believe Ernst Rohm had been executed under Hitler's direction. A smear campaign was launched and awful things were said of Rohm to justify his disposal. They said he was a homosexual with a thing for young boys. Was it true? I don't know. My father didn't agree with it, but he understood things were changing and he evolved with the changes. My father later remarked, 'Well, if Rohm had to die for the greater good of the German nation then so be it; it was God's will!'

When the Hitler Youth movement began, all the children of Germany were encouraged to join. It was not like you had to join early on, but if you did, it could prove favourable to you compared to those who did not or resisted joining. My father made my brothers join the Hitler Youth and I followed them some months after. He bought us all of our uniforms and encouraged us to do our utmost in all activities within the movement. Father became obsessed with Hitler. I'm not sure what mother really felt, as she never said much about it, she just went along with it all, as did many.

Father would come home drunk on many occasions after being present at Hitler's speeches. He and his friends would come in, falling through the door, onto the floor in a giggling heap. He would say to me, 'Come here my girl, where's a hug for your father?' Yet, when sober, he rarely expressed any emotion towards me. He would show me off to his friends, 'Look at my beautiful girl' he would say to them. He would make me sit on his lap and run his fingers through my hair and stroke my face. I felt like a prize horse or something and did not appreciate being pawed by all these drunken men. Mother did not intervene and she stayed out of the way. Even when I looked at her with eyes beckoning to get me away from this she didn't do anything. She was frightened, I guess; afraid of the man she was supposed to be in love with. I recall one evening father coming in pissed, as they say. He could barely stand and was being held up by these friends of his. It was the same routine: 'Come here my girl!' He would be patting his lap for me to sit on. I would sit on his lap and he would go through his routine again. Only this time, he kissed me on the lips and I recoiled from him. I think this embarrassed him as he pushed me down from his lap and told me to get out of the room and 'go to your mother!' Again, my mother saw this, but said, nor did, anything about it. Father and his friends would be in the next room with my brothers. They would be singing patriotic German songs and you would hear choruses of 'Sieg Heil'. It would go quiet for a moment as one of them struggled to open a bottle, then I'd hear my father announce a toast, 'To Germany, to us and to our friend Hitler!' My happiest moments were ones snatched with my friends. My one friend had a garden and in the summer we would sit out and play games at a table. Her parents were lovely and brought out tea and sweet pastries for us.

Chapter Six

The Swines Rejoice, 1934-1938

The rise of Hitler and the Nazi Party to absolute power in Germany is a well-documented subject and a detailed explanation here would be wholly unnecessary. In brief, the Nazis' ascent to power was a steady affair. Hitler proved a popular figure in German politics, as a former soldier and self-professed man of the people. His attributes as an orator and a politician was without equal at the time. By the end of July 1932, the Nazi Party had gained 13,745,000 votes [37.3% of the German electorate] and secured 230 out of 608 seats in the Reichstag. This meant that the Nazi Party was the largest single political party in the German Parliament and, as such, able to choose the President. This fact aside, there were still many complex events leading to Hitler becoming Chancellor on 30 January 1933. The conservatives, who had assisted Hitler's rise to political power, were convinced that they could control the Nazi Party. Hitler's critics had described him as a mediocre copy of Italy's ruling dictator, Benito Mussolini.

Clearly, the threat that Hitler posed was not taken seriously enough and the Nazis were able to manipulate their way to creating a dictatorship in Germany. After the death of President Paul Von Hindenberg, in August 1934, Hitler and his party acted quickly to consolidate their power. All political opposition was brutally suppressed, to the point that no one dared to vent their opposition to the Nazis, and all other political parties were outlawed. Gone were the days of rival political groups fighting and rioting on Germany's streets; the political discontent that had blighted German society during the previous decade appeared to vanish overnight. People's wellbeing soon depended upon their loyalty to the Nazis. You were either with the Nazi regime or you were against it; there was no middle ground in Hitler's 'new Germany' under the Third Reich.

The political events of 1934 came as a terrible shock to Melitta Jorg, who was holidaying in the USA when she learned the news that Hitler and the Nazi Party were now responsible for running Germany. She wrote in her journal:

> This day could not have begun in a more beautiful way. Everyone else was sleeping in and I was taking breakfast out on the veranda. The boy came and dropped down the usual bundle of daily newspapers and I was slightly reluctant to leave my toast, boiled egg and orange juice to go and fetch them. However, I felt a strange compulsion that morning to get off my backside! As I placed the newspapers on the table I almost spilled my orange juice over them, as I recoiled at the proclamation that Adolf Hitler was now ruler of Germany. Of course, there were rumblings of Hitler and the Nazis for some years, but I never believed the conservatives for one would allow this ogre and his thugs to seize power. From what I read, it was the acquisition of absolute power by default. Poor old Von Hindenberg, his death could not have had more serious consequences for Germany. How the Nazi swines must be rejoicing. This is a disaster, as the Nazis will soon show their true colours; they will emerge from the shadows of Hades with their racism and violence. Free speech and opposition will be destroyed by this monster. God, I felt so happy when I awoke to the dawn chorus and the warm sun beginning to rise over the hills. Now I feel sick and I thrust my half-eaten piece of toast in my orange juice in anger and disgust. I light a cigarette, then another, and then another after that. Mother joins me at the breakfast table. She can sense my anger and asks me what's wrong. I pass her the paper with the image of the ogre emblazoned upon its pages. As mother reads, I draw heavily on my cigarette and utter the words, 'Fucking Hitler!'

The ruling elite of the Nazi Party consisted of many of Adolf Hitler's friends and associates, either from the military or his earliest political activities. These friends and associates would soon become household names to millions around the world. They were gifted various offices within the Nazi government and it is clear that many of them were not up to the task. This would become quite obvious in later years, when each office began vying for the Führer's personal favour. Notable Nazis such as Martin Bormann, Rudolf Hess, Heinrich Himmler and Herman Goering were desperately seeking to please their master more than the others, and this would have a detrimental effect upon the Nazi war machine's ability in later years.

Of all the leading players within the Third Reich, perhaps the most colourful was Hermann Wilhelm Goering. Born 12 January 1893, in Rosenheim, Bavaria, Goering became a distinguished and highly decorated aviator during the First World War. This was no surprise to those who knew him well, as he was often described as an undisciplined and reckless individual, two attributes that successful fighter pilots often have. His childhood had often been described as lacking in parental love, but Goering found the rigid structure of military life easy to assimilate. Despite health issues, even in his youth, Goering was undeterred and became an airman in the German air corps in 1915. He had effectively deserted from the infantry unit he had been serving with from the outbreak of the First World War and was persuaded to join the air corps by none other than his friend, Bruno Loezer, who would go on to become a flying 'ace', with 41 'kills' to his name. Goering's first sortie in the air corps was as Loezer's observer and together both men distinguished themselves in the reconnaissance role. Goering himself went on to become an 'ace' fighter pilot, credited with 22 'kills' by the end of the First World War. Goering had met Adolf Hitler in the 1930s and the two appeared to have an immediate connection. The friendship with Hitler flourished and Goering became involved with the NSDAP more or less from its inception. When Hitler and the NSDAP came to absolute power in 1934, Goering rose to become the second most powerful man in the Third Reich. However, his early health issues left him with an addiction to morphine, something that would blight him for most of his life. He became indulgent and bloated, possessing an eccentric taste in clothes.

Paulina Rischner recalls the Hermann Goering of the early years:

My mother worked for the Goerings for a short period as one of the maids. My mother once took me along to his house, saying that this man was one of the most important people in our government and I might see him if I were lucky. I only went the once with my mother and recall her knocking on his study door. She had to always knock before entering to clean the room. If no one said to come in, she was told to not enter the room. On this occasion, a voice from within the room boomed, 'Come in!' My mother opened the large study door to a scene of opulence. I was momentarily taken aback by the drapes and the paintings, chandeliers and silverware that surrounded his huge desk. My mother asked if it was alright for me to stand by the door while she cleaned the room. He smiled and replied, 'No, no, please come in.' Goering was not wearing his uniform, but his dress sense was somewhat eccentric. He was wearing what I recall as being like something from medieval times. A white shirt with frilly sleeves or something it was. He had gold cufflinks on and was sat at his desk. He resembled a big toad. He stood up and came over to me, shook my hand and asked my name. He then asked me if I might like something sweet to eat, but I would need to ask my mother's approval first. My mother agreed and said, 'Of course, it is fine, sir.' Goering left the room for a couple of minutes before returning with a china plate of cakes. He asked me to sit down at a small table in his study and said, 'Help yourself.' While my mother cleaned, I sat and ate cakes in Goering's study. It is all so unreal when I reflect on it all now. He didn't come across as evil or anything and his manner was extremely courteous and pleasant. Everything he said was said with a huge smile and genuine affection. I ate several of the cakes and was only interrupted when my mother had finished cleaning his study. Even then, Goering insisted I take the cakes with me before we set off for home. He wrapped them in a bundle for me and patted me on the head and waved us off. I told father when we got home and he couldn't believe it. 'What, you had cakes from the great Goering in his personal study? You are one very lucky girl.'

I found it hard to associate that kindness with the horror and murder that was later revealed and that he without doubt had been party to.

Hermann Goering was complicit in many of the extreme policies of the Third Reich. He had been involved early on in the leadership of the Sturmabteilung, or SA and, although he denied being anti-Semitic, the evidence to the contrary is overwhelming. Goering would later become Commander-in-Chief of the German Luftwaffe [Air Force] and was instrumental in masterminding the German Blitzkrieg in Europe.

The persecution of Jews in Germany had begun to rear its ugly head in the years prior to the Nazis' seizure of power. Wealthy Jewish families, such as the one that Melitta Jorg belonged to, had sensed the impending danger lurking in German society and left the country in advance of Hitler gaining control. In January 1934 the German government banned Jews from membership of the German Labour Front. It was a move designed to deprive Jews of the opportunity to find positions within the private sector and of a number of employment benefits. These measures though were just the beginning. Hitler had far more sinister intentions towards the Jewish population of Germany.

The German economy began to recover steadily, but not at the rapid rate that is often claimed. After the First World War many countries experienced many of the same problems as Weimar Germany, such as high unemployment. The Nazis inherited these problems and came up with ways of resolving them. One method employed to combat high unemployment was to exclude women from as many employment opportunities as possible. Hitler insisted that a woman's place was in the home, not in the factory, office, school or any other work institution. This, of course, reduced the unemployment rate quite considerably, freeing up jobs for unemployed German males. Propaganda was devised to sweeten these measures, making the women feel they were performing a valuable service to their country. Compulsory military service was introduced for all young males. Anyone hoping to attend university was required to have completed some form of youth service or military training and anyone who refused could be denied access to university. Those young men entering compulsory military service were then removed from the employment statistics. Men were also forced into work on the autobahns as labourers, regardless of their skills or education. Any man who refused to do menial labour tasks could be accused of being 'work shy' and the contempt for these individuals was reflected in the severe punishments meted out. There are cases of men threatened with being sent to concentration camps along with their families. Such threats were usually enough to ensure compliance. The significant drop in the unemployment figures under the Nazis was heralded as an 'economic miracle'. By 1934 unemployment had fallen from 5.6 million to 2.7 million. No other European country could boast of such a recovery. To ordinary Germans, as well as the outside world, this reduction in unemployment did appear miraculous.

Ursula Metschuldt and her older brother Rudi were lower-class Berliners. Ursula recalls those early years of economic recovery in Germany:

> Our mother and father never had much anyway. Both fully approved of Hitler's policies, particularly his economic ones. Our mother had been working for as long as I can remember in jobs in shops and she was also an orderly at a local hospital. Hitler insisted all women should be at home where they could free up their occupations for the men who were out of work. Many men did not like the idea of having to do what they termed 'women's work', but it was policy at that time. I did hear of men arguing about this and they were told, 'You must do as the government says or you will be guilty of breaking the new laws.' I remember one man shouting at a Nazi Party official, 'What fucking law I am breaking, you tell me?' A swift blow to the jaw was all it took from the man, who, if I recall correctly, was one of the Brownshirts. It was usually their job to quell any signs of dissent in the community. The man who had been arguing just a minute ago was now on the floor holding his jaw, a trickle of blood oozed from the corner of his mouth. His papers were thrown down at him and again he was ordered, 'You will report to your place of work as instructed, if I have to come back, God help you!'

Rudi recalls with a smile:

Things did gradually improve for us. We started to eat a little
better than what we had under the Weimar regime. We had a
few more clothes, as personally, I felt Hitler was embarrassed
by the state many Germans were in. It was not the Germany
he had envisaged for his people. We were told this in school,
'Be patient and the Führer, Adolf Hitler, will provide for
his people!' There was a lot of propaganda aimed at us in
schooling at the time. Under the old Weimar government,
Jewish and German children went to school together. Once
the Nazis had established power and could make up their laws,
this soon stopped. Do you know, I was in class and it was one
Monday morning in 1934. We had this new teacher and a new
headmaster. He had decorated the walls with these big swastika
flags and three portraits of Adolf Hitler hung on the walls in
the classroom. As soon as we kids entered, we were told by the
new teacher, 'From this day on you will, whenever I enter this
room, raise your right arm and say "Heil Hitler!" At the end
of school, you will do the same before you leave the building.
If you do not, you will have this across your hides!' He then
waved this stick in front of our eyes. He was very strict and
militaristic and not one kid dared ever cross him. The one day,
he said that we must go home and learn our family history as
far as we could go back, so as we could talk about it in class
the next day. Most of us did this eagerly, as we all wanted to
keep in his good books as they say. The next day, most of us
were called up to talk about our parents, grandparents and
great-grandparents. Mine had fought in the First World War,
so I was congratulated and the class was ordered to give a
round of applause. However, one kid who was known to me
back then, began to explain his past and was stopped by the
teacher in mid-sentence. The teacher began asking questions
and it was soon revealed he had a Jewish background. It did
not really matter to me at that time; he was just a kid at our
school who we knew. The teacher began to ridicule the kid

with the words, 'Ah, so we have a Jew in our midst do we? Do you know the Jew is responsible for much of our ills? They infest, they invade, they take and they prosper.' He began to raise his voice as he spoke, 'We Germans cannot have Jews in our presence any longer. I will not tolerate the contamination of young German minds.' Then he shouted at the kid, 'Now get out, get out!' The kid got up and ran out and just as he reached the door the teacher grabbed him by the scruff of the neck and shouted, 'You will not leave this room until you have saluted the Führer!' He made the kid stand and say his 'Heil Hitler' before letting him run on through the door. The kid fled in tears and we did not see him at school again. We all sat there wondering what was going to happen next. He just calmly said, 'The new Germany is for Germans. You young people are its very lifeblood. We cannot allow the Jew to pollute what is our most precious resource, our beautiful, strong and devoted youth!' At that, class was dismissed for the day and we made our way home along the streets. As we walked, posters were being put up. I recall them being Hitler Youth adverts. It was not compulsory at that particular time, but they were always barking at you, 'You will soon be joining us, young man!'

Bella Schonn's father, Ernst, was an unemployed builder's labourer who was overjoyed with the prospect of working on the autobahns. Bella explains:

My father just wanted a job. He was well used to hard work and enjoyed working. When he went to work on the roads we were soon enjoying a better standard of living. After a few weeks, my father was even able to give me some pocket money. As you can guess, this money was spent on sweet treats. Sweet treats had been such a luxury before and being able to go and buy them was a quite wonderful feeling. I remember when father came home from his work; his hands would be raw sometimes from using a pick-axe all day long. My mother would tend his hands like a child's and rub ointments into them. We did feel things were finally getting better for us people in Germany. When we compared Weimar and Nazi Germany there was no comparison. The Nazis at the time were giving us a standard of living with dignity. I know they probably did this to gain more support from the ordinary Germans, but it worked. My father though, initially sceptical of Hitler, soon put aside the politics and just concentrated on his family and providing for us. That's all many Germans wanted; just to be able to enjoy a better standard of living and earn to be able to achieve these things. War was not in my father's blood at all and it annoys me when people have accused us of being a war-like race. Maybe we were all naïve and we should have thought about it more, but by the time many Germans realised the reality of what the Nazis' plans were it was too late. For the time being, it was sweet treats and even holidays for us. After a few months, we even had our first car. This was wonderful. We thought, we can go anywhere we want now.

Helga Bassler, who was interviewed during the writing of *Hitler's Girls – Doves Amongst Eagles*, recalls what some referred to at the time as the 'halcyon years' for German society:

Sundays, in particular, were always special days. When we were young our grandparents always came round to our house late afternoon on a Sunday. They would join us for tea and we would all sit around the table, as many British families would in England. The adults would discuss all kinds of things such as events going on locally and in Germany as a whole. We children would sit and eat our sandwiches and listen to them talk. Of course, much of the conversation during Hitler's early years was about Hitler. My mother and father were patriots, but my grandparents were more sceptical. They were the cursed old generation that Hitler was desperate to silence. My grandparents could see the wrongs, others couldn't. Grandfather would say, 'This business with Jews, this is not the path our country should be going up. This will all end in much trouble and bloodshed. Germany has barely survived World War One; Hitler is a warmonger, can't any of you see this?' My father would, of course, argue. He would not have any of it. Only the intervention of my grandmother would silence the two of them. She would say, 'For God's sake, the two of you; can't you ever talk about anything else?'

Father was the head of our house and whatever he said was right; this was something we had to obey. Father had close associations with some wealthy Nazis. I am not sure if they put pressure on him, as he joined the Nazi Party soon after they came into power. I do know that through the small business he used to run he made donations to Nazi Party funding. In exchange, he was granted certain favours and given certain immunities those that didn't join did not get. He was also a very keen sportsman and enjoyed hunting in particular. He was invited on hunting trips into the Black Forest and other places. I remember Hermann Goering was there once. Though I did not get to speak to him, my father certainly did. My father always took me on these trips with him. I'm not sure why really; maybe I was his favourite as he always gave me more attention than the others in my family. He used to call me his 'engel' [angel]. I liked going on the trips, as it made a change from home and the forests were so beautiful in the wintertime especially. The shooting party would stay in what looked like a castle. It was a 14th century grand home and typically gothic looking. Inside there were suits of armour, wall drapes, silver, paintings, swords and guns on the walls. Oh, it was beautiful. I was given my own chamber to sleep in and a servant to look after me. If I wanted anything, all I had to do was ring a bell.

It was on one hunting trip for wild *sau* [wild pig] that my father sighted one standing in a clearing. My father whispered in my ear, 'Here, you have a go. Take the shot.' As he took the weight of the rifle, I held the rifle into my shoulder, as explained to me and I peered through the telescope. I could see the animal quite clearly and could see its breath in the cold forest air. It didn't run and may have had young nearby.

I carefully aimed at the *sau*, placing the centre of the telescope cross between its neck and the top of its front leg. I gently squeezed the trigger. There was a bang followed by a hefty kick. Through the telescope I saw the animal drop and twitch a few times before lying quite still. My father cried out, 'Yes, *engel*! You did it, great shot!' He picked me off the ground and hugged me. The other men stood in disbelief, '*Mein gott!*' one said. We walked over the clearing where the animal lay dead on the ground. The men examined where the bullet had entered. It had passed right through the animal's heart; it was a perfect shot.

All of the meat was used and the animal heads often mounted for wall trophies. The tusks were also cut out and used for things. At the end of the shooting party, the meat would be evenly distributed amongst the party and we would return home with it. Nothing was wasted; it all went into the cooking pot. Some of it was dry cured and smoked while some was made into sausage. The meat was just beautiful. Those shooters who did not get a kill were somewhat disgruntled. There were rumours that Goering had sharp shooters dotted around the forests we shot in. They were to ensure that any animal he shot at was killed. Of course, this was ridiculous; Goering had been a World War One ace pilot. His marksmanship was without question. He often used a shotgun, which was not ideal for hunting *sau*, but it did the job I suppose. Most of the shooters used army rifles from the First World War or other types; some large-bore weapons. My father's gun was a First World War Mauser, 7.92-mm calibre. The bullet was high velocity and if you hit anything with it, it would most certainly kill it. My father used to say to me, 'If you can bring down wild *sau* you can bring down an enemy.'

In June 1934 Hitler sought to consolidate his power further. The Night of the Long Knives, sometimes referred to as the 'Rohm Putsch', brought about an end to the SA along with its leadership. The German public had expressed concern over the violent and brutal tactics employed by the SA; its usefulness long since exhausted in Hitler's eyes. Hitler was also concerned by leader Ernst Rohm's support and belief in a second revolution in Germany. Hitler and the Nazis viewed Rohm – who had been a long-time friend and supporter of Hitler – and the SA as a threat to their power. From 30 June to 2 July 1934 measures were taken to liquidate the leadership of the SA. A series of extrajudicial executions followed. Members of the SS and Gestapo arrested Ernst Rohm, along with Gregor Strasser – figurehead of the Strasserist left-wing faction of the Nazi Party – former Chancellor Kurt von Schleicher, and Bavarian politician Gustav Ritter von Kahr. Von Kahr had suppressed Hitler's attempted seizure of power in Munich in 1923 and had been an obvious target for some time. All were taken away and executed by firing squad. Rohm's last words as he was arrested and taken away were, 'My Führer. Nein, nein!' In all, some eighty-five people died during the purge although the final death toll was thought to have been much higher. It was a reflection of the fratricidal nature of Third Reich Germany. Rohm in particular was subject to many derogatory accusations. As the later affair with Rudolf Hess revealed, separating truth from fiction was impossible.

Melitta Jorg, now back from her vacation in the USA, wrote to an American friend:

> Sorry to have to bore you with yet more melancholic writings about the events taking place in once beautiful Germany. My love for that country just will not subside, nor will my fear for the good friends we left behind there. I see the Nazis have carried out a purge against those dreadful SA Brownshirts, as they used to call them. Their leader, Rohm, was apparently taken away squealing for mercy, 'My Führer, please! No, no!' Hitler's circle are merely cows and bulls, all ready to be slaughtered upon his request. Did they think this would happen to them? It is great here in London and I love the fellow socialites and the London culture. I am meeting with my aunt Heather and shall try to raise my spirits with a visit to the Savoy for high tea.

Paulina Grier, whose father was serving in the SA, remembers that her father had been caught up in the violence between 30 June and 2 July 1934:

The Hitler Bodyguard and Gestapo had arrested my father. The authorities came to visit our house. They carried out a brief search, asking me and my mother questions. We just wanted to know where father was and when he would be coming home. They just told us, 'He will be released if he is not guilty of any crime against the state. If he is, you may be visiting him in the cemetery!' He returned home after three days. He said they interrogated him for hour after hour. They had beaten him too, as his face was cut and bruised. I heard him tell mother, 'I don't understand this, I am a Nazi, a patriot.' He sat and brooded for a few weeks over what happened, but he understood what allegiance meant. He went out one morning to see about joining the Hitler Bodyguard, as the SS was then known.

By 1935 it was clear that Hitler had no intention of abiding by the terms of the Treaty of Versailles. He, along with many Germans, despised the treaty and blamed it for much of Germany's hardship. On 26 February 1935 Hitler summoned Hermann Goering to a meeting, during which Goering was ordered to establish the Luftwaffe, in defiance of the Treaty of Versailles. Goering set about his task with great enthusiasm. Prospective German pilots had been in training to fly aircraft in an offensive role for some years previous. This training was carried out in secrecy, first in the Soviet Union during the late 1920s, then in Germany itself, in the early 1930s, at the Zentrale der Verkehrs Fliegerschule [Central Commercial Pilots School] under the cover of the Deutscher Luftsportverband [German Air Sports Association], a clever deception to disguise Germany's real military intentions. In February 1935 the existence of the German Luftwaffe was revealed to the world with Reichsmarschall Hermann Goering as its Commander. The Luftwaffe was still a few years away from being the formidable force that it would become through the early years of the Second World War, but one could sense that a monster was awaking. Germany's intentions of rebuilding its war machine were exposed by Carl von Ossietzky in 1931. His revelations earned him the 1935 Nobel Peace Prize. Condemned by the Nazis, he was arrested and sentenced to 227 days imprisonment. His sentence was extended further, during which he suffered beatings and torture during his incarceration, until his death on 4 May 1938. Ossietzky's revelations regarding the Nazi rearmament programme forced Britain to consider its own rearmament options. Hitler had already withdrawn Germany from the League of Nations and the Geneva Disarmament Conference in 1933, and the signs should have been clear to the rest of the world. Britain, fearful of another outbreak of German aggression in Europe, had belatedly begun to prepare for war, but would she be ready to meet the threat posed by Nazi Germany if it came? Gertrud Klumm wrote in her diary at the time: 'Germany is being reborn thanks to Adolf Hitler and the glorious National Socialists. The announcement of our Luftwaffe should send a clear message, particularly to the French, that Germany is coming!' This was certainly a very prophetic statement of defiance, typical of many Germans at the time.

Melitta Jorg retained a close interest in the events taking place in Germany since she and her parents left the country. She recorded in her diary:

> It makes me sick! I am more German than Hitler as I was born a German in Germany; I was raised there until these thugs came into existence. So the new German air force has been revealed. It is no surprise to me and the next thing Hitler will be building ships, submarines, tanks and an army, if he hasn't done so already, under his blanket deception. How can such an intelligent world be so damn blind? I really fear for the safety of many of our family friends in Germany at this time. I feel an uneasy sense that time is running out for them. Mother, father, grandpapa; we have all told them to get out of Germany. They refuse to leave everything they have worked for behind. They want to defy Hitler, but doing so is dangerous, as we know. Being a Jew in Germany now is like being a mouse in the presence of a hungry cat. I wish they would get out, but they won't listen and it is possibly too late now. I am hearing all kinds of nasty things. I do not know how true they are, but knowing what the Nazis have done so far, I would not be surprised as to their authenticity. Damn Hitler; why couldn't someone just shoot him!

-7 By 1936 a beast was indeed stirring in Germany. Although the 1936 Winter Olympics, held in the Bavarian town of Garmisch-Partenkirchen, provided a brief distraction from the events in Germany, trouble was never far away. On 7 March 1936 German military forces entered the Rhineland. It was yet another violation of the Treaty of Versailles. It was the first time since the end of the First World War that German troops had been in this region. Far from expressing trepidation at their arrival, many locals greeted the German forces as liberators. This territorial move in the Rhineland would also prove a useful stepping-stone to Hitler's subsequent ambitions in the east. Hitler argued that he was left with little choice but to remilitarise the Rhineland in response to the Franco-Soviet pact of 1935. The former British Prime Minister, David Lloyd George, stated in the House of Commons that Hitler's actions were entirely justified; that he would have been a traitor to Germany had he not moved to protect his country. When German forces marched into Cologne, vast cheering crowds threw flowers at the soldiers while Catholic priests offered blessings. In Germany, the news was greeted with great excitement; celebrations broke out all over the country. The German people felt that they were fulfilling a destiny, thus reaffirming Hitler's god-like status.

1937 was, in many ways, a pivotal year for Germany. There were of course some events that Germany would rather forget such as the *Hindenburg* airship disaster, which occurred on 6 May at Lakehurst, New Jersey. The *Hindenburg* passenger airship exploded into flames, killing 13 passengers, 22 crew and 1 member of the ground crew. Historians have argued as to the cause of the explosion ever since. Various theories, including sabotage, have all been explored, but it remains a mystery to this day. Melitta Jorg marvelled at her morning newspaper the day after the tragedy. She felt compelled to write in her diary, 'Well, a lot is happening. Hitler's army has entered the Rhineland much to the rapture of its people. The Government in England do not seem worried, in fact the Prime Minister thinks it was actually a good move on Hitler's part. What of this *Hindenburg* business? Seriously, the thought of some flying craft displaying Swastikas landing in the USA! Divine retribution is what it seems and what will Mr Hitler and his Nazi Party make of this disaster? I do feel for the poor souls on board and that unfortunate member of the ground crew who was not quick enough to avoid it as it crashed down upon him. This *Hindenburg* incident is surely an omen and it does not fare well for Germany.'

In July 1936 civil war broke out in Spain. The Condor Legion, under the command of Hugo Sperrle, was formed to provide military assistance to the Spanish Nationalist forces under General Francisco Franco. Aside from helping Franco's Nationalists defeat the Russian-backed Republican side, the Spanish Civil War was used by the German forces to develop their own military tactics that would later prove useful when the Second World War broke out. The German air force used 'terror bombing' for the first time, on 26 April 1937, when it destroyed the Basque town of Guernica, which was being used as a communications centre behind the frontline. The attack on Guernica caused great controversy as it involved the bombing of civilians, resulting in the killing of 1,654 people. Though the Luftwaffe leadership had rejected the concept of terror bombing against civilians during the interwar period, their experiences in Spain led them to utilise it as a means of breaking the will of the people and, by doing so, aiding the collapse of the enemy. Either way, the Luftwaffe and army gained valuable combat experience from the Spanish Civil War and this would serve the German military machine well in the initial stages of the Second World War. The Blitzkrieg principle of an air force working closely with the army on the ground proved devastatingly effective in Poland and France. Soon names such as Adolf Galland, Werner Molders, Hajo Hermann and Hannes Trautloft would become household names known throughout Germany and the rest of the world.

German involvement came as no surprise to Melitta Jorg, as she wrote to a friend:

> Hitler's Nazis, well there they go again. Spain it is now, helping the fascists there. The world needs to understand that they need to act now to stop Hitler. Surely, somebody could assassinate him. Would such an undertaking be plausible and if so, what form of power vacuum would be created by it? I don't know; all I do is watch, listen and despair at the news. If the world were to act now maybe a disaster of far greater

proportions than World War One could be avoided. The world, it seems, is a complacent creature slumbering away in its individual prosperity. I would imagine many Germans feel the same; only they have a sense of empowerment now. Unemployment has fallen, living standards have risen and the people are much happier now than they were years ago. This all has a price, though Hitler's aggression, if it continues, will bring about a catastrophe. You can't tell any Nazi German this, as they will refuse to listen. Before we left Germany I did make a remark to an NSDAP supporter about the future of Germany. He bluntly told me to, 'Fuck off!' What a charming fellow eh, oh well. Your love always, Mel.

The Condor Legion, having sharpened its claws in Spain helping Franco's fascists secure victory, returned to Germany to a rapturous welcome. Hitler was overjoyed with the victory in Spain. He knew that General Franco could not have secured such a victory without German military assistance. German society was relatively relaxed during this time. Many Germans now had jobs and life was steadily improving. Hatred towards Jews, however, had been on the increase since Hitler came to power. For Jewish families still living in Germany, life had become increasingly difficult due to anti-Jewish legislation. The Nazis exploited the fears of the German people to the point where Jews could be randomly attacked in the streets. Jewish homes and businesses became the targets for arson attacks. The Nazi authorities turned a blind eye to the violence. In fact, violence against Jews was openly encouraged.

Hitler's next move was to provoke the destabilisation of neighbouring Austria as part of his plan to reunite his native homeland with Germany. This resulted in the Anschluss [union] of Austria and Germany. Hitler now had designs on the Sudetenland, a region of ethnic Germans that had, under the terms of the Treaty of Versailles, been given to Czechoslovakia. Hitler's expansionist ambitions triggered a crisis in the Sudetenland. Lengthy political discussions between the British Prime Minister Chamberlain, France and the Nazi government followed. With no Czech representatives involved in the talks their fate was effectively sealed and German forces were able to march into the Sudetenland without having to fire a shot. By the end of September it appeared to Germans, and the outside world, that Hitler was an unstoppable force, capable of achieving anything he set his mind to.

The true nightmare of National Socialism became apparent on 9 and 10 November 1938, in what became known as Kristallnacht ['Night of Broken Glass']. Mobs in Germany rose up in an orgy of violence and destruction against Jews all over the country. It was a sickening spectacle as Jewish-owned shops, buildings, homes, schools, synagogues and even Jewish hospitals were attacked. Windows were smashed, littering the streets with broken glass [hence the name]. Many murders were committed during this period. Some estimates put the figure at ninety-one, but a more recent analysis by German scholars puts the figure much higher. The mobs attacked the buildings with sledgehammers and over 1,000 synagogues were burned [ninety-five in Vienna alone]. Some 7,000 Jewish businesses were either destroyed or damaged, and many Jews were dragged out into the street and beaten, sometimes in front of their families. These events sent shockwaves around the world. Many foreign journalists had witnessed the events of Kristallnacht. *The Times* wrote: 'No foreign propagandist bent upon blackening Germany before the world could outdo the tale of burnings and beatings, of blackguardly assaults on defenceless and innocent people which disgraced that country yesterday.'

For Dorothea Hirsch the events of Kristallnacht are cruelly etched into her memory as her mother and father were almost beaten to death by a mob. She recalls:

> They only spared me a beating probably because I was a very young child of just five years old, but these mobs came. They were like hunting dogs on the scent of their prey. They smashed in windows of all the houses and on our street doors were kicked down. The mobs then entered the homes and attacked the people inside, stealing anything they wanted before destroying everything else. I heard the noise outside of many people out in the street, but at the time I thought nothing of it. When I heard the crash of breaking glass, I knew something was very wrong. My parents were in the process of trying to run upstairs to me when men broke in and began hitting them

with sticks or batons or something, I don't know. They were screaming and pleading for them to take everything, but leave us alone and not to hurt us. They kept beating my parents, who fell to the floor. I began to scream and cry, but they looked at me with wild eyes filled with hate and said nothing. When they left, we remained in the house in darkness for some time. Then another mob came in and bundled us all out onto the street. From there, we were taken away and asked questions. My parents were accused of anti-Nazi activities although they had not been involved in any political opposition to the Nazis. The charges were invented as were many; yes we were Jews, but we were German Jews. After a few days, we were on our way to the concentration camp known as Dachau. We knew nothing much about this place until we arrived. Any Jews left behind would soon be rounded up to follow. You could not escape; we were terrified by the sights and sounds upon arrival at that place. We knew it would take all our strength, faith and courage to survive this place. My mother would later die in that hellhole. My parents gave me any scraps of food they had and they went without so that maybe I would survive. I did survive, along with my father, but what a price we paid.

The evil that many had feared would result from Adolf Hitler's Nazi Party was finally being displayed to the world. Still, the world held its breath; still the world did nothing. Melitta Jorg wrote in her diary, on a page clearly stained with her own tears:

'Peace for our time' was a declaration made by British Prime Minister Neville Chamberlain, in his speech concerning the Munich Agreement. As good as Chamberlain's intentions may have been at that time, his naivety all these years later is somewhat embarrassing. The fact that Chamberlain chose the path of appeasement with Hitler merely exaggerated his weaknesses in the eyes of the Nazis.

When Chamberlain left to return home, happy that he had secured terms for a lasting peace between Britain and Germany, the sneers began. Many of Hitler's inner circle made no secret of their contempt for a man they described as weak and who would sacrifice other nations to achieve his political goals. Foreign Minister Joachim von Ribbentrop remarked to one of his secretaries in the days after the Munich conference, 'He came along quietly, like a lamb. He left the same lamb, but one marked for slaughter!' A German journalist who witnessed many of the proceedings during the Munich Agreement wrote:

> Mr Chamberlain is the quintessential Englishman. He is smart, well educated and well spoken. He greets everyone warmly with a friendly handshake, however, he is a politician and this is how politicians are. Some can be bought cheaply; others cannot. He came across as desperate for peace at any price. He came to the Germans, shaking in his smart leather shoes. This did not go unnoticed by the Führer. In this sense, I do not think his people will be entirely happy. I know the English well and I know they are harder people than this. I feel Munich will end the English Prime Minister's career!

The inexorable journey towards another war with Germany could count the Munich Agreement as one of its main staging posts. Theobald Ebner, a German First World War veteran, went out with friends to celebrate after news of the Munich agreement broke. The friends drank beer and began to sing patriotic songs they had learned as soldiers in the kaiser's army. Theobald was out late that night and had to be helped back home by friends. His son, who wrote about these times in a scrap book which still exists today, wrote:

> Father is pissed. Yes, he is very pissed, but he is happy and he will sleep tight knowing that the honour of himself and his comrades, many of whom were lost in World War One, is slowly being restored. Munich shows that England has no desire to cause trouble with Germany. This is good news. Father has just vomited all over the floor, mother is clearing up and shouting at my brothers, 'You little swines, this is no laughing matter!'

The Christmas of 1938 was possibly the best yet for many Germans. The people had more this year due to the country's war economy. Like it or not, the Nazis had begun to make substantial improvements to the lives of the German people. Ingrid Altmann, now a single woman again, wrote:

> We are looking so forward to being with grandma and grandpapa this Christmas. We will all be eating well this year, including the little ones. My nieces have chocolate SS soldiers, tin tanks and fighter planes. I will bake them biscuits in the shapes of birds, deer, boar and swastikas. How the little ones love this time. I am sad for Andreas, but I am so not ready for marriage or babies at this time. I had to tell him things must stop there. There are things I would like to do first before becoming a housewife. He did not take it very well. In fact, he got up and threw a drink in my face. What a pig!

With the introduction of the WHW, or *Winterhilfswerk des Deutchen Volkes* [Winter Relief of the German People], even the poorest of German society could be assured they would be looked after. The WHW was an annual drive organised by the National Socialist People's Welfare Organization to help finance charitable work. With the slogan, 'None Shall Starve or Freeze', the scheme was originally created by Heinrich Bruning in 1931, though Hitler would later claim credit. The WHW scheme ran from October to March every year, from 1933 to 1945. The objective of the scheme was to provide food, clothing, coal and other daily essential items to less fortunate Germans during the hardest months of the year. Bella Schonn recalls:

> We needed all the help we could get when father could not work. In winter, when things were bad, any building work would stop, sometimes for weeks if it snowed or the ice was very bad. The WHW was a wonderful charity scheme designed to ensure no one went without in Germany and no one died from the cold. They gave us food, soap, clothing and coal for our fire. We could all eat enough, had a warm home

and some decent clothes for when we had to go out to school. The winters were pretty hard back then, they could be very, very cold indeed. The importance of having social welfare like that was immense. It saved many from death. The only people excluded from the WHW were Jews. I can remember that quite clearly.

Chapter Seven

1939 - When the Devil Whispered

In 1939 war broke out in Europe and, once again, German aggression would be responsible. This move towards war was Hitler's greatest folly. Although Germany had built up one of the most formidable fighting machines the world had yet seen, she was still not prepared for a war that would very soon be fought on two fronts. By the end of the conflict, countless lives would have been needlessly sacrificed and millions more murdered. By May 1945 Germany would also have suffered what was, in effect, a reciprocal genocide perpetrated by her enemies from the east. She would pay a heavy price for her initial early successes and her attempt to rid Europe of the racial elements considered undesirable in Nazi Germany.

By 1939 Alexander Kohlmann was a sixteen-year-old who, like his mentor, Uncle Frank, was an avid follower of the Nazi regime. Alexander had joined the Hitler Youth for boys some years previously, against his mother's wishes. Under his Uncle Frank's direction, Alexander, or Zander as he was known to his friends, had become more than capable of looking after himself. His mother, Hilde, sometimes despaired at her brother's methods with her son. Hilde was not happy about Frank's involvement in the Nazi Party or introducing her son to Nazi politics. Hilde felt that Hitler would only bring trouble. Whether she was right or wrong mattered little to the young, impressionable Alexander. He, like his Uncle Frank, began to despise the Jewry in their midst, blaming them, as did others, for the problems Germany had endured over the past years. The Hitler Youth fuelled the anger that raged within Alexander and he absorbed their teachings like a sponge in water. He even had a large poster of Adolf Hitler in military uniform on his bedroom wall and would salute it every evening before bed and first thing every morning. Alexander's school life in Hamburg after the death of his father had been mixed.

The other boys teased him about his father's death and he often got into fights. But this did not deter the young Alexander, who was determined to become a soldier in the German Army. He was a dedicated student in class and could recite large excerpts from Hitler's *Mein Kampf.*

Hilde could do little about her son's views other than try to persuade him to get a normal job, find a girl and settle down. Alexander wanted none of this and the more Hilde tried to persuade him, the more he argued with her. Things came to a head one weekend. Hilde and her brother, Frank, had a blazing row and she told him to stay away from her son. When Alexander learned of this he demanded to know why. Hilde did her best to calm him down and explain her fears, but Alexander would have none of it. He threw a cup against the wall in anger, the shattering porcelain flying in all directions. Hilde threw her arms across her face to avoid the splinters. They shouted at one another for a while and Hilde tried to reason with her son, saying she had done her best for him as a child. What really hurt her was what Alexander said next, 'You used to use Jews for money didn't you? Why can't you admit it? When I used to lie awake all those years back after father died, did you think I did not know? You were letting those filthy Jews use you. Why did you do that, why?' Hilde, by this time, was in tears. Alexander grabbed his jacket, storming out of the front door. Hilde let him go. She knew it was hopeless chasing after him while he was in such a temper. She started to care less about Alexander after that, believing that her brother, Frank, had influenced her son beyond the point of redemption.

Women in Germany at this time were slowly being repressed within society. Hitler had his own plans for German women; plans which did not feature the workplace, politics or education. Hitler wanted the women of Nazi society to remain ignorant of everything bar the menial tasks of home life, cooking, cleaning and child bearing. Hilde was painfully aware of this, but as a woman of an older generation, she was seen as a threat to the new German social order. After the altercation with his mother, Alexander walked the short distance to his uncle's home. Hilde knew he would have gone there and was not too concerned when he did not return home by suppertime. She slept fitfully that night, tormented not only by her past but also the deteriorating relationship with her son. She woke much earlier than usual the next morning and was sitting at her kitchen table when there was a knock at the door. She opened the door to a stern-looking gentleman in a black leather coat. She noticed the Nazi Party armband on his left arm. 'I need to discuss something with you, if you will permit me to come in,' said the man. Hilde let him in and he went on, 'There is a problem with your son, you understand. It has been brought to our attention that you argued last evening and that he felt compelled to leave his home to spend the evening elsewhere.' Hilde interrupted him, 'It was fine. Alexander is at his uncle's home and will be home shortly if you need to speak with him.' The man replied, 'It is not your son I am here to talk with, it is you. It has been brought to my attention that you have expressed certain regrets at our government and its leader, Herr Adolf Hitler.' Hilde was slightly alarmed and explained that she and her son just had an argument and that it would soon blow over. The man retorted, 'You must understand that we cannot tolerate those who do not share those views of our government, our leader and that of the German Reich. There are certain policies implemented that, if not adhered to, have severe consequences. Now, am I making myself clear?' Hilde asked the man if he was threatening her, to which he replied, 'If you have nothing to feel threatened about, then you have nothing to be concerned about, do you? We know your history, Fraulein Kohlman. We know your husband was a hero of the First World War and that he fought honourably for Germany. All I am saying is just behave yourself, do your duty as instructed by our Führer and we will all prosper, and you shall not have me visit you again.' Hilde sat and nodded her head in compliance. The man then walked out, giving a Heil Hitler salute before closing the door behind him. It did not take long for Hilde to register that her son or maybe even her brother had reported her to the local Nazi Party authorities for non-conformism. When Alexander did return home later that day he and Hilde spoke little. They stared at each other across the kitchen table. Hilde asked her son if he was alright and he would nod in acknowledgement whilst eating a sandwich. Afterwards he told her he was going to bed. He did kiss his mother on the cheek, wishing her a goodnight before disappearing into his room, which was nothing more than a partition in the living room with a heavy woollen blanket acting as a wall. Hilde was perplexed by her son's behaviour, but had decided to let him go his own way regarding his political beliefs and his desire to become a soldier.

Hitler's desire for conquest was great. He would have taken his people to war sooner had the opportunity arisen and as 1939 progressed so Germany edged towards war. As the Nazi generals plotted the world appeared oblivious to the danger. This war would be far worse than any other in our relatively short human history. Plans to invade Poland were being finalised and a great terror would soon be unleashed upon Europe. Oberleutnant Heinz Mollenbrock, a young Luftwaffe bomber pilot, remarked during an interview at the German Military Cemetery at Cannock, in England, 'We were well prepared for the operations against Poland. We knew the Poles would offer heavy resistance and cause us casualties, but we were under no illusions whatsoever that we would be victorious. We had all resources in place and were put on readiness for the attack. It was just a case of us being told when to go.'

The attack came on 1 September 1939. Poland had little chance of preventing Germany and its ally Russia from invading her territory. The Polish air force was equipped with obsolete aircraft such as the PZL P.11 which was outperformed by the Messerschmitt Bf109 and Bf110 fighters of the German Luftwaffe. Despite their antiquated PZL fighters, Polish fighter pilots shot down at least 110 German fighter and bomber aircraft during the invasion. The Russian invasion of Polish territory did not commence until 17 September, by which time the Molotov-Tojo agreement, which effectively ended hostilities between Russia and Japan, had been signed. The German invasion of Poland came from the north, south and west in a well-coordinated attack. The Wehrmacht made rapid progress as the Luftwaffe spearheaded the assault. Junkers Ju87, or Stuka, dive-bombers were in the air constantly, working in combination with the German ground forces.

Stuka pilot Karl Voght was one of the pilots involved in the initial assault:

> I had flown the Stuka in training flying many times. We practiced the famous dive, but this time we were flying in operations; this was for real not practice. What was the Stuka like to fly in war? Everyone wants to know that question. The Stuka was a big aeroplane considering it had only one engine. It was big and heavy and not a fast aeroplane at all. We had

total air superiority over the Polish battlefront so we had no concerns other than the threat from possible anti-aircraft weapons. We were shown our targets on a map, we conferred, made a few notes and then off we went to do our job. I recall my first attack on a troop concentration. I peeled off as the lead aircraft and, from the corner of my eyes, I could see the other Stukas following me down. I pushed the aeroplane into a vertical dive and opened the throttle full. The sound of the wind around the aeroplane was very loud and you could see the wings almost flex under the pressure of the airflow going over them. Inside the cockpit, we [me and the rear gunner] could not hear the scream of the sirens that made the Stuka so feared. Those you were attacking on the ground would hear them very loud and clear. The Ju87 required a cool nerve and a lot of faith; you were hurtling earthwards toward a speck on the ground, which quickly began to fill your windscreen. I operated the bomb lever and the bomb, a 500lb explosive, was slung forward on a rack then, at the right moment, I would release the bomb which would follow the aeroplane's trajectory in a perfect line. The automatic dive brakes would deploy and pull the aeroplane out of its dive. This, as I say, would be automatic, so even if you blacked out and were unconscious the aeroplane would take care of itself in a sense. It was frightening for the first few missions, but afterwards you got better and more relaxed. We were in action constantly as a spearhead for our tanks, soldiers and artillery. We attacked and they all followed behind us. It was all about speed and hitting the enemy so hard he could not fight back. In Poland, we had every confidence of a quick victory. There was no question about that at all.

The Poles fought fanatically against the German invaders, but resistance was hopeless. With the Russians also involved, the Polish forces were faced with an enemy on two fronts and a war they were unable to sustain. Wehrmacht veteran Karl Heinz Lutz wrote in his unpublished memoir on Poland:

To be honest, Poland for me was of no concern. I viewed France as our real enemy. It was the French who I most wanted to get to grips with. I wanted to test their mettle and their stomach for a fight with us now. Poland served as an experience in my view. I didn't have any problem with the Poles; those Polish soldiers fought as hard as lions. They fought with a ferocity that told us, 'You won't take us easily or even alive.' No, I had utmost respect for the Poles and really felt for them. We had smashed their country and I felt a sense of guilt having to march through it. I often gave people some of my rations. I gave my sweets to the kids there. I just wanted to fight the French; I was desperate to do that. Many of us felt the same; we wanted revenge for Versailles and all of the shit they did to us afterwards. Hate the French you ask me? Oh yes, I hated them. [He asks me to excuse him.] I fucking hated them.

While Poland fell victim to the German Blitzkrieg, in Britain, Prime Minister Chamberlain went on air to make his announcement to the British people. Chamberlain had warned Germany that an attack on Poland would invite a state of war between Britain and Germany. The nightmare many had feared had now become a reality. On 3 September Prime Minister Chamberlain broke the news to the British people in a lengthy speech. On summing up that a state of war now existed between Britain and Germany, he added, 'Now may God bless you all. May He defend the right. It is the evil things that we shall be fighting against – brute force, bad faith, injustice, oppression and persecution – and against them, I am certain that right will prevail.' France also declared war on Germany. One peculiarity of the declaration of war against Germany was that Britain and France had not declared war against Russia for their part in the invasion. Rightly, the Poles felt betrayed. Even by the end of the Second World War Poland would still be effectively occupied by Russia.

As the German Blitzkrieg advanced into Poland, hundreds of thousands of Jewish and non-Jewish refugees fled the devastation, heading east. Their reasoning was that they had hoped that the Polish army would halt the German advance in the west. Many of the refugees had no idea where they were going. Men, women, children and the elderly travelled on foot, bicycles, carts, trucks or any mode of transport they could find. They took only the possessions that they could carry with them. They left their homes and most of their things behind them. Many would never see home again. The exodus of refugees soon began to clog the roads to the east. Many of these wretched souls were ill-prepared for the journey they were undertaking.

Natasha Kizl, now a frail old lady well into her nineties, recalled the journey:

It was a journey from a hell into what became another hell. We fled from the guns and the Stukas, which had levelled our towns and cities to rubble. We were terrified of the Germans, fearful that, if caught by them, we would be executed or put into the camps we had heard rumours about. We trudged miserably east to a backdrop of the sounds of war behind us. We walked all day long and when it got dark we slept in ditches by the roadside. I saw many corpses on the way east. These were the bodies of old people mainly. They were people who were just too weak or ill to go on such a journey. These people fell down, died and they were left where they fell. Birds would sometimes be pecking at the corpses. The birds took the soft bits first, bits like the eyes. As we walked past, I would strain my neck to look, but my parents would pull me away. I was young and curious, but confused at what was happening and where we were going. One morning, at first light, I heard an aircraft above in the sky. I stood up and looked and could see it was a German aircraft. At first, it just did a few circuits and appeared to be looking at us. It did this a few times then came around again, heading vertically towards us level with the road. Flashes came from its nose, followed by the rattle of guns. The German plane was firing at us. Everyone threw themselves down. Parents threw themselves down on top of their children. Sadly, for some, this proved useless and after the German plane flew off there were the bodies of whole families on that road lying dead. I remember the dark red blood on the muddy road. Some of the people died with their

eyes and mouths wide open, as if they had been letting out
a final scream before death claimed them. We continued the
journey east and soon we encountered Russian fighter planes.
These Russian planes came down very low over us, but did not
machine gun us. The nightmare for us was not over by a very
long way. The first soldiers we encountered were Russians.
They told us if we were Jews then we were not welcome and we
would be sent to labour camps to work either for the Germans
or Russians themselves. We thought to ourselves, when will
the world come to our rescue? Will Britain and France come
and save us? My parents just said to me we have to be prepared
for what will be the worst hardships we have ever faced. Father
said that this was just the beginning, but, with HaShem's
blessing, we might just survive. HaShem was the way many
Jews traditionally referred to God. My father did not hide the
fact that our situation was serious. I was frightened, yes, I was
very frightened. I was frightened of the unknown of what was
coming, things we did not know.

The fears this frail old lady spoke of were rightly justified. Jews were not
welcome in Russia; many Russians despised them as passionately as the
Germans. Some areas of Polish society fared better than others under
German occupation. Mirka Lamorska Yarnold, a Polish national with
proud Kashubian ancestry, recalled of her family's time under the Third
Reich, 'We were treated as Third Reich citizens and could not speak any
language other than German. The whole administration consisted of
Germans. The Kashubian people were more or less forced to fight for
Germany against their will.'

The terror that the Nazis inflicted on the Polish people was on an
unparalleled scale. In Pomerania mass executions were a daily occurrence.
Polish intelligence operatives were sought out by the Nazis, as well as
political activists, clergy and those considered of higher education.
Perhaps one of the most disturbing periods of the Nazi occupation
of Poland occurred between October 1939 and January 1940. The
Volksdeutscher Selbstschutz [Self-defence Force] was a paramilitary force
active in Central and Eastern Europe. It consisted of ethnic Germans

who had been living in the eastern territories during and after the First World War. They remained after the First World War as a form of protectorate for the local ethnic German communities and to indirectly serve German security interests. Approximately 100,000 *Volksdeutscher Selbstschutz* were actively fighting the Poles as a fifth column during the German invasion of Poland. They also served as auxiliary elements to the Gestapo, SS and SD during the early phase of the German occupation of Poland. They were responsible for organising locations for the massacres of interned Poles. Many of their victims were, however, executed on the spot; shot once their work had been carried out. One victim recalled of one massacre:

> People who were shot were often finished off with a blow from a shovel or the butt of a rifle. Some were still alive though as they were being buried. Mothers were forced to lie their children down in pits where they were all shot together. In many cases, the girls and women were raped on the ground before their execution. In fact, these beasts were so sadistic that even the Germans were shocked at their deeds.

One German soldier was so horrified that he felt compelled to write a report about it. This report refers to an action that took place in the town of Swiecie. The report submitted by the German soldier still exists today and is held in the German Federal Archives. The *Volksdeutscher Selbstschutz* was actively involved in the persecution and mass executions of Poles and Jews. It is believed that the organisation was responsible for the deaths of 10,000 men, women and children. This may seem a relatively small number when compared to other Nazi atrocities, but considering they were active for a relatively short period of time and disbanded by the winter of 1939-1940, this figure is shocking and it is likely that they were responsible for even more murders than those recorded. Many of these men became active within the ranks of the *Einsatzgruppen* [Task Force], which was responsible for the murder of thousands of innocent people in the east. Many of the *Volksdeutscher Selbstschutz* members would transfer to the SS or Gestapo by the spring of the following year and thus continue to visit murder and mayhem upon the Polish population.

Many of the ordinary Wehrmacht [German Army] soldiers were horrified by the work of the *Einsatzgruppen* in the east. One young army corporal witnessed first-hand the work of these so-called 'Task Forces':

We approached what had been a small village in Poland. We were told that the 'Task Force' had been through and sorted it out. As we approached, the first thing I remember seeing were rats that had been feeding on the corpses scatter in all directions. The smell was revolting and you had to cover your nose and mouth; it was that bad. I cannot even begin to describe what it was like. It was a pitiful sight, the small bodies of dead children who had been shot. Most had been shot in the back or the back of their heads multiple times. As a soldier, I could examine a body and know what kind of weapon had been used too. These people had been killed by sub-machine guns and at close range. They had been left where they had fallen and left for the rats to feed on. Many of the homes had been looted and then burned. What did I think to myself on seeing this? I thought to myself, 'This isn't war, is it?' What these bastards have done is something we are all going to have to pay for. It was murder, pure and simple. I noticed one of our men just stood with his hands on his hips surveying the scene. He just said, 'Oh, fucking hell!' He was looking down at the bodies and shaking his head in disbelief. Some are so sickened by the sights and smells they vomit onto the ground. All around, you hear men vomiting and the wet splashing sound of vomit hitting the dry earth. As we move off, I notice another rat scurrying across the dirt track before us. The thing drops something on the ground. As I get closer, I stop to see what it is. I realize that it is the finger of a small child. It was very delicate and must have been from the body of a female child. This place was a vision of hell itself. 'Is this what our war is all about?' I thought. I just had an uneasy feeling about all of this. Where was it all going? I knew that God would not be on our side from that day onwards. We had entered into a pact with the devil. In that village, on that day, the devil whispered.

Many of those who served in the *Einsatzgruppen* units in the east during the Second World War are still alive today. What are their opinions of their actions today? Do they suffer remorse or regret for their actions? Horst Vitalowski was part-German part-Polish by birth. A National Socialist, he joined the Task Forces in the east, as his knowledge of where Jews and suspected dissidents were living was second to none. I learned about Horst from his son who was happy to talk about his father's past, 'If there is anything you want to know, you can ask my father yourself, just call him on the telephone.' I made a phone call and the old man on the other end recalled his service in Poland. 'I was not with the Task Forces, as they were known, for very long. I knew where all the Jews lived in my locality and I knew where the traitors lived also. I was able to direct our mission effectively to where it was needed. For me, there was never any disparity between the races of Jews, blacks, gypsies and traitors. To me they were all the same and I hated them all equally.' The voice on the end of the phone was obviously that of a very elderly German male, but it had a sense of menace about it. I had never experienced this before in any of my contributor interviews. It was a voice devoid of regret or conscience at taking part in the killing of innocent people. Their only crime had been a religious or cultural difference that was contrary to that which he had believed in. Even his son remarked, 'When dad dies it will be a good day as he was not a good man to us, my mother or anyone really.'

Stanislaw Maksymowicz was a truly remarkable, brave and resilient Polish soldier. He was born on 14 January 1914. As a young man, he had been active against the Russians in the Polish-Soviet war of 1920. His daughter, Mariska Dickinson, explains:

> The earliest stories I recall my father telling me was when he was a boy. A priest had instructed him to take potatoes to the Russian soldiers. Before he took the potatoes to the Russians, explosives were placed inside of them. When the Russians placed them in their fires to bake them they would obviously explode, killing and wounding the Russians. It is difficult to think that at such an early age he was involved in sabotage. He told us many terrible stories of things that had happened. He could barely bring himself to talk about the things he saw.

More often than not, he just described them as 'terrible things'. When the Germans invaded Poland in 1939, Stanislaw was serving as a Corporal with the Polish 25th Infantry Division. The 25th Infantry Division, though heavily depleted by the time they reached Warsaw, fought valiantly in the defence of the city. Stanislaw was taken prisoner of war shortly afterwards. He was stripped of his decorations by his captors and transported to a prisoner of war camp in Weikendork, Austria, until 1944. It was in 1944 that Stanislaw made a daring escape attempt. Through sheer determination and some assistance from the local resistance fighters at various stages, Stanislaw finally made it to England. The exact date of his arrival is not known. What is even more remarkable about Stanislaw is that he survived the Katyn Massacre. The massacre was perpetrated by the Soviet secret police [NKVD, or Peoples Commissariat for Internal Affairs]. Though the killings took place at several different locations, the massacre is named after the Katyn Forest, where some of the mass graves were first discovered. The number of victims attributed to the Katyn Massacre is 22,000. Victims included Polish military officers, intelligence agents, gendarmes, landowners, saboteurs, factory owners, lawyers, officials and priests. The killings were sanctioned by NKVD chief Lavrentiy Beria, and approved by the Communist Party, including Soviet dictator Josef Stalin himself. Stanislaw managed to escape the massacre, but was left with nightmare visions, which would stay with him all his life. He recalled, 'Women and girls were savagely raped before they were shot dead. I also remember seeing a huge pile of shoes, obviously from the victims of the massacre. Even after the war, it was considered unsafe to return to Poland. Returning home to Poland after the war was out of the question. Being under Soviet control, if you did go back you, risked being arrested by the Soviet authorities who would execute you. In fact, many only returned in 1995 when the last of the Russian military left Poland.'

It is often an overlooked factor that the Soviets were equally complicit in committing acts of genocide in Poland during their early alliance with the Germans. It is a sad chapter in Polish history and Poland would indeed become a country synonymous with the word suffering. Not only was Poland left devastated by the German and Soviet invasion, she would also soon become the foundation of some of the worst of the Nazi concentration camps. These camps would soon become household names to locals and to the outside world. Nazi death camps such as Auschwitz-Birkenau, Chelmno, Majdanek, Sobibor and Treblinka would symbolise everything about Nazi terror in Europe. For Poland, the nightmare had just begun. Her occupation would be a lengthy one. Many Polish nationals were able to escape the Germans and flee to Britain. Many of these Polish nationals joined British military units, including the RAF, where they fought with great bravery and distinction, but it would be some years before they could take their revenge on the Germans on their own soil. Poland was in a sense the birthplace of the Nazi genocide. The fighting and resulting mass murder that would later emerge from the war in the east would be on a scale hitherto unseen in the civilized world. Even at the end of the Second World War in Europe, Poland's fight against occupation and oppression would not be at an end. She was, it seemed, a country that would be fighting for its own survival for as long as it continued to exist.

Chapter Eight

Blitzkrieg on France

In response to the Nazi aggression in Europe, the BEF [British Expeditionary Force] had begun its formation back in 1938, in readiness for a possible war with Germany. The French and British governments had pledged to defend Poland following Germany's invasion and, with the expiry of the ultimatum on 3 September 1939, they declared war on Germany. The BEF began its move to France in September 1939. The British forces assembled along the French-Belgian border as part of the French *1er groupe d'armees* [French 1st Army Group]. This was the period that became known as the 'Phoney War'. The reason for this was that most of the BEF were initially engaged in the digging of field defences on the French–Belgian border. Many British soldiers were lulled into a false sense of security that war might not happen after all. Sergeant Francis Child of the Royal Artillery recalled:

> We actually became quite bored and spent much time checking our equipment and making sure the guns were kept clean and things. If we weren't doing that, we were digging bloody holes and trenches. You can only do that sort of thing for so long, then you start to get very bored. We didn't even see any Luftwaffe aircraft at first and yes, it all seemed very phoney indeed. Of course, when the Germans did attack we bloody well knew about it. The speed with which they moved at was startling and the dive-bombers were merciless.

The German invasion of France began on 10 May 1940. Blitzkrieg tactics, which had proved deadly in Poland, were employed against the British and French. The Luftwaffe would attack, followed by German armour and infantry, all working as a single cohesive weapon. It was devastatingly effective in these early European campaigns. The German attack came as a shock, as Sergeant Child recalls:

The German artillery was very good, I had to give them that. They put heavy, accurate and consistent fire down on us. Casualties soon began to mount and wounded men had to be evacuated away from the battlefront. You saw their injuries, some with legs or arms missing or some without a mark on them. You just prayed you wouldn't end up as one of them. All the time, the Luftwaffe attacked. The lads would say, 'Where's the fucking RAF; why the hell are they not here shooting these bastards down?' Many of us began to feel we had been abandoned to our fate. We did see the odd RAF Hurricane or Spitfire, but most of the aircraft in the sky above had black crosses with swastikas on them. They certainly weren't fucking ours! Those Stukas were the worst of all. They resembled vultures those things did. They would show up and circle over you, weighing things up and then all of a sudden, they would be diving right above you. They used to make this screaming sound as they dived into attack. I was told specially fitted sirens in the wings made the screaming noises. Why would anyone want to fit such things to an aircraft? The Stukas sent men into blind panic, as there was nowhere to take cover from them, as we began to retreat towards the town of Dunkirk. The Stukas often machine gunned you if you were caught out in the open and when they flew past their rear gunner would also take a squirt at you. If you were lucky you didn't get hit. It was all about luck really. We got into Dunkirk and it was a case of, 'Right, what the fucking hell are we going to do now? Are we going to swim home?' The Germans were advancing and there we were, stuck on a beach like sitting ducks while the Stukas picked us off. It was an absolute miracle that all those little boats and ships back home came out to get us. Every conceivable size of ship and boat came out to us. There was a lot of panic at times, as everyone wanted to get on a boat back to Blighty. I swore if I made it alive off that beach and got back home I'd never complain about the English weather ever again. We were in long queues and waded out almost shoulder deep to the boats as they came in. The water was freezing cold and took your breath away. You could do nothing but stand in the water and wait your turn, shivering your arse off. We watched as the Stukas attacked nearby shipping. Some were near misses; others direct hits. It was a horrible sight. We were picked up by a big vessel and had to climb a scramble net up the side of the ship to get on board. As soon as we were aboard, we were wrapped in blankets and given hot cups of tea. That tea never tasted so good and as we pulled off I felt a huge sense of relief. The thing was, I knew that Blighty would cop it next. The Germans would come across the Channel and invade in massive numbers. And then what? It was a terrifying time for us all back then.

It was during the BEF's retreat through the Pas de Calais region of France, during the Battle of Dunkirk, that British forces would experience first-hand the brutality of the Nazis. On 27 May 1940 soldiers of the 2nd Battalion, Royal Norfolk Regiment, had become isolated from the rest of their regiment. They found themselves trying to defend a farmhouse in the village of Le Paradis from the crack Waffen SS Totenkopf [Death's Head] Division. The British soldiers put up a spirited fight, but were hopelessly outnumbered, outgunned and soon out of ammunition. Their only option was to surrender to the superior German forces. The SS soldiers ordered the British out of the farmhouse. They came out in a line with their hands raised in the air. What happened next must have been simply terrifying for the British Prisoners of War. They were led across the road to a wall where the SS soldiers cut them down with machine guns. Of the ninety-nine British soldiers who came out of the farmhouse to surrender, ninety-seven were killed. Both of the survivors were injured, but managed to hide until being discovered and captured several days later by regular German soldiers who were sickened at the sight of so many dead prisoners.

The Waffen SS [Waffen means 'weapon' in German] became synonymous with Nazi terror during the Second World War. Their unquestioning loyalty to the Führer, combined with their obedience and dedication to their duties, made them the most feared combat soldiers of the war. Having started out as Hitler's bodyguards, they were soon drafted into a combat role, though this was not without its problems. In Poland, for example, the regular army felt that the SS performed poorly. The SS soldiers took far too many unnecessary risks and suffered a higher casualty rate compared to the regular German army, or *Heer* as it was known. SS Officers also came in for criticism; many *Heer* officers felt the SS officers were unsuitable for combat command positions. As the war progressed, so did the efficiency of the Waffen SS. By the end of the war, not all Waffen SS units would be guilty of committing war crimes, though units such as the SS Leibstandarte Adolf Hitler, SS Totenkopf Division and the 12th SS Panzer Division Hitler Jugend [The Hitler Youth Division] would end the war with the blood of thousands on their hands.

Gefreiter Karl Lutz had relished the chance to fight the French in battle. He had already earned the award of the Iron Cross 2nd Class for bravery in action in Poland and was now eager to join the battle against the French. He finally got his chance in the fighting on the Maginot Line. The Maginot Line was a series of fixed concrete fortifications, obstacles and weapons installations that had been built by the French in the 1930s, specifically to deter the threat of invasion from Germany, but it was an outdated and ill-considered idea. Rather than engaging this line of defence directly, the Germans simply went around it. The German invasion forces punched a hole through the Low Countries, bypassing the Maginot Line. Another factor that the French had not given serious consideration to was a German advance through the 'impervious' Ardennes Forest. Given the difficult terrain of the Ardennes, the French did not suspect that their German invaders would attack from the north and so German forces were able to effectively split the French and British defensive fronts. The British were forced to retreat and the subsequent Dunkirk Evacuation, or 'Operation Dynamo', saved much of the British Expeditionary Force. A few French units escaped with the British, but most were abandoned to their fate. *Gefreiter* Karl Lutz wrote:

> The French did not have the stomach for the fight. It was good getting to grips with them. It was a case of firing shots; getting

close. Our bayonets showed our intent and this was often
enough to secure their surrender. We knew our superior tactics
and the greater will of the German soldier would prevail. Yes,
we have violated the supposed neutrality of Belgium, but that
is war. We do what we have to do in order to gain victory. This
monumental task has taken our armies just six weeks. Yes, in
six weeks, we have defeated the French on their home soil. The
25 June 1940 is a day I shall cherish and remember for all of my
life. We have conquered the French and now we occupy their
land. The Führer is overjoyed!

When Hitler received notice from the French government that it wanted
to negotiate an armistice, he decided it would take place at Compiegne
Forest. Compiegne had been the scene of the 1918 armistice and Hitler
wanted the signing of a new armistice to take place in the same rail carriage
where the Germans had signed the 1918 armistice. The rail carriage used
in 1918 was removed from the museum where it had been on display
and transported to Compiegne. Although the Germans denied that this
action was designed to humiliate the French, this was clearly the case.
Witnesses reported Hitler's mood on that day as 'emotionally mixed'. As
the rail carriage was placed on the exact spot it had been in 1918, Hitler
arrived and placed himself in the chair in which Marshal Ferdinand Foch
had sat when he addressed the delegates of the defeated German Empire
in 1918. Hitler sat impassively through the reading of the preamble. In a
gesture of contempt for the French delegates present, he got up and left
the carriage, leaving the negotiations to his *Oberkommando der Wehrmacht*
[High Command of the Armed Forces], Chief General Wilhelm Keitel.
Many French citizens were under the impression that the German
occupation of their country would be short lived. The French believed
that Britain would soon return to liberate them, but as time elapsed even
the most confident citizens became pessimistic.

Anti-Jewish laws were soon imposed upon the French territories now
under control of the Third Reich. These laws mirrored those in effect in
Germany. Jews were deprived of their civil rights, including the right to
employment and many were fired by their bosses as a result of the new
laws. Jews were also forbidden to work as teachers, journalists or lawyers.

Soon they were being incarcerated in internment camps in southern France. The numbers of Jews in these camps swelled with the addition of those deported from other regions of France. All Jewish assets were seized, including property, businesses, personal effects and money. The Vichy State oversaw much of the administrative tasks regarding Jews, as well as organising anti-Jewish propaganda. Jews were obliged to register and lists were compiled. These lists would prove invaluable to the Nazi authorities when the future round-ups and mass deportations began. Later on in the German occupation zone, all Jews aged six and upwards were required to wear a yellow star on their clothing. As the French began to come to terms with the German occupation, Hitler was turning his attention to Britain. Hermann Goering, chief of the Luftwaffe, stood with Hitler as they both gazed out across the English Channel towards the white cliffs of Dover. Goering, ever the ebullient one, was boastful and confident that, once unleashed, his Luftwaffe would secure a swift victory for Germany. Goering's confidence was, however, somewhat premature. The 'Mr Toad' of the Nazi hierarchy had greatly underestimated the resolve of the British.

Chapter Nine

Britain's Fight for Survival

Hitler understood that he would have to defeat Britain in order to achieve his military ambitions in Europe. He had hoped that once Poland, France and the Low Countries had fallen Britain might sue for peace. He was wrong. With the downfall of Prime Minister Neville Chamberlain, came Winston Churchill, a very different character who would offer no concessions to Hitler and who vowed to fight, whatever the cost. His 'British Bulldog' spirit helped galvanise the population to prepare for the onslaught that everyone knew was coming. From a tactical perspective, the German invasion would largely consist of large-scale air attacks and attempts at creating a blockade from the sea. For the first time, the Luftwaffe would be flying across the English Channel into an organised defence. Britain had excellent radar equipment along its south coast that would detect the approaching Luftwaffe bombers and fighter aircraft. The information would be relayed directly to the RAF stations, which would then scramble fighters to intercept the enemy aircraft. Britain also had an air force equipped with their latest Supermarine Spitfire and Hawker Hurricane fighter aircraft. While these two remarkable fighters were undoubtedly one of the most important assets of the British defensive strategy, they were not the catalyst to victory that is often stated. The German Blitzkrieg strategy was missing its infantry and armoured components, both vital elements in the previous victories over Poland, France and the Low Countries.

Melitta Jorg wrote to a friend in America regarding the situation Britain was facing at the time:

> It would appear that, for the time being at least, I shall not be visiting you again, my dear. With the hostilities now firmly about to begin in our own backyard, mother and father believe

it would be tempting fate to continue travelling back and forth to America. They are worried the Luftwaffe or Kriegsmarine may attack even neutral shipping. I would not put such actions past those dreadful Nazis. I am very concerned about the German war machine now assembling across the English Channel. They will do everything within their power to land on these shores and enslave us. If they do succeed, then we are finished; we will most certainly be sent to concentration camps. There is a strange atmosphere of anticipation, yet we are going about our daily lives as if there is nothing wrong. The beaches down south are now out of bounds. Most have barbed wire across them and are quite possibly mined, I don't know. As much as the urge to skinny dip takes me sometimes, I feel it is safer to travel the short distance to Milton Keynes. There is a fine place there with woods intersected with many deep and shallow freshwater pools. The place is something of a little paradise and we go there when it's hot. Of course, mother and father are often embarrassed. They don't feel it is polite or within etiquette to cast one's clothes off to the wind. For God's sake, they have seen me naked before many times, so why should it worry them so? As for anyone else, I do not particularly care, as I can't have that bad a physique with all the wolf whistling that seems to emanate from the offices and work places in London whenever I walk out. We may travel up to Scotland soon as father is sure the Germans will attack London. He has so many contacts in this country we could stay virtually anywhere we like. If London should be attacked we may leave for Scotland or anywhere else that father considers being safe. He can be dreadfully paranoid about my safety, but I do see his point. Oh well, at least we're an island; the Germans can't just swim across the Channel! I will write again when I have something juicier to tell. Love Always, Litta.

For a period of time, life in Britain did continue with an air of relative normality. However, everyday items were soon subject to rationing; petrol being one of the first commodities to be controlled. Soon virtually everything else would also be subject to strict control. People were encouraged to grow whatever vegetables they could. These measures were vital to prevent Britain starving as the war dragged on.

The first German intrusion into British air space had occurred earlier, on 7 September 1939, when Heinkel bombers neared the east coast of England. No bombs were dropped and the enemy aircraft turned for home. The turning point for Britain would come on 10 July 1940. This date was to herald the infamous struggle for survival referred to as The Battle of Britain. There have perhaps been more individual histories written on this single campaign of 1940 than any other in military aviation history. Oberleutnant Heinz Mollenbrock, a twenty-year-old Dornier 17 pilot, recalled:

> We again felt confident in the ability of our aircraft to do the tasks we were asked to do. In the early phases of the Battle of Britain, or *Die Luftschlacht um England* [The Air Battle for England], shipping in the English Channel and around the Channel coast was attacked with bombs. We also attacked places on the coast where there were shipping centres, places such as Portsmouth. Things began to become more intense as the battle wore on. As pilot of our aircraft my job was to fly the aircraft, get to the target, drop our bombs and then fly it back home. We each had an individual task to perform; yet we worked as a team also. On 1 August there was a shift in tactics, as the fighters were instructed to eliminate RAF Fighter Command. This was, they hoped, achievable through decoying the Spitfires and Hurricanes up where the Messerschmitt fighters would then be waiting to pounce on them from altitude. Next thing for us was the RAF airfields. We were given instructions to wipe out the RAF airfields in the south of England. RAF infrastructures were also subject to attack from our bombers. Soon, we were also attacking factories constructing aircraft or making components for them. Initially, we were successful in our operations. We were given a target and we would go and bomb that target; it was as simple as that. The Dornier 17 was not a bad aircraft, but it was only really a lightweight bomber

and could not carry the very heavy bomb loads that some RAF bombers could carry. In my personal opinion, we should have invested at least in some four-engine heavy bomber aircraft. I think had we done so, we may have achieved more in terms of results. We had the experienced pilots and to a degree the equipment. Tactically, however, we were very much let down.

Much has already been written about the Battle of Britain, so it needs little explanation here. There were, of course, four initial phases to the battle. When the Luftwaffe first attacked Britain, their targets were ports and shipping in local waters. The Luftwaffe soon became committed to destroying the RAF and its airfields, largely in the south of England. It was the south that bore the brunt of the fighting. The Luftwaffe attacks were both consistent and devastating. Fighter Command of the RAF was losing aircraft and pilots at an alarming rate. The Luftwaffe fared little better, suffering high losses, especially amongst the bomber crews. Clearly, these losses could not continue on either side. It was a case of who would break first. Yet the break came from a purely tactical error made by Hitler himself. A Heinkel bomber crew became disorientated, dropping their bombs on the City of London instead of the allotted target of the nearby docks. They could have had no idea of the implications this would have on the outcome of the battle. Britain retaliated by bombing Berlin the next night. Hitler was furious, vowing to wreak a deadly vengeance upon London and other cities in the UK. What Hitler did not realize was that the RAF was already at breaking point. Had the Luftwaffe maintained its attacks on the airfields in the south of England, they would have defeated the RAF within two weeks.

On 16 August 1940, twenty-year-old Heinz Mollenbrock and his crew of three climbed up into their Dornier 17z of 3/KG2 [KG stood for *Kampfgeschwader*, or Bomber Group]. Heinz strapped himself into his pilot's seat and the crew prepared for take-off. There were thirty-six Dorniers on this particular raid, flying in close formation at 16,500ft. Heinz described what happened as they approached London:

I was leading the last three Dorniers when we were attacked by RAF fighters. The first attack scored hits on our aircraft and it sounded like being in a car with someone throwing stones against it. One of our engines was hit by machine-gun bullets and this engine soon became inoperable. We were attacked three or four more times by what I recognised as a Hawker Hurricane fighter. My comrades, *Gefreiter* Reinecke and Gollob, fell dead in their positions. I was hit by .303 bullets in the right arm and left shoulder. The aircraft began to lose control and I knew I had to get out of it quickly. My wounds meant that this was quite some struggle. I managed to get out, I fell and felt the rush of the wind around me. I pulled the cord, my parachute opened and I ended up in a plum tree in an orchard on a farm. I was badly shocked and in a lot of pain from my injuries. Some people from the farm came to my aid and I was taken to hospital until I had recovered enough to be transferred to a prisoner-of-war camp. I later discovered that we had damaged one of our attackers with our 20mm Oerlikon cannon. This gun was fitted as a suppressive fire weapon to be used against anti-aircraft positions. I was repatriated later, but faced more operations on my damaged arm and shoulder. The injury still gives me considerable pain to this day, though I am grateful to the people that came to my aid in the orchard. My dead comrades went down with the Dornier.

I corresponded regularly with Heinz during the mid- to late-1990s, finding him, in many ways, a man of contradictions. He had the habit of telling me that no one would be interested in the kind of research I had been doing at the time on German military and social history of the Second World War. Yet, at the same time, he assisted a number of notable UK-based aviation historians, which seemed odd to me. The last meeting I had with Heinz was in the summer of 1999, at the German Military Cemetery at Cannock Chase, Staffordshire. Heinz had returned to the UK to pay a visit to his dead comrade's grave. He stood momentarily, just looking down at the stone. The emotions he must have been feeling at the time were clearly visible. I took a photograph of him as he walked among the rows of white gravestones in the cemetery. He reiterated with a slight hint of a smile, 'No one is going to be interested, you know!' I replied,

'Well, that's your opinion, Heinz, and you are entitled to it, but I disagree.' I carefully grasped his hand, shook it and then I left him at the cemetery. That was the last contact I ever had with him. Heinz Mollenbrock died peacefully at his home near Kiel, Germany, in December 2007. All that is left now are the group of letters and pieces of correspondence that he sent me over the few years we were in contact.

With Hitler's insistence that the Luftwaffe attack London, the tactical advantage was unwittingly lost. It would prove to be a major error of judgement. Without securing air superiority of the skies over southern Britain, the proposed German seaborne invasion could not go ahead. Operation Sea Lion was cancelled indefinitely. It was, in a sense, Germany's first defeat of the Second World War. As the Battle of Britain reached its conclusion, a new battle would begin; one that would take terror to new levels. It would be indiscriminate and everyone, men, women and children, would be in the front line. On 7 September 1940 the Luftwaffe's bombing campaign against British cities began. Joyce Smith recalled that fateful day:

> That day the Germans changed tack, didn't they? They stopped hitting the RAF and turned to bombing our cities. I had a relative who had been at Biggin Hill, the RAF airfield. He said they'd had a terrible time of it and had been hit really bad. So in a way, I knew even as a child what to expect. The first attack on London came on 7 September. From that point on my family of my brother, mother and father had a well-rehearsed routine every time the air raid siren went off. We just went into our kitchen and got under the large, heavy kitchen table. That table was solid as anything and had belonged to my grandmother. We had an Anderson Shelter in the garden, but it was bloody cold in those things and the damp made your clothes wet and they were just uncomfortable, so we stayed in the house under the table. The raid of the 7 September didn't affect us at all, though it was pretty noisy with all those German bombers overhead and the 'ack, ack' guns firing away at them. The shrapnel from the exploding 'ack, ack' shells would fall from the sky and you could hear them hit the tin roof out the

back; it used to make a hell of a racket. My dad caught some young lad climbing onto our shed roof one afternoon to pinch some shrapnel that had been up there. Dad pulled him down and gave him a thick ear before sending him off. Shrapnel was like money; you could take it to school and trade it for things. We also had this Jack Russell terrier; now he used to know when the German planes were coming ten minutes or so before the air raid warning went off. He would sit up bolt upright, his ears pricked and he would start barking, then run off into the kitchen and curl up under the table. The first time he did this we took no notice of him, but the next we were right behind him. I think it was always a gamble staying in the house, but we got hit. All I remember is being under the table; there was this tremendous explosion and all this stuff came crashing down around us. The table protected us, but all around was rubble and we couldn't get out because of it. There were a few chinks of light shining though some gaps, so we knew we wouldn't suffocate and luckily there was no fire. The dog barked incessantly and rescue workers worked their way towards us. After what seemed an eternity, we were rescued without any injury. We were a bit shaken by our experience, but my younger brother had a good tale to tell his pals at school. I remember dad swearing, and he never swore in front of us kids, but he did that day [she laughs]. He said, 'Well, fucking hell. I think I have actually shit myself!' It was a good job my mother did not hear his expletives, as no matter what the situation she hated bad language.

The Blitz on London steadily intensified, along with bombing campaigns on other British cities such as Birmingham, Coventry and Liverpool. Coventry in particular was a major target for the Luftwaffe as it was an important manufacturing and engineering centre for the war effort. It suffered the most concentrated air attack on a British city during the entire Second World War. On the night of 14 November 1940, the Luftwaffe dropped 500 tons of high explosive bombs, 30,000 incendiaries and fifty huge parachute mines on the city. A new exploding incendiary bomb was also being trialed by the Luftwaffe for the first time. The German bombers, flying at 6,000ft above the burning city, could smell the smoke in their crew compartments. *Unteroffizier* Karl Retschild, a Heinkel bomber gunner, had a first-hand view of the destruction below from his position in the forward nose of the aircraft. He watched in awe as death and destruction fell on the city. He recalled:

> It reminded me of when I was young. I would sit and watch the fire as the coals burned. The city below glowed like hot coals and this lit up the inside of our aircraft with a red- yellow glow. I remember thinking 'God help those people down there'. It was war though and we had a job we had to do. When we landed back home there was little talk, no shouts of joy or celebration. We were deep in our own thoughts about the raid. The High Command were happy, as it was a success; the destruction caused by our bombs had been significant.

As dawn broke over the city the next day, the destruction became apparent. There were traumatised people everywhere. Some wandered around in a daze, others were crying hysterically. Children were so terrorized by the experience that many were seen digging into rubble with their bare hands trying to make tunnels to hide inside. There were even, amidst all the horror, some moments of humour. One man recalled being pursued down a street by a knee-deep lava flow of boiling hot butter. The dairy had been hit by bombs and the contents soon boiled over into the streets outside. The official death toll figure was 554, but the real figure could have been higher as many people were missing and remained unaccounted for.

Melitta Jorg put pen to paper in her journal about the latest Nazi terror:

> It would appear we beat the Luftwaffe's plans to invade Britain. Now they are going to try to bomb us into submission. With London under daily attack and now other cities becoming a target, I hope Britain can maintain its resolve. It's going to get an awful lot worse before things get better. If we can hold it together and defy Hitler, as Churchill insists, we may just

prevail. I have seen the destruction wrought by the bombs. It's very frightening indeed. Can we go on like this? I'm not sure and all we have is hope.

Melitta also penned a hurried note to her friend in Scotland, which read:

We are in the grip of the Nazi fist at this time. They are trying to reduce us all to rubble. We have to carry on and take this and defy whatever they throw at us. There can be no alternative way of life. If we allow Hitler to win, at some point he will invade and then where will we all be? I dread to think of such a time ever coming. Father wants me to marry. I've not known the young man for very long and I have my reservations. He is serving in the RAF and is quite charming, as many of them are. We do appear to annoy each other at times. Just little things really, but is it being 'unladylike' to spit your lover's fluid from your mouth post oral? He seemed annoyed and gave me all the talk about such an act is 'unladylike'. Can you believe? I told him that I heard no such complaint as his phallus passed my lips! In fact, you know I could have placed a pistol between his balls and he would not have noticed! I think father despairs of his 'wayward daughter', as he now calls me. He thinks I drink and socialize far too much. He tells me I should calm down and I reply, 'Father not even marriage can save me now.' [ha ha.] As you can imagine, not that you know father, he is not best pleased with me right now. I am not some beast that needs to be tamed. Hopefully, the current situation with the war may provide him with some greater distractions. [I live in hope, ha-ha!!] Yours Always, Litta.

The Luftwaffe did not have things entirely their own way during the initial phase of the Blitz. The anti-aircraft batteries took a heavy toll on the night attackers. In the daytime, the RAF made concerted efforts against the Luftwaffe, along with the anti-aircraft defences and barrage balloons. Night fighting tactics in the RAF were thankfully fairly advanced by the 'Baby Blitz' of 1943. Reliable Air Interception [AI] radar had been developed in the form of the AI MK.IV. This had a range of 20,000ft down to a minimum range of 400ft. The radar had been fitted to a number of RAF single-seat fighters such as the Hawker Hurricane and the Bristol Blenheim twin-engine light bomber. These were, however, interim measures replaced by the purpose-built night fighter versions of the Bristol Beaufighter. The Beaufighter was a twin-engine fighter with a heavy armament of four 20mm Hispano cannon and six .303 Browning machine guns. The two-man crew consisted of the pilot and his radar/AI operator. The AI operator was positioned behind the pilot within a perspex observation dome. The radar/AI operator was also responsible for loading fresh magazines into the four 20mm cannon. Interception of an enemy aircraft was a complex process. The night fighter had to be vectored into the vicinity of the enemy aircraft before its AI radar could detect it. The AI operator would have a small CRT [Cathode Ray Tube] display before him. He would use all his skill to decipher the information from the CRT screen and relay it to the pilot. The AI operator effectively guided the pilot into visual range of the enemy. This sounds relatively simple in theory, but the reality was very different; it was an incredibly dangerous undertaking. Having guided the pilot onto the target, it was then up to the pilot to make a visible identification. This was achieved by looking for signs of an enemy aircraft up ahead. Turbulence from propeller wash was one indicator that an enemy aircraft was up ahead and the dull light from engine exhausts was another. The pilot would then approach the enemy aircraft from astern and slightly below. He would actually position his aircraft beneath the enemy, looking for the tell-tale signs such as shape, engine configuration and, of course, the black crosses beneath the wings. Having established the identity of the enemy aircraft, the intercepting night fighter would throttle back until the target was a few hundred yards in front. The pilot would then switch on the light of his gunsight and fire a full two- to three-second burst into the enemy aircraft, which was often enough to bring them down.

For the crew on the receiving end, escape from their burning plane was more often than not impossible. Some Luftwaffe aircrews managed to bail out and survive to tell the tale, but the German Military Cemetery at Cannock Chase in Staffordshire is testimony to those who didn't make it. The people of Britain were elated every time a German plane was brought down. There were no tears for the corpses of the dead crews. Many civilians were of the view that what the Germans were doing was tantamount to a war crime. Hitler and Luftwaffe chief Goering had underestimated the resolve of the British people. Amidst all the death and destruction in the towns and cities of England, people were determined to continue fighting, regardless of what the Germans threw at them.

Worse was to come in the later years of the war. With the onset of the V-Weapons offensive of 1944-45, a new terror was emerging which would bring death and destruction from the skies. By June 1944, the first of the V-Weapons made its terrifying debut in the war against Britain. The term 'V' refers to *Vergeltungswaffen*, the German word for 'reprisal' or 'vengeance' weapon. The first of the V-Weapons was the V-1 Flying Bomb, a pulsejet-powered cruise missile. Once launched from their launching sites in occupied France, the weapon would follow the fixed trajectory of its launching ramp. These were aimed towards London and the pulsejet motor contained enough fuel for it to reach its intended target. Once over the target, the motor would run out of fuel, the engine would splutter then cut out and fall to earth. The 1,870lb warhead was filled with Amatol-39, creating a very substantial blast on impact. The V-1 was totally indiscriminate, having no guidance mechanism to enable it to fall on a specific target or area.

One of the worst incidents concerning a V-1 weapon was the Weald House bombing. At 3.37 am on Friday, 30 June 1944 a V-1, which had been fired at by anti-aircraft guns near the English coast, was damaged. As exploding anti-aircraft shell fragments pierced its thin metal skin, the V-1 began to lose control. The weapon approached the edge of Crockham Hill Common in Kent, where it struck a tree. This impact with the tree deflected the V-1, which cartwheeled through the air before crashing into Weald House. The explosion shook nearby homes, rousing locals from their beds. One recalled: 'The night sky glowed red above the direction of Weald House.' At the time, Weald House was being used as a refuge for evacuated children. The blast demolished the house, killing twenty-one children and eight female staff. The youngest of the victims was eleven-month-old Christopher N. Ansell. The V-1 offensive would continue until the Allies overran their launching sites.

The V-2 was a completely different kind of terror weapon for which there were no countermeasures. The V-2 was the world's first intercontinental ballistic missile. It could be towed by a special vehicle to a specific site where it could then be launched. The V-2 carried a 2,200lb Amatol-filled warhead of which 910kg was actual Amatol explosive. With a range of 200 miles and a maximum speed of 3,580mph, the first anyone knew of the missile's approach was when its huge warhead exploded. The total number of fatalities caused by the V-Weapon attacks on Britain was given as 6,000, with a further 1,800 injured. The Nazi plan had originally been to use the V-Weapons in saturation attacks upon Britain. Thankfully, their entry into the Second World War came too late for that plan to have been made feasible. The Luftwaffe would continue with its efforts, but would be constantly frustrated by the stubbornness of the British people. Things were extremely hard for the British, but they were winning their fight for survival. Melitta Jorg wrote of the V-Weapons in her journal:

> They are horrible these things. Only these things could have been conceived within the mind of a Nazi. They buzz across the Channel coast, then, when they arrive over the city, their engines cut out and the things fall to earth. When they hit the ground the explosions are immense. One day they were coming over on and off throughout the whole day. It makes one's preoccupation with one's underarm hair a very trivial worry indeed. Yes, as the bombs rain down, there I am topless before the mirror, shaver in one hand and a small piece of soap in the other. I couldn't imagine a greater turn-off for a man than seeing a girl stretched out upon the bed awaiting him with black fluff showing from her underarms. A girl should try her best to maintain that manicured perfection, so fuck the Luftwaffe, fuck Hitler, fuck the V-1s. Just fuck them all really!

Chapter Ten

Norway - Heaven and Hell

Peter Weiss served with the Wehrmacht in Norway. He was stationed near Oslo in 1940, after the German occupation of the country began. His son made contact with me through mutual friends as he felt his father's reminiscences might be of some use to the research work I was conducting at the time, in the summer of 1999.

At the end of the Second World War, Peter Weiss, in his own words, 'Inexplicably ended up in England'. He had only ever intended to visit some old friends who had settled here. During his time in England, in and around the city of Oxford, he met an English girl and the two soon fell in love. After some initial complications, which took some time to resolve, Peter moved to England, leaving behind everything he knew in Germany. Peter married his sweetheart and the couple settled down to a relatively quiet life in Oxfordshire. The reason his son made contact was that he had often had access to many of his father's keepsakes from his time in occupied Norway. The keepsakes were in the form of notes that Peter had written on his service, plus several small books containing various writings. There were also some dried, pressed flowers, which had been collected in Norway. Peter's son explained his father had some interesting reflections to share so we agreed to meet at Peter's home, hoping to learn more about the German occupation of Norway.

When I arrived one beautiful Sunday morning, Peter and his son had a box with bundles of letters, medals and photographs all neatly arranged on the kitchen table. We shook hands, cups of tea were made and then we settled down at the table. Peter began thumbing through old photographs. I noticed that his hands trembled and his fingers, stained yellow from tobacco, were barely able to grasp the photographs:

This is me near the city of Oslo. I was just an ordinary Wehrmacht foot soldier that spent most of his time cleaning up after the officers, being shouted at, performing guard duties; things like that. For me, the war in Norway was a relatively quiet affair early on in the occupation. We had the odd British reconnaissance flight to contend with, but these boys flew so high and fast you barely saw them. All you could hear was the faint growl of a Merlin engine as a Spitfire, painted in its blue paintwork, would pass over at very high altitude. Messerschmitt fighters would be sent up to try to intercept. I don't think they were very successful in this task though. When I first arrived in Norway we did not see much of the population as we were busy sorting out sleeping quarters and other administrative tasks. After a while, we did venture out into the nearby city of Oslo. It was a beautiful place, which made you feel that you were anywhere but at war. As we were out walking around off duty, taking photographs like tourists, we became familiar with many of the local people. I recall one young girl. You must understand that this memory is a painful one for me. You might think I am stupid, but, at the end of it all, we all have deep emotions and this one is more a haunting than an emotion. The girl was the same age as I was. We caught one another's eye, as strangers sometimes do and we exchanged smiles. I never thought I would see her again, but I saw her frequently in the town after that. After many such times I finally plucked up the courage to ask her to join me for coffee in one of the local cafés. I was shocked when she smiled and said yes, so we arranged a day and time and we met for coffee. The officers did not always like us getting too familiar with the locals. We were warned not to cause any problems with them and be discreet. Even though our officers were doing much the same as we were, we still had to keep these things low key, as they say.

When we met up at the coffee shop, I ordered our drinks and pulled out a chair for the girl. She said her name was Astrid, but I somehow felt this was a covering or fictitious name she had given me. She explained she came from Denmark originally, where she was born, and her family had moved to Oslo some years ago, when she was around six years of age. She said her family was moderate regarding the Hitler regime and she hoped that the Germans would not bring too much trouble to Norway; that it would remain merely a quiet occupation, void of any violence. I asked her if her parents knew who she would be with today and she remarked that she had not told them. She then asked of my family back in Germany, where I had come from. It was mainly nervous small talk on that first meeting. When we parted company, I asked if I could see her again and she said she would let me know when she saw me next. I took her hand, kissed it on the knuckles and returned to my barracks.

The next few weeks were torture; all I could think about was this girl. Her face was constantly on my mind. Oh, she was beautiful. We would be sent out into the populace on what were foot patrols and I would be looking out for her all of the time. Clearly, I was not thinking about my duties and the other guy with me, an older guy named Jochen who came from Oberndorf, would be talking and then nudge me as I had failed to answer him. I would apologise and ask him to repeat his question; it was quite funny. We were out one day, late in the afternoon in the town, and there she was, walking towards us with a small basket in her delicate hands. My spirits immediately lifted and my heart began to race as I greeted her and asked her if we could meet when I was next off duty that week. She smiled at me and said, 'Yes, of course.' We arranged to meet at the same place; the little café just on the edge of the town. As she walked away, Jochen then said, 'Well, that explains everything doesn't it, you rascal Peter!' We laughed and he commented, 'Well, you certainly have an eye for a lovely girl, don't you.' He then took out a photograph of his sweetheart back home in Germany. As he gazed lovingly at the small black and white photograph of the pretty blonde girl he said, 'When this war is over, I am going back to her and we will get married.' We walked back to the guardhouse in good spirits that evening and reported nothing of note happening; everyone happy.

On my day off, which was a Saturday, we met at the coffee shop and she said, 'I want to show you some of the real Norway and for that we must head up there.' She pointed up into the mountains, which were covered in trees and the distant peaks capped with snow. I was surprised at this girl's stamina as she strode up the wooded hill. I was out of breath, even though I considered myself fit. We stopped momentarily and I took a photograph of her; in fact I took more. I could not stop clicking away at this girl. We walked and chatted about the war and our hopes for the future when it was over. We stopped and sat on a large boulder, and it was at that point I told her I found her captivating and I could not think of anything else. I was sorry, but I had fallen head over heels in love with her. We met many times afterwards and I would always meet her at that same rock in the woods. I think it must have been almost seven months when we again went up the hill into the woods where we would talk, kiss and yes, do other things. There was one day we met and she seemed different, somewhat distant with me. I told her again I was very much in love with her. She smiled at me, then peered into the distance and seemed lost in her thoughts. I asked if she was alright, she took a deep breath and said, 'I really do like you Peter, I think you are sweet and caring, but I don't think my family would ever approve of us having a relationship or you living here. What happens when you have to return to Germany or if you get killed somewhere? What would I do? We would be faced with so many problems.' She then took my hand and I caressed her soft fingers, my eyes were welling up with tears as I had never felt this way about any girl I had been with before. She placed a finger under my chin, lifted up my head until our eyes were level with one another's. 'Please don't be upset. Don't make this any harder for me, Peter. You will find someone else when you get back home and you will forget all about me. This is my home, where

I belong and I don't think I could ever leave this place. Even when the war is over, it could be dangerous for you to be here. Not everyone likes the Germans here and it might not be safe once you are here alone without your army.' I knew what she was saying made sense and she was probably right. As I looked into her beautiful blue eyes, I tried to stop sniffling. She leaned forward, kissed me on the cheek and told me that maybe it is best for us both we never meet again. She said, 'Let's just enjoy this moment and remember it forever in our hearts.' As we walked down the hill through the woods she stopped to pick small flowers and collected pretty pebbles. As we neared the town she stopped and gave me the small bag containing the flowers and pebbles. 'These are for you, Peter, and something to remember me by. If only things were different, but they are not. Please don't be angry with me or hate me.' I took the small bag and again we stood and stared into one another's eyes, only this time tears were running from her eyes. She again took my hand, leaned forward and placed a tender kiss on my lips and said, 'Goodbye Peter, please be safe and return home to those who love you.' She turned and walked away and I watched as she disappeared down the hillside path amongst the trees and late afternoon shadows. For a few minutes, I held my head in my hands and I cried like a child. I hoped she might return, but as the shadows grew longer it began to get dark and I had to get back to the barracks. I walked the short distance back with my mind in turmoil.

In the course of my duties, the strangest thing of all was that I never saw Astrid again. I looked out for her each time we were in or around the town, but it was like she had never existed. I even went into the coffee shop and asked the owner if he knew where Astrid lived. I described her in fine detail, but the lady and old man in there said they didn't know who she was and didn't know any girl in the town of that name. I received notice that I was to be transferred to another part of Oslo where there had been some problems with Norwegian resistance groups. We would be required to take part in patrols into the countryside. I packed my things and we were loaded onto a transport vehicle and we left. As we drove through the town I looked out for her, but in vain. Jochen said, as we left the town, 'Maybe the resistance have got her. They don't take kindly to their people fraternizing or collaborating with the occupying forces and you should know this, Peter. You may have put that girl in great danger, you know. For God's sake, don't ever allow your emotions to run away with you again.' Jochen was right; I knew in my heart of hearts he was. I hoped that she was alright and maybe had left to visit family elsewhere where we had no chance of seeing each other again. She lives now only in my memories.

This was a heart-wrenchingly sad story. By the time Peter had finished relating it, he was clearly very upset. But why? He had found love afterwards and had married; a union that bore him two fine sons and a daughter. Why was he so upset about this girl he had met in Norway so long ago? He went on to explain:

She was not just any girl. There is something else I was not going to tell you, but what is the point of not telling you now, after all these years. Does it matter anymore? As I have said, for the most part we were ordinary soldiers mingling with the population. As the time passed a resistance movement began to emerge and we were all involved, or had an obligation to root out members of the resistance. We were involved in some large patrols that then went out into the Norwegian wilderness. The forests and mountains were where these resistance groups were hiding out. We went out for several days into the hills searching the area and for the most part we saw very little other than the wildlife there. I loved nature, which may seem peculiar, so I did not mind relinquishing the luxury of a bed at night to get out into it. We had no fear of anything, as we were well armed for our task. We found numerous small areas, which we believed had been campsites for partisan fighters. These were nothing more than just small areas where campfires had been lit several nights previous. When examined, the fires were found to be reasonably fresh. Those who had lit them could not have been very far ahead of us. From that point on, we used stealth as we went forward. We kept talking to a minimum and at night we did not light fires. The next morning, a few members of our platoon had sighted people moving around in the thick forest ahead of us. We immediately took up a tactical formation to outflank and surround these people. We moved forward with our rifles cocked and ready to fire. We observed five to six bodies moving around and they appeared to be washing themselves near a small mountain stream. All of a sudden a scream of 'Halt!' broke the silence. The figures, obviously startled, then tried to escape, making a break to run and then shots rang out. I saw two of the figures drop to the ground, dead. Another one was shot a few minutes later after a brief pursuit. The three others escaped into the forest. We went back to the bodies to check them for any documentation or anything that may have betrayed their intentions. I was horrified that two of the three bodies were young females. One lay face down and the shot that had claimed her life had hit her square in the back. I turned her over and immediately recoiled in horror, shock and disbelief. I dropped my rifle, covering my mouth with my hands, as I felt like I was going to be sick. This young girl's body was that of the one that I had fallen in love with; it was the girl that had been known to me as Astrid! My mind was in utter turmoil. A comrade helped me to my feet and joked, 'What is the matter with you, my friend? Yes, she is very pretty is she not, but she and her friends may well have killed us had we not got them first.' Of course, I said nothing at all about this to anyone. Only my friend Jochen knew about this. I told him about it later and naturally, he was not sympathetic at all. He told me to keep quiet and say nothing to anyone and he had hoped I had learned a valuable lesson here. He said, 'In future you keep your heart in a box and your dick in your pants!'

The small bag of pebbles that Astrid had collected, along with the small book containing the flowers she had picked, all neatly pressed within, were now sentimental, if chilling, keepsakes which were too painful for Peter to reflect upon. They lay open on the kitchen table and, as Peter reached over and picked up the small book of pressed flowers, I noticed a tear, which ran past his thick-framed glasses down his cheek. He shook his head while carefully placing these keepsakes back in the box. His son then took them and put them back in a cupboard somewhere in the living room. He returned and comforted his father with a hand on his back. It was at this point the strangest thing happened. Peter, who had been speaking in perfect English throughout this meeting, sat with his head in his hands and uttered the words, 'Das tut weh!' I thought little of it, but before leaving, I asked his son what it meant. He said it meant, 'This hurts', in German.

On the way home from Oxford I reflected on this meeting. It was certainly one of the more interesting ones I have conducted over the years. I can only ascertain from Peter's reaction that the wounds we had opened that Sunday morning were still very much raw and painful. His story illustrated perfectly the dangers of fraternising with the locals in occupied areas.

Norway was not a willing satellite to Germany's military ambitions in Europe in the Second World War, but she would soon become strategically important to the German war effort. A stunningly beautiful and seemingly quiet backwater, it was all too easy for the young soldiers of the Wehrmacht to become distracted. The German occupation of the country began on 9 April 1940. The Elite German *Falschirmjager* [Paratroopers] were dropped in and seized the aerodromes at Oslo and Stavanger. There was some initial armed resistance while the king and pre-war government escaped to London. Civil rule in Norway after the German invasion was taken over by the *Reichskommissariat Norwegen* [Reich Commissariat of Norway], which collaborated with a pro-German puppet government. Norway was immediately subject to many of the Nazi laws imposed on other nations under German rule. Considerable efforts were made to ensure that the country's economy and social welfare programmes remained unaffected by the occupation; this proved unsuccessful and Norway lost all of its trading partners.

Germany could not compensate for the country's lost import and export trade and the Norwegian people soon faced the prospect of starvation in their own country. This is where the true resilience of the Norwegians came to the fore. They began to grow their own crops and reared their own livestock. In city parks they grew potatoes, cabbages and other hardy vegetables. Fishing and hunting became a widespread pursuit amongst the population, even by those who had never fished or hunted before. Norway was the most heavily fortified country during the Second World War, with a ratio of one German soldier for every eight Norwegians, and there were approximately 6,000 SS troops stationed in the country, under the command of *Obergruppenfuhrer* [Senior Group Leader] Wilhelm Rediess. At the beginning of the German occupation, there were approximately 2,173 Jews in Norway. A total of around 765 would lose their lives as a result of the German occupation. The deaths of Jews in Norway resulted from extrajudicial execution, murder and suicide, and 742 were sent to concentration camps.

Katherine H. Jorgensen is a friend and fellow military historian who lives in Nottoden, in Norway, and who has a passionate interest in the history of her country's occupation during the Second World War. Katherine was able to provide some unique photographs relating to the Norwegian resistance, which soon grew in her country. Deep in the forest outside Nottoden is evidence of Norway's struggle against the Nazi occupation in the form of a small resistance fighter's camp. Seeking out the long-forgotten relics of the Second World War in Norway is not without its dangers. During one hike deep into the forest to find a resistance camp, Katherine was confronted with a female moose with two young calves; a potentially dangerous situation and only averted through her knowledge of her surroundings and the local wildlife. Ignoring the natural desire to run, Katherine backed away, slowly giving the startled animals space to move away. Katherine explains:

> The site where the former resistance camp lies is so well concealed you could walk past it without knowing it is there. The forest is very dense in the region and the camp has been left exactly as it was the day it was abandoned. A wood hut stands on the site and within it all of the original contents are

still present. During the course of the Second World War in Norway, the Germans sent frequent patrols out into the forest to search for the resistance groups who sought sanctuary within it. This particular camp was one whose existence was discovered by a German patrol. A gun battle broke out between the Germans and the resistance fighters. A number of resistance fighters fell in the battle that ensued. The camp, untouched by time, now remains as a silent memorial to those brave men who fell fighting for our country. Nothing has been looted; everything is left exactly as it was on that fateful day. Curiously, while the resistance fighters were occupying the hut, they drew pornographic images within it. These images still remain daubed upon its walls.

Norway is also famously connected with the German Bismarck Class Battleship, *Tirpitz*. In early 1942 *Tirpitz* sailed to Norway, primarily to act as a deterrent against any proposed Allied invasion, but also in order to intercept Allied shipping convoys to Russia. Her presence in the area forced the British Royal Navy to commit substantial resources in order to contain her. The Norwegian deep-water fjords offered a high degree of protection for German shipping. The overhanging cliffs offered cover and protection from any Allied aircraft. Heavily armed flak ships were brought in as extra defence. Nearby, Luftwaffe aerodromes offered fighter support should an attack be detected by coastal radar. Despite these precautions, many attacks were mounted on German shipping in the fjords, some of which were among some of the most dangerous missions carried out by the RAF. RAF veteran Flying Officer Ronald Moore recalled:

I flew Beaufighters [a twin-engine heavy fighter] in World War Two. We were based up in Scotland, flying regular sorties across to the fjords in Norway to attack shipping. It was immensely dangerous trying to get at the ships. You had to fly in low, weaving around the mountains with their overhanging cliff ledges. This was not easy at speeds of 300mph or more. The flak ships would be firing their guns at you and you would generally use your four 20mm cannons to try and suppress the flak. If you were lucky, you could get in, hit one of the ships with bombs or rockets, then get out in one piece. Then you had to fight your way back home, as the Luftwaffe would be circling above waiting for you to come out. I saw so many of our aircraft crash, killing the crews on board. Norway was such an important factor in the Nazi war effort, the pressure had to be maintained upon her. Not many are aware of just how important this beautiful part of the world was to the Nazis or just how hazardous missions there were.

RAF Lancasters eventually sank the German battleship *Tirpitz* in its Norwegian lair on 12 November 1944. The Lancasters dropped 12,000lb Tallboy bombs, two of which scored hits on the ship. A third 12,000lb Tallboy bomb missed the *Tirpitz* yet the resulting explosion and shockwave was so immense it capsized the ship. It was reported that over a thousand German sailors lost their lives in the sinking of the *Tirpitz*.

Perhaps one of the more sinister elements of the German occupation of Norway was the fact that it was used for the production of heavy water [deuterium oxide]. Norsk Hydro had constructed a facility at Vemork for the purpose of the commercial production of heavy water in 1934. The deuterium oxide produced was primarily a by-product of fertilizer production at the site. The site had the capability to produce some twelve tons of heavy water per year. Though heavy water is not dangerous in itself, its production was one of the vital components of the Nazi nuclear weapons programme. Heavy water acts as a neutron moderator, slowing down neutrons so that they are more likely to react with the fissile uranium 235 than uranium 238, which captures neutrons without fissioning. Heavy water was an essential coolant used in Pressurised Heavy Water Reactors, or PHWRs. Germany's first efforts at producing an atomic bomb began in 1939, just a few months after nuclear fission had been discovered. Hitler's invasion of Poland had inadvertently taken the initiative away from the Germans' research into nuclear weapons as many notable physicists were drafted into the Wehrmacht. Furthermore, academics within the nuclear research field were generally thin on the ground due to the expulsions

Above left: The only known photograph of Hilde Kohlman. (*Courtesy of the Kohlman Family*)

Above right: Melitta Jorg, described by her family as a 'charming socialite'. (*Courtesy of the Jorg Family*)

Below: Alexander 'Zander' Kohlman, on left in picture, holding an axe. (*Courtesy of the Kohlman Family*)

Above left: Paulina Rischner in the foreground, pictured at her older sister Helena's wedding. (*Courtesy of Paulina Rischner*)

Above right: Anna and Trudi Kohlman. This photograph of the girls was taken after the war. (*Courtesy of the Kohlman Family*)

Below: Ingrid Altmann, pictured with her brother, Horst, and their mother, Monica, outside their home in Munich during the Second World War. (*Courtesy of the Altmann Family*)

A young Helga Bassler poses with a friend. (*Courtesy of Helga Bassler*)

Paulina Grier, on the left, in the garden with her friends. (*Courtesy of Schondt*)

Former Luftwaffe KG2 Bomber pilot, *Oberleutnant* Heinz Mollenbrock, photographed during the author's meeting with him in summer of 1998, at the German Military Cemetery, Cannock Chase, Staffordhsire, England. (*Author's collection*)

Karl Voght, Ju87 'Stuka' pilot. (*Courtesy of Karl Voght*)

Two French soldiers' graves, taken by a German soldier after the fall of France. (*Author's collection*)

Four Messerschmitt Me110 heavy fighters pass overhead a German convoy somewhere in Russia in 1941. (*Author's collection*)

Above: German machine-gun
crew somewhere on
the Eastern Front.
(*Author's collection*)

Right: A child gives a
Nazi salute in Warsaw.
(*Author's collection*)

Above: Girls of the *Bund Deutscher Madel* performing a foot inspection. (*Author's collection*)

Below: Hitler Youths pose for a photograph before boarding a train in Germany. (*Author's collection*)

Above: Hitler Youth boys photographed at a sports tournament in Germany. (*Author's collection*)

Below: Ukrainian civilians who have been rounded up in a forest clearing. Many were killed by the Nazis or sent to slave labour camps, though the fate of the people in this photograph is not known. (*Author's collection*)

Left: Hans Joachim Pluschka.
(*Author's collection*)

Below: Hitler Youth *Streifendienst*
(SRD) certificate. The owner of
this one was fifteen years old.
(*Author's collection*)

Ergänzungsamt der Waffen-ᛋᛋ   Stuttgart-O., den 30. 11. 42.
Ergänzungsstelle Südwest (V)   Gerokstr.7

SRD - TAUGLICHKEITSBESCHEINIGUNG

Dem HJ - Angehörigen _____

geb. am 25. 6. 27

wohnhaft zu _____

wird bescheinigt, daß er lt. ärztl. Untersuchung für den

SRD-tauglich befunden wurde.

        Der Leiter   Der Führer des Bannes
    ᛋᛋ-Untersuchungskommission

    ᛋᛋ-   mführer.   Rudi Arnold
                                                 Oberscharführer

Above: The resistance fighters' hut at Nottoden, Norway. (*Courtesy of Katherine H Jorgensen*)

Right: German Flak-gun crew, on the Norwegian coast during the Second World War. (*Author's collection*)

This photograph of a young man hanging from a post was taken in Greece or Yugoslavia. It was found enclosed in a letter sent home from a German soldier. (*Author's collection*)

The face of terror; a concentration camp inmate. (*Source unknown*)

The barbarity of the war in the East. The frozen corpse of a German soldier, allegedly being used as a signpost. (*Source unknown*)

The Ten-Thousand-Yard Stare. A pistol in one hand and a trench shovel in the other, a German soldier returning from a close-quarter fight with Russian soldiers in the East. (*Source unknown*)

Siegfried Strelow, aged seventeen, in 1944. He was killed in March 1945, in the fighting in Silesia. A needless sacrifice. (*Courtesy of Hanna Rees*)

Hanna Rees (born Kaufholz). Pictured with the author's grandson, August 2017. (*Courtesy of Tina Hayward*)

Above: Photo taken by a German soldier of destruction near Normandy, France, in 1944. (*Author's Collection*)

Below: This photo shows vapour trails from Messerschmitt Me262 jet fighters intercepting B.17s of the US 8th Air Force, over Germany in 1944. (*Author's Collection*)

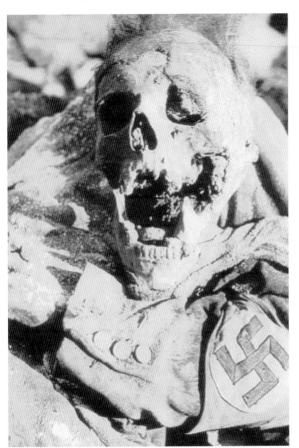

The incinerated remains of a German soldier exemplifies the horrors of war. (*Courtesy of WW2 In Pictures*)

Josef Kramer, photographed after his arrest. (*Source Unknown*)

Right: Wiener Katte surveys positions once occupied by American troops outside Aachen. (*Author's Collection*)

Below: Russian troops loading Katyusha rockets for the final assault on Berlin. (*Courtesy of WW2 In Pictures*)

Young German girl drinking a hot cup of tea given to her by an Allied soldier 1945. (*Courtesy of The History Place*)

The face of despair. A young German girl stares from the window of her home during the depression years. (*Source unknown*)

that had occurred in Germany upon the Nazis' seizure of power. Many of the best physicists and mathematicians, who could have proved vital to the Nazi nuclear project, were of Jewish ancestry and most had the good sense to leave Germany early on.

The only way to effectively halt the progress of the development of the German atomic bomb was through sabotage. In February 1943 a team of SOE – [Special Operations Executive] trained Norwegian commandos succeeded in destroying the production facility at Vemork. The attack was rapidly followed up with bombing raids by the RAF, forcing the Germans to cease their operations and transport the remaining consignment of heavy water to Germany. This was also thwarted in a remarkable sabotage operation mounted by the Norwegian resistance. The ferry, *SF Hydro*, loaded with the supplies of heavy water, was sunk by explosives on Lake Tinn. The supplies of heavy water sank to the bottom of this deep lake where they still lie to this day. Had Germany succeeded in producing an atomic bomb there can be no doubt she would have used it. The first target for such a weapon would have most likely been Soviet Russia. The USA would have also been on the list of potential targets. Although Germany did not possess a bomber capable of carrying an atomic bomb to the USA, she was certainly working on the feasibility of building one that could. Britain, too, may well have found itself on the list of targets. The prospect of an atomic bomb being dropped on London during the Second World War would have been too horrific to comprehend. It is due to the bravery of the Norwegian people that the terrible scenario of a nuclear-armed Nazi Germany never materialised.

Chapter Eleven

A Thorn in the Bear's Paw

1941 would be a year that many Germans would look back on as the beginning of the end. Germany had initially been successful in its early military campaigns in Europe, yet had failed to defeat Britain. This was a grave error and one that would return to haunt the leaders. Italy had joined Germany as an ally against Britain and France, on 10 June 1940, but her involvement in the war would be very limited. Italy became more of a liability for the German military as the war progressed and Hitler was forced to allocate precious military resources to support the failing Italians. The Italian people themselves soon grew weary of the war and Mussolini's aspirations of restoring the Roman Empire in North Africa and the Mediterranean. The Italian dream of a new Roman Empire was snuffed out by 1943, when Italy surrendered to the Allies. As one former British soldier, Phil Prior, once told me, 'The Italians were not a bad people. They never wanted war in the first place. Many of the Italian POWs I met were just happy that it ended when it did. They were sick of war by that point.' It was in late 1941 that Germany's Asian ally, Japan, attacked Pearl Harbor, thus bringing the United States of America into the Second World War. The industrial power of the USA would prove a vital factor in victory over Japan and Nazi Germany. That same year Hitler began to look seriously at his options in the east. Plans to invade Russia had been drafted as early as July 1940. Russian dictator Josef Stalin had no reason to fear German aggression at the time. Germany and the Soviet Union had previously signed a non-aggression pact, guaranteeing political and economic interests for strategic purposes. The German invasion of Russia would prove to be Hitler's greatest gamble, and his ultimate undoing.

Operation Barbarossa was more an ideological exercise. Hitler believed he could conquer the western Soviet Union, which could then be colonised by Germans, with the indigenous population retained as slave labour. Barbarossa was the beginning of one of the most notorious episodes of the war. It would lead to the slaughter of many thousands of Russian people and later to the reciprocal murder of German citizens captured by Russian troops. Operation Barbarossa was launched on Sunday, 22 June 1941. It was initially a success, but was soon exposed as a foolhardy endeavour. Although Nazi Germany was militarily strong, her resources would become stretched well beyond their capable limits. Worst still, Germany now faced war on two fronts; a military commander's worst-case scenario. Hitler exacerbated the problems faced by his armies in the east by wresting command from his generals and staff in the field. Hitler's interference in military matters would be a source of considerable frustration throughout the execution of Germany's war. When Barbarossa began, the Luftwaffe again were at the spearhead of the operation. Hauptmann Heinz Knoke, a Messerschmitt Bf109 pilot, recalled his first offensive flight against an airfield in Russia:

> We caught them totally by surprise. Many of their aircraft were on the ground and we strafed the airfield with our 20mm cannon and machine guns. I recall a Russian anti-aircraft crew running to their gun. No sooner had they climbed up onto it, I had them and the gun in my sights. I pressed the button to fire my 20mm cannons and watched. As the cannon shells scored hits all over the gun and its crew, I watched as they were thrown from the gun by the force of the exploding shells. They fell dead to the ground and I looked down on them as I passed overhead. I called them 'Ivans' [the Russians]; that is the name I called them after Ivan the Terrible, the 15th Century Prince of Moscow and Tsar of all Russia. I will admit I did not like them and I have explained why in my book [*I flew for the Führer*, originally published in 1953] as you will know.

As the Luftwaffe laid waste to the antiquated Russian Air Force on the ground, those that did manage to take off were soon shot down. In an interview before his death, in 1993, Heinz Knoke explained:

Many of the Russian aircraft then in service were obsolete types, such as the Polikarpov. These were no match for our excellent Bf109 fighters and all it took was a few bursts of machine-gun fire to shoot them down. As we had destroyed their air force largely on the ground, they had to rebuild. This later became a problem, as the new Russian aircraft were far superior. They had some good aeroplanes later on which could hold their own against many of ours.

The German land invasion of the Soviet Union was the largest invasion force in military history. In all, some four million Axis personnel were involved, which is why Hitler could at least be initially excused for his optimism. Some of his generals expressed concern privately that perhaps Germany was not ready for a sustained war with the Soviet Union. Others felt that a quick victory would be at hand. Paulina Rischner's brother, Kurt, was one of the Wehrmacht soldiers involved in the invasion of Russia. One could argue that he was one of the lucky ones. Three weeks into the invasion, Kurt Rischner was severely wounded by an artillery shell that killed five of his comrades. His family was notified that he had been wounded and that he would be repatriated back home for further treatment and convalescence. Pauline recalls:

We received the news that Kurt had been injured. At first we knew nothing and father tried to get information, but was frustrated by the clerks in the army who couldn't tell him anything. We soon learned that Kurt's injuries were quite extensive. Shrapnel had sliced through his legs, damaging his leg bones. We were told he may not walk ever again. We had an anxious wait for him to come home, or rather to arrive at a hospital near where we were living. When we were told we could go and see him, we were not sure what to expect. We arrived at the hospital and were directed to where Kurt was. He had been placed in a room on his own as we were told he regularly cried out through both pain and nightmares. That first time we saw him we all burst into tears. He had been drugged up to the eyeballs and barely knew who we were, and appeared disorientated by his surroundings. An officer came and told us one of his legs had to be amputated below the knee while the other one had been saved. There was still a risk of infection setting in, and the other leg having to be amputated, but we were told only with time can we tell. The weeks dragged on for us and we visited Kurt every day. I felt sick when his dressings were finally removed. The stump of his left leg looked like a sausage; it was horrible. The other was badly scarred by shrapnel. As Kurt lay in bed an officer came and awarded him the Iron Cross 2nd Class for his bravery in action. The officer talked with Kurt for some time before leaving. He said to us, 'You should be proud of that boy!' When he went, Kurt just looked at the Iron Cross and placed it on his bedside table. My father remarked at what an honour it was to be awarded such a coveted medal. Kurt just looked at him vacantly then turned his head to look out of the window. Kurt did get better and the damaged leg healed well, which was down to our excellent medics at the battlefront. In fact, Kurt told father to send his Iron Cross to the medic who treated him at the front, as he didn't want it. He left the hospital on crutches and he was never quite the same again. His personality seemed to change overnight. He would lose his temper quickly. He wasn't the brother I knew anymore. He settled down with a civilian job, married, and even had kids, but he still wasn't quite the same after getting hurt in Barbarossa.

Herbert Schiller was another young soldier who served in Operation Barbarossa. He was a twenty-one-year old serving with a Waffen SS armoured unit. His daughter, Heidi, supplied me with copies of some of the memoirs he had written of his experiences. Herbert Schiller died in 1987, after battling a short illness. The first piece of Herbert's memoir is as follows:

Russia, well here we are finally. The land of the Bolshevik, how do I describe it? So far, an endless horizon of mosquito-infested grassland, swamp and maize fields. The clouds of mosquitos are incessant and it drives you mad. A man can scratch until he bleeds in this place. I ask myself; what exactly are we conquering here and what are we gaining? We encounter clusters of what can only be described as run-down tin roof dwellings mostly made of wood. As we approach, the noise of the Panzers [Tanks] frightens the inhabitants. They flee in terror and the children squeal like piglets as they run through the long grass. We showed them no mercy; a machine gun opens fire and it is all over. I've seen it time and again. Their houses are burned and usually a few shots from a 2cm Flak [anti-aircraft gun] with its incendiary ammunition is enough to set them ablaze.

Incidents such as the one described by Herbert Schiller were not uncommon during the invasion of Russia. Even the Luftwaffe was complicit in acts that could be considered as war crimes against the Russian populace. Another former German soldier, who did not wish to be named here, recalled:

This Luftwaffe truck pulled up to our camp one afternoon. Several guys jump out of the back and the guy sat beside the driver jumps out, slams the door and shouts, 'Does anyone want to come hunting with us?' Most of us just sat there and thought, what are you on about? There is nothing to hunt here. We just smile at them and say we would rather stay here and rest. One of our guys said, 'Okay, I will come with you. Where are we going?' These Luftwaffe boys just jumped back in, so he got in with them and they drove off, leaving a huge cloud of dust behind them, which annoyed us even more. The guy who went off with them later returned and he did not look very happy. He later told me what happened, 'We drove to this place, around six miles away from our camp. There was a large cluster of trees and when we walked inside the trees there were a group of people huddled together in there. They were told to run and there were shouts of, "*Schnell! Schnell.*" As the people got up and ran, the guys I had come with grabbed their rifles and gave chase. I stayed rooted to the spot. I was shocked by it and couldn't believe what I was seeing. I heard lots of shooting in the direction where the people had run. When the Luftwaffe guys returned they made remarks. One said, "This is what we call hunting here!" Another sarcastically said to me, "What's your problem; you are not a fucking blond *arsch* [slang for a homosexual], are you?" I didn't hang around, in fact, I refused a ride back to the camp and I walked back. On that walk back I felt sickened. This should not be happening as this what I had seen was murder not war. The fury of these guys was frightening.

As the German forces pushed into Russian territory, they encountered many civilians, including young girls and women. German soldiers were reminded of the racial hygiene laws regarding sexual encounters with girls and women in the east yet there were cases of rape. Exact figures are difficult to ascertain, but they are nowhere near the scale of that later inflicted upon German women and girls at the end of the war in 1945. Some officers turned a blind eye to the rape of Russian females while others strictly forbade it. It appears to have been another case of, 'do it, but don't get caught doing it'. Herbert Schiller's memoir extends further to reveal:

It was not so unlike us shooting rats in a barn. Hate absolves all conscience and, as a young man, I possessed sufficient hate and I had no conscience for what I did at that time. I did what I was ordered to do. We were given a location to go to on a map and told to erase it from that map. There was always a momentary surge of adrenaline as you watch your comrades kick down doors to the houses. A grenade would be hurled in through a door or window. There would be screams followed by explosions and the rattle of sub-machine gun fire. They would come out of one house and then move onto the next house. Killing became a normal course of action. We were all beginning to break emotionally after a short period of this. At the time, I felt no pity as a young man; only in later years with a family of my own did I think about the things I saw and the fact that I had also done some terrible things. I was a part of it and I was there with them, watching it happen. I could not have stopped it had I wanted to. They would have shot me dead too, I think. It has troubled me for a great many years and I cannot remove the images from my mind.

The Russians proved to be an exceptionally tough and resilient foe. They withdrew entire factories back from the German advance, despite having virtually no food, and the death toll amongst the Russian population was extremely high.

As the German invasion progressed, more sinister elements began their work. Alexander Kohlman had left the Hitler Youth, aged eighteen, in 1941. He left with glowing reports from his seniors. He had proved to be an excellent boxer and sportsman, showing great enthusiasm and courage in all of his endeavours. He underwent his military training, learning to master the standard German Army rifle, the 7.92mm Mauser K98, the Luger pistol and standard hand grenade. Alexander was very keen to become a soldier and hoped to graduate to the ranks of the Waffen SS. He had proved himself a good leader who commanded the respect of others. His mother, Hilde, despaired at her son's interest in becoming involved in the war. Neither was she happy that her son appeared to thrive on violence and the anti-Semitic views that the Hitler Youth had instilled in him. Hilde's brother, Frank, who had mentored the young man, reminded him that in the world of National Socialism there was no room for weaklings, traitors or pacifists. Alexander's selection for the Waffen SS was virtually assured. He fulfilled the criteria of being born to pure German stock, he was physically fit and strong, and was a well-indoctrinated individual. He joined the ranks of the SS Das Reich Division and would soon be heading to the Eastern Front. Hilde was slightly shocked by Alexander's appearance when he returned home for two weeks prior to leaving to fight. Gone was the scruffy shirt jacket and trousers in which he had left her, replaced with a smart black uniform with polished black boots. His hair was cut short, perfectly manicured, and the young man was clean shaven. He told his mother he would be joining his unit in the east soon, but did not tell her when he would be leaving.

The morning he was due to join his unit, he got up much earlier than usual, leaving a note for his mother on the kitchen table. When Hilde woke that morning she saw the letter. It needed no explanation. Alexander had gone off to his war, eager to prove himself against an ideological enemy in the east. His letters home were somewhat vague as to his activities. His great-granddaughter was able to fill in some of the gaps by providing some things he had written when he returned home after being wounded in 1943. Many of Alexander's private papers were written hastily in pencil, often when he was alone. He kept most of his writings in a small, locked box crammed with his Hitler Youth proficiency certificates and awards. There was also a black Wound Badge, War Merit Cross 2nd Class with swords, an Iron Cross 2nd Class and a small Walther handgun with ammunition in the box. Alexander's daughter and great-granddaughter went to much time and effort to translate for me anything they felt might be suitable for inclusion in my books. In one piece of text, Alexander describes the following event:

> This morning I saw for the first time our first live enemy. We captured around thirty of them and many were wounded, some seriously. The wounded were separated from the fit ones and taken away. I later heard from a jubilant Sergeant that they had been shot. The Russians looked at us, bedraggled, but one big fellow looked at me contemptuously. I challenged him to a boxing match, to which he agreed. As my friends and other members of the unit looked on, we fought. My opponent was strong as an ox, a real credit to his race. My blows soon prevailed and I felled him a number of times before he refused to get up anymore. We soon tired of our sport and the prisoners were taken away to the rear area.
>
> Our panzer [tank], one of the Panthers, needs a little maintenance and as a crew we work with the mechanics to make any repairs that are necessary. Usually, it is the damn tracks that fail on this machine. They can be broken by enemy artillery fire quite easy. The enemy know this and often target the tracks to immobilize our panzers. One crew got out during battle to repair their tracks when the Russians sent mortars on

them. They were all killed. If this happens in battle we are to remain inside our panzers, at least until it is safe or the area secured. If it is not safe, another panzer will come to our aid. Just a few days ago we rounded a corner flanked with trees. I made the novice error of just rounding the corner when I should have cut around it. Sure enough, in the trees, I saw the muzzle of a Russian artillery piece pointed menacingly at us. I shouted to my driver, 'Full ahead, full ahead!' We drove straight at the gun and its crew were frantically trying to load a round into the breech block as our Panther hit it. There was a terrible crash as we hit the artillery gun and we were thrown around violently on impact. We drove over the gun, crushing those who were not quick enough to get out of the way to death. We swung around, firing our machine gun and killing the other Russians as they tried to make their escape. One of the Russians was lying on the ground, fumbling with what may have been a grenade. I ordered our driver to reverse until we were on top of the Russian. We should have just machine-gunned him, but I ordered our driver to slew the Panther left to right. The Russian was crushed to death beneath the tracks. We got out and checked our Panther and she is fine, no damage. The artillery weapon was turned upside down and quite mangled; the bodies of its crew squashed into the mangled remains. To me they now looked like mincemeat. I notice that caught up in the tracks of our Panther is the mangled remains of a severed arm. We leave it where it is as none of us want to mess around trying to remove it. We were very lucky; had that artillery gun crew we had encountered earlier been more alert and fired on us, it could have been the other way round. Our mothers would have been getting death notices, not theirs. Complacency is deadly in this place.

Before nightfall we form up with our comrades. We make a fire and put the pot over it. Anything we have, we throw into the pot and cook. We have driven through many farms and so we are not short of rations. We take whatever's there: potatoes, corn, flour and things. We even have a few chickens, which are a considerable treat for us. Gunther spent some time chasing them down. It was hilarious to watch and I have to give the chickens credit; they dodged and outmanoeuvred him with great expertise. He grew angry and then hurled himself upon one of the chickens. In a split second, the bird turned and he fell flat on his face. In the end frustration made him draw his pistol. He stood and fired several shots, killing the chickens. How we laughed at him though; it was such a funny thing to watch, and the squawks of the chickens as they ran from him! We approached one farm a few days ago and fired some shots from our machine gun into the buildings. One caught fire almost in an instant. Our infantry moved in, firing into the buildings before entering, but the farm was empty. Everything had been left behind and the people must have fled our advance. We took anything that was of use and then set the buildings on fire. The main dwelling proved a stubborn structure. As we moved out, I ordered my driver to go through the building. I closed the hatch and, like a good fellow, my driver did as he was instructed. You cannot hear much over the noise inside a panzer, with the engine and gears moving, but you could hear the crash as we ploughed through that building. When I looked back through my command position, there was nothing left but rubble and broken wood.

We make good momentum and any resistance is met with blind fury from our panzers, artillery and soldiers. The enemy constantly fall back and there is a worry that there may be some left behind that we haven't seen, causing us problems. The security divisions are coming in and doing a good job of neutralising the threats in our rear areas. They rarely take prisoners, and who could blame them. It bothers me not that they kill all they find as this is war. The security fellows have a very tough job in this vast place. We covered many kilometres without too many problems. Again we stop and camp, write letters home and prepare meals between us. I was sitting in the shade of our Panther one afternoon. The heat was intense, the air filled with biting insects. I watch as *Gefreiter* Korscher tries to cook and keep the swarming pestilence around him from getting in the cooking pot and his face. He curses the place constantly. When we eat later, we pick all kinds of bugs and flies out of our food. We all smell like vagrants from our dirty uniforms and the heat. Inside the Panther there is little respite and it is very hot in there. As we sit in the shade of the Panther, our forces bring a line of captured Russian soldiers who walk past us. They walk with their hands on their heads. They are taken a few hundred metres away and ordered to stop. Shovels are thrown at them and they are ordered to dig trenches. They are there digging these trenches for most of the afternoon. When the trenches are dug deep enough they are ordered to jump in them. The cocking of automatic weapons is heard then the rattle of machine-gun fire follows. Was I shocked by this? Not at all, as this is not a civilized land. We are moving towards a great battle and we will emerge victorious.

The great battle that Alexander speaks of in his narrative was the Battle of Kursk. Alexander's SS Das Reich Division was involved from 11 July 1943, alongside the SS Totenkopf and Leibstandarte divisions. Their objective was to smash through the Russian lines at the village of Prokhorovka, breaking the flank of the Russian defensive positions. The German forces had begun to falter in the east. They had lost the fight for Moscow that took place from 2 October 1941 to 7 January 1942. Further military disasters would soon follow. The Battle of Kursk would be a defining episode on the Eastern Front in the context of the Second World War. The German forces were confident of victory; they had superior equipment, tanks and artillery, as well as the Luftwaffe providing massive air support for the battle. The sheer scale of the Soviet defence, however, was to prove decisive in overcoming the Germans' advantage. Alexander Kohlman was to experience first-hand the reality of war when his unit began its involvement in the Battle of Kursk. Until this point, the war had not troubled him in any way. Alexander's daughter had sought out one of his comrades to ask what he was like during the war. The response was not a flattering one, he said:

Your father once observed a village at a distance with his binoculars. The village lay several hundred metres to the west of our position. Alexander's face had this curious twitch, much like how a wolf might observe its prey from a concealed position. He scanned the horizon a few more minutes before slamming down the hatch and ordering our driver, 'Go forward to that village!' I had a slightly odd feeling about what might happen next. We were approximately a few hundred metres away from this village when Alexander ordered the driver to halt. He then ordered a high explosive to be fired directly into the houses. The loader rammed an explosive round into the breech and the breech was shut. I aimed the gun and fired as instructed. Through the gunsight I watched the round impact. It destroyed the houses as if they were nothing but matchwood. There may have been women and children inside, but he did not care about that at all. To be honest none of us did at the time.

Alexander's war would soon change when, during the early phase of the battle, his tank was hit hard, either by fire from a Russian tank or an anti-tank round. As he described:

All I remember was directing my crew up a hill which we crested. I could not see any enemy as I scanned the area in our path. I ordered my driver forward and there were Panthers on my left and right flanks. These began firing at targets that I could not make out. There were two farm buildings right ahead with trees to the left. I ordered my gunner to fire a 7.5cm shot into these trees. Before he had even a chance to load and fire the round there was a tremendous bang. A shower of sparks followed the bang and these hit my face, causing some burning pain. Smoke obscured the view for some seconds, but then daylight was visible. I looked down and could see our driver had a large slab of sheared-off armour plate that had sliced clean through his body mid-thorax. This was where the daylight was coming in from, where this piece had sheared off.

He was dead and there was much blood. There was a little smoke starting to come from the forward area too. I saw the remains of the machine gunner who was down in the hull. There was not much left of him, just gore, like his body had been smashed against the inside of the panzer. I knew that we had to get out of the panzer as quickly as we could before any ammunition exploded inside. My gunner was unconscious and his head was bleeding, but I dragged him out of the tank and rolled him off onto the ground. The radio operator was shaken up, but he had got out, along with my loader. Both had concussion and mild head wounds, but otherwise they were fine. I broke some of my gunner's ribs rolling him out of the panzer, but it was better that than remaining inside. I dragged my wounded comrade as far away from the panzer as I felt safe. My other comrades followed, helping each other along. Our tanks rolled past us and the noise of battle could be heard in the direction they were heading. We reached some cover in a slight ditch and collapsed inside. As I lay in the ditch, looking skyward, I could see aircraft high up in the air, dancing like flies. These were our own fighters engaging Russian planes. As I lay in the ditch with the others, I felt pain for the first time in my face and my right arm. Blood was oozing from my jacket sleeve. Initially, I felt no pain at all, even when I dragged my comrade from the panzer. I tried to remove my jacket to see what damage had been done, but the pain was so bad I couldn't do it. Then our soldiers appeared and a medic was rushed over to us. They cut the arm off my tunic and I could see the arm of the tunic was wet with blood. My arm too was soaked with so much blood I could not see a wound. The medic told me I had multiple bone wounds that would need urgent attention. He bandaged me up and, along with the others, we moved to the rear. I was okay and could walk, but our gunner could not and had to be carried on a stretcher. The other survivors of my crew were just mildly concussed. They were given some water and medication and cleaned up. They rested for a few hours before being told to report to the front as they were considered fit for duty. I argued that if they fix my arm, I could return to duty also. It was with a heavy heart I made my report, only to be told I would be evacuated to hospital for an operation. After this, I would be sent home to recuperate. If I could pass fit after my arm had healed, I could return to my unit, but this would be out of the question for a long time I was told. I was so angry about this. On my way to the hospital, I sat in the back of the truck with my right arm heavily bandaged and in a sling. We drove past a long line of Russian prisoners. I was so angry I drew my small pistol that I had with me at all times. With my left hand I drew the pistol, aiming it into the group of prisoners. I squeezed the trigger. I hit one of them and saw him drop to the ground. Had I killed him? I don't know and I didn't care at that moment. I was seething with anger and there were five other fellows in the back with me. They just looked at me expressionless and never said anything. I put the pistol back into my tunic pocket, rested my head in my arms and cried.

When I arrived at the hospital, I was rendered unconscious while the doctors repaired the bones in my damaged right arm. The arm was then set in a kind of splint, which was very unpleasant as it could not be moved at all and I felt it looked stupid. I felt like some kind of clown with this thing on. As I recovered in hospital, one of our officers came to visit and he presented me with the Iron Cross 2nd Class. Arrangements for my transport back home were then discussed with me. My mother had been informed about my injury. I dreaded going back home back to the dreary civilian atmosphere I knew would be waiting. I knew it would drive me fucking mad. I had no choice in the matter, as I was no use to the army in this state. Later, I learned that the great battle we had embarked upon was a loss. We had lost so many good soldiers and panzers. Those Russian devils appeared in ever-increasing numbers with their own panzers. I spoke with my friend, Jochen, later about the battle and he said it was slaughter everywhere. The Soviets drove their panzers, crashing into ours in suicidal attacks, firing at point blank range, burning hulks everywhere, mangled corpses. Jochen said it was a vision of hell. He was like me; he was very angry and wanted revenge for his suffering. Jochen had suffered injury to his legs but could walk and run and had made a good recovery. They would not allow him to serve on frontline duty and was offered duty in the rearguard section. He said to me, 'Maybe this is something you might think about later?'

Alexander Kohlmann headed back to Germany to convalesce from his wounds, but many of his friends in the Das Reich Division would never return home. The initial successes of the German forces on the Eastern Front gave way to a series of setbacks from which the Germans would never recover. The failure at Kursk was just one element in the equation. Germany's military incursions into the vastness of Soviet Russia had proved fruitless. The severe winters had also taken a heavy toll on the Germans since the launch of Barbarossa; equipment became inoperable and men froze to death. The Russians, on the other hand, used the winter weather to their own tactical advantage. Infantry *Gefreiter* Gerhard Neuhoff wrote of the Russian winters:

I dreaded them more than going into combat with the enemy. The weather killed men in a matter of hours. The temperatures could drop as low as minus fifty or sixty below freezing. The wind would blow hurricane force at times, making these temperatures totally unbearable to most humans. Your rifle would freeze solid, making it impossible to maintain, load and fire. Vehicle engines would freeze to the point where we would have to try and light fires beneath them in order to be able to start them. Sometimes they would not start at all. I saw men slowly die from the cold. It was an agonising death and most would die with a grimace upon their faces. Some of the men appeared to have smiles upon their faces. I was told that when you die from extreme cold, the moment of death feels warm and you smile, thinking it's over, but this is the very moment you die. We tried everything to keep warm and keep our feet free of frostbite, but it was not easy. The Russians appeared unaffected by the weather and used it to their advantage all of the time. I lost a number of toes to frostbite and in the end I could barely walk. I had to be evacuated out and I am sure had I not been I would have died at some point. I came close to just giving up numerous times. The extreme cold does that to you. It was only the thought of my mother and father crying at my loss that kept me going. I imagined them receiving the news and how it would have driven them mad with grief. There was no way I could just let go and die in that place. Even though there were many times I just wanted to be free of the torment of the freezing cold, wind and snow. The snow falls so thick; it buries everything, even aircraft. If a man falls unconscious, he can die and never be found in the snow. The eastern front was truly a horror only those there could ever comprehend or understand.

It can be said that the German campaigns in the east were a thorn in the bear's paw, but the initiative now lay with the Russians. With lend-lease equipment arriving from Britain and America, the Russian bear began to rise to its feet again. She began to produce new fighter and bomber aircraft which were far superior to the antiquated ones the Luftwaffe had destroyed on the ground during the early phase of Barbarossa. They were also producing new tanks in their thousands. They were mass produced and far from pretty, but proved deadly against the German tanks. The Russian commanders would exploit the lost opportunities and tactical blunders made by the Germans. Hitler's constant interference in his generals' military planning also aided the Russians greatly. The Russians had suffered intolerable cruelty and hardship under the Germans; now they would steadily gain momentum and show no mercy to their German enemy.

In England, Melitta Jorg rejoiced at the news of the German failures in the east. She wrote in her journal:

It is so very gratifying to read the press reports that the Nazis are taking such a battering in the east. They have failed in every respect and rumour has it that Kursk will be the nail in Hitler's coffin. I was taken to celebrate and helped myself to father's cognac. So, I went into the library and drank a few glasses by the fire. It was fine until I tried to stand up. It was a case of, 'Oh dear, Melitta, you are a bit pissed [again]!!!!' Father will not be happy if he finds out, but he is away on business in Oxford for a few days, so, with luck, he will not discover this episode. If he does, I will never hear the end of it. I can assure you I am no alcoholic; I am not beyond control. I don't even drink a lot, it's just I get pissed very easily indeed [he, he]! I am not sure that the young RAF boy, Albert, is the one for me. He is incredibly sweet and good looking but his domestic skills are severely lacking, I'm afraid. It's rare to find any man who, after making love to you, actually bothers to fold up the clothes they've cast onto your bedroom floor, especially the underwear. I cannot bear the post-coital clearing up, or the fact he lights himself a cigarette and doesn't offer me one. My legs and thighs hurt too. He has this thing for bending me into all these positions, that it's much like the gymnastics classes father tried to enrol me in when I was nine years old! It's a good job Hitler cannot read this as, right now, he would be saying, 'Listen to this dirty Jew!' What propaganda my writings might produce in his or Goebbels' possession? Anyhow, to the point. I couldn't continue any relationship where I am any man's run-around. Either way, I will be breaking the news to him next time he calls. In the meantime, I will continue my ramblings as I am sure that someday someone is going to read this and the titillation will provide some welcome distraction from some melancholy episode [he, he].

Chapter Twelve

A Brief Flirtation with Murder

My past has always been a closely guarded secret kept within my family. I always felt it better to keep things this way, due partly to the mutual misunderstanding that society has these days regarding the war. When my three children were at an age where I could sit them down and tell of my past, I did so. Even so, they were sworn to secrecy; not that I had been guilty of any crime, because I hadn't, but because few children could say that their mother had been an *Aufseherin* [female concentration camp guard] at the infamous Auschwitz concentration camp in Poland. Yes, it came as a shock, but when I explained everything to them and told them the whole story, they understood.

This is what I was told by the now very elderly Katrina Roth, who had been a close friend of one of the women I had interviewed for my first book, *Hitler's Girls – Doves Amongst Eagles*. It was perhaps the most eagerly anticipated interview I had conducted in a very long time. I had all kinds of ideas as to what I would be told and braced myself for a catalogue of horrors. What I learned was quite the opposite in some ways. Katrina's father was a serving officer in the German army and he took Katrina, her sister, Alana, and mother, Gudrun, to a new German settlement in Poland. Katrina takes up the story:

I just remember from a young girl, my father being in uniform and being a soldier in the army. We were raised as a National Socialist family. My father expected us to read various Nazi Party publications and, of course, we all had our own copy of the *Mein Kampf* book written by the Führer, Adolf Hitler. After supper each evening, if my father was home, he would sit and expect us to read him passages of the book from memory. He kept saying it was important we learn it by heart if we were to excel at school. My education was very good and I did very well at school overall.

I had joined the *Bund Deutscher Madel* [League of German Maidens] in 1939, the year the Second World War started. I was fifteen then. The BDM was like your English Girl Scouts organisation. We had a medical fitness test prior to being accepted. My father provided papers going back three generations to show our blood purity. He bought uniforms for my sisters and me. To have a uniform was quite something back then as not every girl's family could afford one. The BDM was quite politically orientated; a mix of current political doctrine as well as the standard activities of first-aid proficiency, gymnastics, fitness, health and beauty, and things. On camp, they even taught you skills such as how to make a fire, what foods you could find and survive off in the woods and forests. I always looked forward to summer camp with the BDM. All my friends were with me, so yes, it was good. We were expected to put maximum effort into every single activity we did on camp, and at the meetings back home. If you worked hard you received proficiency certificates, awards and badges that you were then permitted to wear on your uniform. If you really put your mind to it and worked hard, they would even make you a BDM group leader, which was quite some honour for a young lady back then. Within a year I was a BDM leader, in charge of a troop of 30–40 girls. Of course, my father thought this was wonderful. With regard to our racial teachings, we did not associate with, or recognize, Jews or Gypsies as a part of the human race. Homosexuals, prostitutes and Jehovah's Witnesses were also classed as a non-human species. Of course, we understood they were human beings in the physical sense, but not in the moral sense, if you understand. This is how we were schooled throughout National Socialist Germany in the Third Reich. We accepted our teachings as those of our country's leaders. My father, also being in the German army and a Nazi Party member of many years, made such beliefs even more commonplace. It was all around us in our society, at school, at home, the BDM; everywhere you looked.

Our family were well aware of what was happening to the Jews in German territory. I knew they were forcibly removed from their homes and jobs and had their possessions confiscated. The camps I had also heard about, but the murders were not mentioned, not at first anyway. Our father never made any secret of the camps, and I guess this is because he felt Germany would never have to answer to anyone for it. Of course, he was wrong, though. I later fell out with my father and we never spoke again. I felt that I had been manipulated and lied to. Something I began to realise when my father orientated me towards becoming involved with what he termed 'a great duty to the German Reich'. He always used to say that when I tried to read books on poetry and science and things. He would say, 'Why do you read this rubbish? This will be no good to you, my girl!' I wanted to be a vet and work with animals, and he told me he would help me get a job working with animals. Only the animals he was referring to were Jews.

I completed my Reich Labour Service in 1942. It was really good. I had a placement on the land and again my leadership skills were recognised. I was placed in charge of the girls and there were quite a few of them to keep an eye on. When we first arrived, many were a little homesick. I heard some of them crying in the night, as we all slept together in a kind of dormitory building with a corrugated metal roof. I would get up to see who was crying, ask them what was the matter, and try talking to them to make them feel better. I had to remind them they could not display infantile behaviour. It was harsh, I know, as some of the girls missed their parents, but it was my job; to maintain their wellbeing and morale and keep them working hard whilst maintaining discipline. We didn't have to get up early, but the work was hard at times. We worked in the fields harvesting the crops, cleaning out stables, milking cattle, exercising horses and helping with maintenance around the local farms. Once that work was done, we also helped prepare our own meals. By the end of each day, we were really tired. We had a wash, then ate our meal and then got changed, ready for bed. We could do some reading before bed, but whatever we read had to be approved as being suitable. It was my job to ensure that girls did not read anything that was not permitted suitable by the state. We could talk amongst ourselves too, as girls still do. We were not allowed to wear any makeup, lipstick, or paint our finger- or toenails either. We wrote letters home to our parents and sometimes we could make corn dolls, or other things, which we could send them as gifts. On Saturday afternoons we could go into the local town. If there was a cinema there, we could go in and watch a film. The films were often boring but the news films were quite exciting. There was also a lot of propaganda being shown in the cinema. All this was quite normal to us, though. Even when the *Wandering Jew* was shown, we watched it impassively. Some girls were scared by the film, as it portrayed Jews as monsters that could spring up from anywhere and pounce on young girls from the shadows. We would all link arms if we went out at night and woe betide anyone who tried anything on with us! Yes, we had some good times, and we girls became lifelong friends and we were pretty close.

When I returned home from my Labour service with yet more awards and praise, I wanted to go on to study to become a vet. I loved animals, even though we were never allowed to have pets, as our father always said no. I once found this stray cat. It was a poor thing and very skinny, but very friendly, so I bought it home with me, hoping I could persuade my father to allow us to keep it. When my father discovered it he took it by the scruff of its neck and I thought he was just going to throw it out of the house. He went through the back door into the yard with the struggling cat and drowned it in the water butt in the backyard. He then said, 'Do you not understand, my girl, we are at war? We cannot afford to feed you children and a stray animal. It is the way of nature to remove the weak, my girl. Now, do you understand?' I couldn't help it; I started to cry at the sight of that poor cat lying dead. He then started shouting at me again, 'Don't you dare cry, my girl! Now, pull yourself together at once. Dry your eyes, and you can bury that animal!'

Some time after, my father came home and said to me, 'So, you want a job working with animals, do you?' I said, 'Yes, please, father', and was quite excited at the prospect. 'Well, I can arrange this for you, my girl', he said. I actually thought he was serious when he said it, but once the day I was due to start my job working with animals came, I realised just what he was talking about. It was one morning in August of 1943. My father often went to his work with the military in a big black car with two other junior officers and a guard. I thought it odd, but got in the back seat of the car with the guard and we drove up the drive from our home and onto the road. I just stared out of the car window as we drove. We went through the town of Oswiecim and all seemed normal as people went about their business. I saw many German soldiers with their rifles over their backs walking around; some were drinking coffee at cafés; all seemed quite normal. Then we came to a military checkpoint where we had to show our identity papers. The sentry obviously knew my father and the other two officers with him and, after checking the papers, he waved us through with a salute. The barrier lifted and we drove up this road and, as we did, huge barbed-wire fences with guard towers came into view. I could see guards with dogs walking around the perimeter and the buildings. I knew where this place was; this was the Auschwitz concentration camp. I had heard about the camp, but I did not even know my father 'worked there', as he put it. He just used to tell us he was involved in local security operations for the state, and it was none of our concern.

The way we came into the camp was not the infamous main entrance where inmates were brought in by rail under the sign '*Arbeit Macht Frei*' [work sets you free]. There was much activity within the camp, which to me back then looked absolutely immense. It stretched for as far as the eye could see. We pulled up outside what looked like a barracks building. My father got out the car and said, 'You will find plenty of animals to work with here, girl. Now come on, get out of the car and follow me.' We went into the barracks and I was introduced to this very stern, frosty-looking woman I guessed was in her mid- to late-twenties. She wore a uniform with a cape and I noticed she had a whip of some sort coiled up and attached to her belt. My father said to her, 'Don't take any nonsense from my girl. She is your responsibility now; just show her the ropes.' I was taken away, measured up, and issued with my uniform. Yes, the uniform looked smart, but what was I doing here, I thought. I asked the woman if they had kept animals here, as this is the work I wanted to do. She laughed so much that she had to cover her mouth with both her hands. It made me feel stupid, so I asked her, 'What is so funny, Frau?' She was still laughing when she said, 'Animals? You want to work with animals, Fraulein? Oh, this is just so funny, is it not? Did your father not explain?' I shook my head and told her, 'No, explain what?' She then replied, 'Oh, come on, Fraulein. Seriously: take a look out of the window and you will see that here we are surrounded by animals: Jewish ones, Gypsy ones, sexual deviant ones, anti-National Socialist ones, religious ones. They are all out there, out that window, Fraulein!' I looked through the window and all I could see were wretched-looking people with shaven heads, wearing the characteristic striped pyjama-like clothing. Maybe I had been naïve, but this shook me to the core. The sheer scale of this place was intimidating, along with occasional whiffs of an unpleasant smell, which seemed stronger some days more than others. I thought at first that maybe the sewage system had blocked or something. God, I was such a stupid, naïve girl, wasn't I? I just couldn't believe this place was real. We had all heard that the undesirables of our society had been taken to concentration camps. I pictured these places as being like communities where the people were just segregated from our own. It came as a shock, but here

I was with the reality dawning upon me. I was told to put my uniform on, which I did, then I was shown to the guard quarters. It was a long, wooden-construction building with a metal roof. There were beds arranged in rows along its length. A heater was at the one end and its chimney went up through the roof. I was allocated a bed and told 'this one will be yours'. I tried to explain, 'I will not need this as I will be going home with my father later.' I was told, 'I am sorry, but I am afraid not, Fraulein. You are now a member of the staff. Your father has personally signed the papers and you are now in the Führer's service.' I felt both angry and scared, but I could not just run away out of the door and out of this place. I asked the woman guard, 'What will I have to do here?' She said, 'It's simple; you will be assigned duties and you will carry them out without any questions. Is this clear, Fraulein?' I nodded to her, and she barked again, 'Yes or no, Fraulein?' I swallowed hard and said to her, 'Yes, Frau, I understand.' She just said something like 'good'.

I was shown the various duties by other female camp guards. They rotated us sometimes, so we did not become too familiar with one person. The personalities were mixed, but most had a rabid hatred of Jews. Most had volunteered and they laughed when I told them how I got here. 'Oh, dear, dear, dear', the one said to me, 'You have certainly landed in the shit, haven't you?' Our tasks revolved mainly around the women inmates at the camp. When they were moved from one part of the camp to another, we escorted them. We did the same for women inmates on work duties outside the camp. I soon learned that the unfit were disposed of in gas chambers. The unfit could be old women, old men and those with a physical or mental impediment, or children. I also soon learned that even the fit, if they were Jews or Gypsies, went to the gas chambers. I was instructed that I should shout '*Schnell! Schnell!*' [Faster! Faster!] and that if any fell behind the others, I should beat them without hesitation. I dreaded this task, as the last thing I ever wanted to do was inflict further pain upon these wretched people, who were suffering enough as it was. Many of them were in appallingly bad condition and were literally bones. Many were not far from death either, by being worked to death in nearby factories. We were shown the gas chambers and told how the killing was carried out. Again, I thought 'this can't be real, surely'. There was no way out and I was as much a prisoner in this place as they were, until our days off, when we could go off camp.

My first day off camp was a Sunday. As soon as I left the place, I got a lift back home. I confronted my father and we had a terrible row where he nearly struck me across the face. Only mother managed to calm him down. I told him I did not want to return to that dreadful place and that its role was for the mass killing of the inmates. I asked him why he did not tell me about this. Father just shouted at me, 'Oh, my girl, you really are a genius, aren't you?' Mother became upset and shouted, 'You two, please stop this now!' I had no choice but to return to that place and was only there up until February of 1944. I was frequently told off for not being hard enough in my services. I was also asked what my father might think of me; him being a serving officer. I was told that I should not feel empathy for the Jews there. They would say, 'Imagine if the boot were on the other foot. Don't you think they would do the same to us?'

On my next leave, we went into the town again. I went with some of the other women. They were all eager for a good time and it was just a relief to get out of that place. We went to this bar in the town, which was full of German soldiers, officers and administrative staff. We went in, sat down, and men would come up, wanting to buy us drinks. Of course, we didn't refuse their hospitality. I had never really drunk alcohol much and after a few glasses of wine I was quite drunk. As the night wore on, there was much drunkenness and singing, and I found myself sitting on the lap of this one young soldier. I was drunk and admit that he was a bit too old for me, but at the time I didn't care. I had my arms around him and he put his hat on my head. He started kissing me and, with not a care in the world, he undid my blouse and had his hands all over my breasts, squeezing and tweaking and rubbing. I had been with boys in the past, but never had a proper boyfriend. I was drunk, but remember a lot about the evening. The other girls were all with boys doing much the same. Some left to go outside and I remember the boy I was with pushed me off his lap, grabbed my wrist and literally dragged me outside. At that moment I didn't care; I felt giggly and happy through the wine I had drunk. We ended up in some trees on the ground, which was damp and musky. He quickly pulled down his trousers and then proceeded to pull off mine. He fumbled with the remaining buttons on my blouse and managed to pull some of them off. He stood before me and more or less demanded that I suck his cock. I told him I had never sucked any man's cock before. What if I did it wrong? He pushed a finger into my mouth and, moving it back and forth, gave me instructions on how I should suck a man's cock. I took him in my mouth for some minutes until he withdrew. He pushed me down onto the ground and had sex with me. It felt good, but he did not last very long and, as soon as he was done, he got up, pulled up his trousers, put his jacket back on and just walked off back into the bar. I lay there for a few minutes with my head spinning and began to feel sick. In fact, when I tried to stand up, I ended up falling into some bushes. I rolled down an embankment onto the road. The other women I was with saw me and came running out. They were all laughing and one said, 'I hope he used something, Katrina!' I looked at her and then felt that nauseous sensation in my gut. It slowly built to the point where I just bent over and vomited several times on the spot. Before we all moved off, I saw the soldier who had just had sex with me, coming out of the door with another girl. They were running into the same trees, presumably he was going to fuck her too? We all walked back to the camp, laughing and singing, some of us kicking off our shoes as our feet hurt so much. I had to stop several times on the way back to be sick. I felt really ill and my head hurt. We walked into the camp to our hut and the other girls helped undress me and get me into bed. I was completely gone in seconds and was roused by the other girls in the morning. I got up, looked into my small mirror and just saw a mess. I was pale, my hair was all over the place, and my brain was pounding in my skull. I told myself I would never do that again. In fact, I told the other women I had been with I'd never do that again. One said, 'That is what they all say!' What we did off duty was our own concern, as long as we didn't cause any trouble for the local authorities. Our seniors were all fucking men on the camp and drinking with them in their private quarters, so nobody cared as long as you were discreet. The next time we went off duty, I chose not to drink, as I did not want a repeat of the last time. Getting drunk in bars was not good, as it was easy to end up pregnant, or even getting raped. I heard of some other young girls who had dated our soldiers and had been literally forced to have sex with them. They particularly liked the young girls of 18-20 years of age. My drunken night in the inn all made sense now. Nothing changes, does it? They get you drunk with the sole intention of fucking you afterwards. I remember going into the town with one of the women and this man came up and sarcastically said, 'You two are with *Der Schadel-Kader!*' [The Skull Squad].

The winters in Germany were cold, but in Poland the cold felt different. It was a freezing cold that entered your bones instantly. The temperatures dropped to minus five, ten, twenty and down to minus thirty some days. At night it was worse; ice would form in the huts, particularly on the insides of the windows. We had a fire, which we put coal and wood into, and this would keep the chill off to a degree but it was only small. It was like these wood burner things you get today. A square cast iron bottom where you put coal or wood into and a chimney that rose up and vented through the tin roof. In winter, your bedclothes often felt damp. I wore a thick woollen gown to bed and two pairs of thick, winter army socks. In the morning you'd get up and try and wash, but the water was solid ice in the basin. I woke up on Christmas Morning, 1943, got out of my bed and went to the window of our hut. The window was thick with ice on the inside. With the heavy woollen cuff of my nightgown I rubbed away at the frosted glass, creating a circle of melt, which I could then look through. I could see inmates trudging around outside in the freezing minus twenty-five conditions. We were lucky; we had the small fire in our hut. The fire burned all night and kept the worst of the freezing air away. Even so, it was bloody cold in that hut, so how did those people feel out there, some in bare feet? I looked across the way towards the crematoria. Smoke billowed out from the chimney like ghosts ascending heaven. I scratched my leg with my foot as I stood looking through the melt, my arms folded, shivering. I closed my eyes and thought 'I could be anywhere now'. I could even be back home as a little girl during carefree days. Only that faint, sickly-sweet smell of decaying human flesh combined with smoke reminded me that I was closer to hell than I ever was home.

I did witness cruelty and violence against the inmates during my short time in that place. I later gave statements to members of the Allied authorities concerning the ill treatment of inmates. I saw women prisoners falling over then being beaten. Some of the guards used whips or riding crops to hit inmates. Others used their fists or their boots. Sometimes, they would pick up anything they could find to beat a prisoner with. One was hit repeatedly with a section of an iron bar once. That prisoner died on the spot, staining the snow around her body red with blood. A few weeks after Christmas of 1943, I came down with a sickness infection. I was treated by the camp physician, who gave me medication and ordered bed rest. I had never felt so ill in my life. I developed a fever, vomited, and shivered all day and all night. My weight began to plummet and this was very noticeable as I was normally only nine stones anyway. My father was called and he insisted I see his doctor back home. They wrapped me in blankets and carried me out into the car. The journey home was agonisingly long, spent crouched up on the back seat. My father talked incessantly, but I cannot remember a word he said to me on that journey. When we arrived home, I was carried up into my own room and my father called his doctor out immediately. He spent some minutes examining me and ordered me to be rushed to the nearest hospital in the town, as I was very gravely ill and could die if not treated properly soon. They thought I'd just caught influenza or something at the camp and that it would pass. I was rushed into the hospital, where again I was examined and pumped full of injections and tablets. I was diagnosed with typhoid, which I had probably contracted from the camp. In places, it was very unsanitary and we were ordered not to touch certain things, or have any physical contact with inmates, due to the risk of disease and lice, etc. I spent some time in the hospital before being sent home to recover. It took a long time until I felt better, could eat properly and gain back weight I had lost. I had dropped down to six stones, but the inmates at that camp weighed far less than that, and were expected to go and work, often in the freezing winter conditions. In the summer, the threat of disease increased and thousands died of disease at that place.

My father was frightened by the fact that I came close to death. He seemed to change after that and tried to be kind. I hated him, though, and I could not look at him in the eyes anymore. I never went back to the camp, and me, my sister and mother moved back to Magdeburg in Germany, under our father's orders. We couldn't get away from Poland quick enough. It felt like heaven to be back in Germany, despite the bombings, which were occurring daily at that time. Am I haunted by that place called Auschwitz? I was not there very long, thankfully, but I did not kill or beat anyone, or even force anyone into a gas chamber. But, yes, I have ghosts from that place in my mind. I remember that Christmas of 1943. I went out on my camp patrol and I saw this child sat on a step, crying, with her head in her hands. I was going to try and comfort her and ask what the matter was, but how could I ask such an obvious and stupid question? It was Christmas Day and the child was in Auschwitz and all alone, with no parents, brothers or sisters; just on her own. Whenever I think of that child I feel sick to my stomach. Did she survive? I'm not sure, but I hope that maybe she did. The question of my own guilt is simple. I was guilty of being at that place, but it was not my choice. I do not condone or support what happened there, as I knew it to be wrong, whatever our political, religious or cultural beliefs may have been.

I left home and, although I wrote to and met up with my mother, I could not forgive my father for what he had done. As I said, I never spoke to him again, even though he tried writing me letters. I never read them and threw them away. When he died, I did not even attend his funeral. To say that there was too much bad blood between father and daughter was an understatement. I know he was questioned on his activities after the war. However, he was not linked to any murders or criminal activity, so they let him go after questioning him. The only other information I have is that he fled the camp, returning to Germany before the liberation. It did not take the Allied authorities long to catch up with him, though, as papers with his address on were discovered. He was involved in junior administration and not the high flyer he made himself out to be. I underwent questioning and so did my mother. My sister was also questioned and everything corroborated with what I had written in a statement. They were happy with what they were told. Even our neighbour came forward and told them, 'Her father was a bastard. Thought he was a better man than everyone else. Do you know he even drowned her cat?'

After the war, I worked with farm animals. I had wanted to become a vet and I suppose I succeeded in a small way, as I became an assistant to a local veterinarian practice. I managed to secure my own apartment above a baker's shop. I made some new friends in a new town and eventually settled down and got married. My husband and me divorced some years ago, but we have remained friends and we have two children. I do feel personal guilt that I lived while so many died at a place I worked at, and in the capacity of a camp guard. It's a heavy burden, but I would never have gone there on my own free will. After the war, I was told the death figures which occurred at that place. It's a stain one can't erase from the conscience, but people will still say I'm an evil person, which I know I am not. This is why I have remained silent all these years. The mutual misunderstanding you might encounter is enormous. It is my generation's burden, regardless of what historians may think or say. The world today is full of warnings and still full of war. What would be my message to young people today? I would say to them, let politicians fight their own wars; let them see for themselves the death and destruction that takes place under the orders they give. Let them suffer instead of the people or the minorities that they oppress. Let children and young people be independent thinkers instead of political scapegoats. Above all, beware of any political figure or party that tries to influence youth in order to further their own political ambitions. These are where the real monsters lurk.

It has to be noted here that most of the German women who entered the concentration camp system to become guards, administrators, staff cooks, etc. did so voluntarily. Any young female displaying a particular ruthlessness within the BDM was often nurtured towards this occupation. Many would remain unrepentant after the war to any wrongdoing. Martha Pohlmann, who served in the capacity of a female camp guard at Ravensbruck, said of her time in that infamous camp:

In my opinion we were waging a war based upon the very survival of our racial and cultural ideology. In this endeavour, there was no room for mercy. We were, in a sense, soldiers of another kind. Men would laugh, and I know some of the males in our society at that time attempted to look down upon us. Yes, we wore bras and knickers, but we carried out our duties as efficiently as any man. I was issued with certain orders and I obeyed them to the rule. I did not question anything; I just acted without conscience or remorse. There were no regrets, as the will for the preservation of our German race was the prerequisite to all of my personal actions and involvement. Prisoners were driven much like cattle to their deaths. I became numb to the fact that, in my duty, I was effectively helping to kill people. It was just a job, a means to an end, to securing Germany's future Reich. Many nations have pursued similar tactics throughout their history. The winners of these wars then label such acts as genocide or mass murder. They demonise those who were also never involved, so what does it matter in the end? That is my personal opinion as a believer in National Socialism. Yes, I am a Nazi. I was born a Nazi, under Nazi Germany, and I will always be one and shall die a Nazi. That is something I cannot escape from if I had wanted to.

Martha Pohlmann died in 1990, a lonely old woman. Her daughter disowned her after discovering her Nazi past. Her daughter did not want to be named, but said:

When I discovered my mother's brief flirtation with murder I was horrified. I say 'brief' because she was not in the camp system for long, as she fell pregnant as a result of her liaisons with a male staff member on the camp. This man, whoever he was, was my father. I never learned his identity, as my mother would never say. I don't care who he was anyway; he was probably a murderer too. I knew my mother had been a Nazi. I found paperwork hidden in a box once, and I read through it. I was just a child then, and I didn't really appreciate its implications. It was only later, when I was older, that I asked my mother about this paperwork. She told me there was none and that she had burned it. I wanted to learn the truth, so I asked my grandparents, who were reluctant to tell me anything also. It was only when my mother had to go into hospital for an operation on her hip that I tore the house apart to search for the documents I had seen in that box. I found them, hidden loose under my mother's mattress. When I read them it just confirmed what I had already feared. She had been in the SS, and she had been active at the Ravensbruck camp for around a year and a half. There were many handwritten notes that appeared to glorify the war, and some other writings, including love letters from a man, possibly my father. The letters were full of filth in many cases, and they made me sick. My mother had obviously been proud of her work. I confronted her in the hospital and she got angry and told me, 'Oh, shut up, will you!' I replied, 'No, I will not shut up. I want the truth!' In the end, after much arguing, she told me. I sat in the room with her as she stared impassively at me and I just thought 'Who are you? You are nothing more than a stranger to me'. We began to argue again and a doctor came in to see what was going on. My mother shouted, 'Get her away from me!' There was no mother and daughter relationship after that. I kept in touch with her, but not in the normal way that any normal daughter would. I basically disowned my mother because I could not deal with the fact that she was not sorry. She may not have killed anyone, but was she guilty by association? I don't know. When she died, I felt a slight sense of relief, but it was still a stain on me, wasn't it? I never had any children, as I felt for a long time this world is no place to bring any child into. I live by myself quite happily, and I am a regular churchgoer. I believe in God, in the sense that we all go somewhere after we die. I also think if we have committed acts of evil we have to recompense for those deeds. At least I can pass with a clear conscience. Many from the Nazi era would not have that luxury.

Very few women who served in the concentration camp system would come forward to discuss their past. Perhaps many did have things to hide. As a historian, when I first began my research into areas of German Third Reich history, I was quick to learn certain facts. Our intrusions into the past can be much like tearing the scab off an otherwise healing wound. To bring this chapter to a conclusion, I felt that the quote made by Stefanie Engeler was apt regarding the female concentration camp staff: 'We were not soldiers in the combat context, but one soldier did say to me in a bar once, "You don't wear a military uniform and call yourself a civilian now, do you?" That remark stuck in my mind and he was right, wasn't he?'

Chapter Thirteen

The Annihilation of Races

The word holocaust is one most people around the world are all too familiar with. It is a word often used out of context today. The Holocaust of the Second World War was undoubtedly one of the worst in human history, but there are other examples prior to the Second World War. Many ask, what's the difference between holocaust and genocide? Both terms are used to describe mass killings carried out with the conscious intention of destroying an entire race of people. Political, religious and social ideologies have, throughout history, all played a part in acts of genocide, particularly in warfare. Holocaust was derived originally from the Greek word 'Holos', meaning whole, and 'Kaustos', meaning burned. In Greek, its historical explanation refers to a sacrificial offering. Since 1945, the word has been used specifically to describe the mass murder of millions of Jews and other targeted groups by the Nazis, but if the Soviet massacres of German men, women and children during the closing stages of the Second World War are to be understood then we have to apply the word in its wider meaning.

In Germany, the Holocaust can trace its roots back to the earliest beginnings of the Nazi Party. Under Adolf Hitler's direction, the fledgling NSDAP [National Socialist German Workers Party] became more violently anti-Semitic as it gained more support. Violence was commonplace at the early Nazi Party meetings. The SA, or Brownshirts as they were known, were the original tool for the perpetration of violence in German society. They actively sought out members of the Jewish community, who were then subjected to verbal and serious physical violence. Gypsies, Jehovah's Witnesses, homosexuals and people of non-German ethnicity were all targeted, and political opponents, along with pacifists, also became the target of violence. As the Nazi Party grew in size, so did its appetite for violence. Physical attacks on these groups soon worsened and resulted in murder. Should we be so surprised that the war Hitler had so badly wanted ended in the way it did?

When one examines all aspects of the Second World War did any particular country suffer any worse than another? Every country suffered to some extent as a result of Nazi aggression in Europe. Clearly the peoples of Eastern Europe suffered horrific violence, depravation and cruelty at the hands of the German forces. The seeds of the Nazi Holocaust, although nurtured in Germany itself, were certainly sewn in the blood-soaked soil of the east. With the liquidation of the Warsaw Ghetto – that began in October 1940 and ended in May 1943 – there followed an orgy of sadism, violence and murder. Many of the Jews living in the Warsaw Ghetto would not survive to see the forced-labour camps that awaited many of them. When the German forces arrived, many men, women and children were killed on the spot, or died as a result of their brutal treatment. Survivors recall seeing young girls dragged by their hair down flights of stairs, to be beaten and kicked when they got to the bottom. Some were stripped and humiliated by the SS soldiers, while others were taken away out of sight to be raped and shot. Babies were tipped from their beds and bayoneted, or left where they were to slowly die.

To begin the real journey through the Nazi Holocaust, we have to examine the first mass gassing of human beings, at the Belzec camp near Lubin, which took place on 17 March 1942. The SS built the Belzec death camp for the sole purpose of implementing the then-secretive 'Operation Reinhard'. This was the codename given to the Nazi plan to massacre the majority of Polish Jews in the General Government district of German-occupied Poland. It marked the deadliest phase of the Holocaust and introduced the extermination camp as a means of destroying European Jewry. The codename was chosen in honour of one of the most senior figures in the execution of the final solution, Reinhard Heydrich. Heydrich was a senior Nazi official during the Second World War, holding the rank of SS *Obergruppenführer* and General of the Police. Heydrich was also chief of the Reich main security office. He was considered so dangerous that an operation was carried out to assassinate him in Prague. Though he was not killed instantly in the attack, Heydrich died eight days later from blood poisoning. Hilde Buchner's father was an old friend of Reinhard Heydrich. She recalled going to the Heydrichs' home on numerous occasions before the Second World War:

> I went there with my father. Heydrich had his children there but none were interested in playing with me. They were much like their father and appeared selfish, vain and arrogant. Heydrich's wife was nice and she would come and talk with me. Heydrich himself was a rather strange looking man. He was very tall, with a long face, sharp, beady eyes and large, pointed nose. His hands were like those of Nosferatu. He had very long hands and they reminded me of a rat's paws. He would acknowledge my presence, smile and say hello, but I don't recall him ever having any conversation with me. He just talked with my father about the then political situation in Germany and how he hoped the future might pan out. It did not surprise me later on how he became so high up in the ranks of the Third Reich. I could imagine him being a cruel, ruthless man when necessary. There was just something very cold about his whole personality, even though he frequently smiled. It turned out he was not only one of the most evil men in the Third Reich but history, too.

Another of the Operation Reinhard extermination camps was Sobibor. By the war's end, a minimum of 250,000 Jews would have been murdered at the Sobibor camp, under the command of the notorious Franz Stangl. The third extermination camp in use under Operation Reinhard was Treblinka. Located in a forest north-east of Warsaw, the camp was in operation for the purpose of mass murder up until October 1943. It is believed that between 700,000 and 900,000 Jews were killed in the gas chambers of Treblinka. More Jews were murdered at Treblinka than at any other Nazi death camp during the Second World War. The Treblinka camp was under the command of Irmfried Eberl from 11 July 1942 to 26 August 1942. The loathsome Franz Stangl then took over command from 1 September 1942 to August 1943, when Kurt Franz, who took command from August 1943 to November 1943, succeeded him.

When the Treblinka camp began its murderous operations, a small number of Jews were spared; kept alive purely in order to dig the graves for their own murdered people. In 1943, the bodies of dead inmates were ordered to be exhumed and then burned on open air fires, along with the bodies of any new victims. The killing operations at Treblinka ended in October 1943 following a revolt by the *Sonderkommandos* in early August. The *Sonderkommandos* were work units made up of death–camp prisoners, usually Jews. They were forced, under threat of their own deaths, to aid in the disposal of gas chamber victims. The Treblinka camp was dismantled ahead of the advancing Russian army. The Nazis even built a house on the site and had the ground ploughed and landscaped in an attempt to hide the evidence of the genocide that took place there. Such attempts at covering up the mass murder that occurred at Treblinka were futile.

Soviet Major Lieniev Ivavanhovich was 23 years of age when he witnessed the site where the Treblinka camp had stood. He wrote:

> They [the Nazis] had gone to some considerable efforts to hide their criminal activities at the camp. It had been almost spirited away and nothing left. There was just this watch-keeper's house and the grounds around it were freshly landscaped. Yes, they had done a very good job, so they thought. The one thing you cannot hide is the smell of death. The soil and air around that place stank of rotting corpses. They could not hide the smell of murder. Just poking around the ground, human remains could be unearthed. Some of the remains were partially cremated, while others appeared quite fresh. Did they really think we would not discover what deeds they had been involved with there? I felt disgusted and sickened as the sheer scale of what had happened there became apparent. Oh yes, I was going to keep going and go all the way into Germany, and, yes, I was going to make them pay. I wanted as many Germans to suffer for this as possible.

The basic method used to murder inmates in the Nazi death camps, particularly in the gas chambers, was a cyanide-based pesticide that had been invented in Germany back in the 1920s. This pesticide was called Zyklon [Cyclone] B; its main ingredient being hydrogen cyanide. The two

German firms, Tesch/Stabenow and Degesch, were responsible for the production of Zyklon B, having acquired the patent from the IG Farben chemical company. Tesch supplied two tons of Zyklon B per month, while Degesch supplied three quarters of a ton. The companies that produced Zyklon B already had extensive experience in fumigation techniques. The use of Zyklon B to eliminate rodent and insect infestations in enclosed spaces meant the chemical could readily be adapted to kill human beings. Zyklon B came in the form of small pellets or discs that were packed into metal tins. The directors of the two firms producing Zyklon B also advised on the best means of using it against humans, including ventilation and heating equipment. Naturally, the directors denied all knowledge of this after the war. Two of the Tesch partners were tried and sentenced to death in 1946, while the director of Degesch received a five-year prison sentence. Hans Stark, who was a registrar of new arrivals at Auschwitz, gave an account of a gassing using Zyklon B. He recalled:

> Maximillian Grabner, who was the head of the political department at Auschwitz, ordered me to pour Zyklon B into an opening on the roof of the gas chamber building. There were two openings in the gas chamber roof and, during a gassing, Zyklon B had to be poured through both openings simultaneously. The victims in the gas chamber below were a transport of 200-250 Jews. There were men, women and children in there. I wore an army issued gas mask to prevent inhaling any of the harmful chemical myself. I poured the granule form gas mixture through the opening in the roof. It trickled down over the victims as it was poured in. They all started to cry out terribly as they realized what was happening by this stage. I did not look through the opening once the Zyklon B had been poured in as the door had to be shut straightaway. There was a lot of screaming coming from inside the gas chamber. After a few minutes all went silent and it was obvious the people inside the chamber below had died. After around fifteen minutes the gas chamber doors were opened. The dead lay all over the place, some entangled with one another. It was a dreadful sight to have to witness.

The dosage of Zyklon B used to kill humans in the gas chambers was approximately 300ppm [parts per million]. This dosage will kill humans in fifteen minutes or so. The gas chambers were relatively small, enclosed spaces with no lights inside. Once the chamber doors were slammed shut there would be total darkness. There would be some momentary light as the small doors were opened prior to the gas being poured in. For those inside the terror would have been unimaginable. The effects of Zyklon B exposure are far from pleasant. Zyklon B attacks the brain and heart first. A severe burning sensation is experienced by the victim, usually in the chest area, rapidly followed by seizure and convulsions. Death is not always instantaneous. Some Holocaust victims took more than thirty minutes to die from Zyklon B exposure. Zyklon B was also used in clothing delousing procedures at the death camps. Delousing required much higher dosages and longer exposure periods. Typical delousing dosage was approximately 16,000ppm, requiring an exposure time of around seventy-two hours. It was discovered insects, including lice, were remarkably resilient to the effects of hydrogen cyanide.

Bergen Belsen was another infamous Nazi death camp. It was in operation from 1941 to 1945. Belsen was located in what is today Lower Saxony, in northern Germany, and was originally established as a prisoner-of-war camp. By 1943, parts of Belsen became a concentration camp. The commanders of the camp during the war were Adolf Haas, who was commander from April 1943 to 2 December 1944, and Josef Kramer, who held the post from 2 December 1944 to 15 April 1945. Around 20,000 Russian prisoners of war and 50,000 inmates perished at Belsen. The camp soon became severely overcrowded and the lack of sanitation caused outbreaks of typhus, dysentery, tuberculosis and typhoid fever, which claimed the lives of more than 35,000 people in the first few months of 1945, shortly before and after the liberation of the camp. The British 11th Armoured Division liberated Belsen on 15 April 1945. The British soldiers were appalled by what they saw upon arrival at the camp. There were approximately 60,000 inmates inside, many of whom were little more than skeletons, barely able to walk, while some were lying on the ground, unable to stand or walk and visibly close to death. Many were very gravely ill due to the camp conditions, the brutal treatment of their guards and inadequate nutrition. Evidence of cannibalism was also discovered where inmates, driven insane by starvation, ate parts from corpses. There were an estimated 13,000 rotting corpses lying unburied within the camp. Belsen was a sight that anyone who witnessed it would never forget. Michael 'Mickey' Thornley, a mechanic with the British 11th Armoured Division, recalled:

> You could smell the place long before you got anywhere near it. The stench was absolutely putrid. It was just an unbelievable sight, it really was. When we arrived and went in there even the living looked like some kind of walking death. There were people who were so emaciated they could not stand, speak or acknowledge anything. They were just too weak and many would not survive long, even after the liberation. The filth in that place was disgusting. For the number of people inside the camp there was no sanitation at all. There was shit and open sewerage pits everywhere. Flies compounded the problems, spreading disease and infection to the healthy. It was like a hell on earth and there was no way else of describing that place. It was full of what were walking dead. We got the camp commandant, that bastard Kramer [Josef Kramer]. Oh God, there were more than one of us who wanted to kill the bastard there and then, but we couldn't. Had nobody been around and I found him first, I would have gladly strangled that man to death with my bare hands. Kramer was loathsome, a real beast, and we heard all about him after he was hanged after the war for crimes against humanity. Yes, Belsen was a hell on earth in every sense. I recall seeing this big open pit. It was full of what was obviously human carrion. It was a putrid, stinking, writhing mass of flies and maggots. I just thought all of this was once human beings with lives, dreams, hopes and aspirations. They had lived, loved, laughed and cried and now here was all that was left of those lives. This was their sepulchre, murdered and cast into this indescribable hell. Seeing the bodies of small children was particularly hard. We made the camp guards clear the rotting bodies and put them in a burial pit. The remains were so badly decomposed that when the guards picked them

up, fluid would spill out over them, and arms and legs would just fall off. Yes, some of those camp guards began to vomit and I would just shout at them 'You get on with it', in German. I also said to them 'You are all going to hang for this!' I was rabid with anger at these bastards and what they had done here. Before we moved off, it was all filmed and photographed. I had a look around and found a small child's hair clip on the ground. It was just metal with a pink plastic flower attached to it. There were still a few strands of light brown hair attached to the clip. I knew this was the hair clip of some little girl who did not escape this hell. I thought of how frightened she must have been and how she met her death. Was she shot, beaten or did she starve or die from the filth in this place? I don't know. I just put the hair clip in my pocket as I couldn't bear the thought of leaving it behind in this place. When I got home to my wife, Lizzie, I took it out and showed it her and told her all about Belsen. We both sat and cried for a few minutes. It was my wife, Lizzie, who took the hair clip to church with her the following Sunday morning. She was a dear, sweet lady and wanted the local vicar to bless it. She felt it came from a tortured soul and felt that whoever she was would somehow find peace through this. It was just a gesture we felt was right. For those of us who had seen Belsen it made many of us ill. The smell for one thing was just so appalling it made you vomit. The smell of rotting bodies permeated my clothes and I couldn't wait to get away from that place and wash all my kit as it stank of death. I never took any photographs when I was there, as I didn't feel it was appropriate. It was a place of mass murder, so I left the photography to those official army photographers whose job it was to document the horrors. It was also filmed make no mistake. We made sure it was all recorded, so no one could say it didn't happen. What made it worse; they even had fucking women guards there. We were told some of them were guilty of murder and abuse, so they were all rounded up. None of them had the look of what you would call normal women. They were horrible-looking specimens and what you'd expect to find in a place like this.

Buchenwald concentration camp was established on Ettersberg Hill, near Weimar, Germany, in July 1937. Its idyllic surroundings of beech forest, from which the camp took its name, was where heaven and hell met. It was to be the largest of the concentration camps on German soil, following the opening of the Dachau concentration camp four years previously. Buchenwald was an infamous setting for mass murder and genocide. Prisoners from all over occupied Europe and Russia were sent to the camp. Inmates included Jews, Poles and other Slavic citizens, the mentally ill and physically disabled, religious and political prisoners, Freemasons, Jehovah's Witnesses [then referred to as Bible Students], common criminals, homosexuals and prisoners of war. They were all initially used as forced labour for local armaments industries. Between April 1938 and April 1945, around 238,380 people of various nationalities, including 350 Allied prisoners of war, were incarcerated in Buchenwald. The commanders of the Buchenwald camp were SS-*Oberstrumbannführer* Karl-Otto Koch [August 1937-July 1941] and SS-*Standartenführer* Hermanm Pister [1942-1945].

The horrors that took place at Buchenwald included the hanging of prisoners from trees. Walter Gerhard Martin Sommer was a notoriously depraved and sadistic guard at the Buchenwald camp, who earned the nickname the 'Hangman of Buchenwald'. It was Sommer who allegedly ordered Otto Neururer and Mathias Spannlang, two Austrian priests, to be crucified upside-down. When Sommer ordered people to be hung from trees, he directed that they be hung from their wrists, which had first been tied behind the victims' backs. The technique, known as *Strappado*, not only caused excruciating pain, but also prolonged the death of the unfortunate victim. There is a part of the forest near the Buchenwald camp that became known as the 'Singing Forest'. It received this name after the screams of the victims that once could be heard. Summary executions were carried out on an indiscriminate basis. Inmates were also experimented upon with various vaccines, including a trial vaccine to combat epidemic typhus. Many of those who were forcibly injected with this vaccine died. Poisons of various types were also administered forcibly to inmates at the camp. The reasons for the poison experiments are unclear, but so are the many other similar abuses that occurred within the camp. It was recorded by one inmate that four Russian prisoners of war were forcibly administered an alkaloid poison. The reason being to determine the level of toxicity required to kill a human. The four men were given a dose of the poison that failed to kill them. It was said the four men were then strangled in the crematorium and later dissected. Inmates were also subjected to trials involving white phosphorus. White phosphorus, in its military application as an incendiary compound, is deadly; should just one tiny pellet fall into the palm of your hand, it will burn all the way through to the other side. It is also known that any victim exposed to white phosphorous can spontaneously combust, even hours after the victim's initial exposure. White phosphorous, which is still in use today, is a particularly deadly chemical. All manner of barbaric acts were carried out in many Nazi death camps, but the levels of cruelty reached at Buchenwald were without equal.

Conducting research into the death camps is inherently difficult. Often those who do have information are reluctant to talk. Amongst many former camp guards, and other personnel who served at Buchenwald, there appears to be a code of silence. It is often the case nowadays that great-grandchildren discover pasts that have been carefully hidden for decades. One woman I spoke with many years ago discovered a diary that had belonged to her great-grandmother. The woman was stunned to discover that her great-grandmother had worked in some capacity in the Buchenwald camp. She asked not to be named here, but recalled:

> The diary, which had belonged to my great-grandmother, was amongst her things which I inherited after her death. The book had been in a large locked box and my mother gave it to me. My mother didn't look at it so she had no idea either. The writing was at first a little hard to decipher, but I soon understood what it was all about. There was a piece in the text that referred to the crematorium at Buchenwald. My great-grandmother had written that, during the winters, it was bitterly cold in the camp and they would try and hang around in the crematorium while bodies were being burned, as it was nice and warm in there. She said that many of the bodies went into the ovens still alive and that she saw them moving prior to being burned. She also wrote that a large number of

women inmates had been brought to Buchenwald from the Ravensbruck camp to serve in the camp's brothel. She noted that sexual slavery was rife within the camp. She wrote that she knew of many supposedly confirmed male Nazis who sought sexual favours from certain female Jewish inmates. The Nazi males were particularly interested in the very young Jewish females.

The woman who now owned this diary felt such shame on learning the dark secrets within its pages that she destroyed the book. The total figure of innocent human beings murdered at the Buchenwald camp is not clear. An approximate figure quotes that 56,545 people were murdered at the camp. The actual figure could be significantly higher. The existence of the Nazi death camp system would not be revealed to the world in all its horror until 1944, when the Russian Army liberated Madjanek and other camps in the former Nazi-occupied areas. There could be no denial as to what purpose these camps had been built to serve. When Buchenwald was liberated the crematorium was discovered. The ovens used to cremate the corpses were overflowing with bones and other human waste. Another former death camp guard, who would only give his name as Karl, now 88 years of age, recalled: 'Most of us in the camp system were eager participants in the killings. There was no question of remorse then or now. What was done was done and there is no point in denying it. Whether you killed an inmate with your own hands, your boots, a weapon or just depriving them of food or water, it did not matter. Each method resulted in death at some point.'

There were, of course, many forced-labour camps in operation in the Nazi-occupied areas. In miserable conditions, suffering abuse and starvation, inmates died in their thousands in these places. Inmates of the forced-labour camps were slowly worked to death. Some of the corpses from the death camps were also used as human anatomical specimens. Jewish skeletons were collected with the intention of creating an anthropological display. The logic behind such a display was to showcase the differences and alleged racial inferiority of the Jewish race. The intention was to house the collection at the Anatomy Institute of the Reich University of Strasbourg, in the annexed Alsace region, where the initial preparation of the corpses was performed. The *Reichsführer* of the SS, Heinrich Himmler, sanctioned the idea. Himmler possessed a morbid fascination for anatomical relics associated with what he termed the 'sub-human races'. Human organs, particularly brains, were easily procured from the death camp system for the purpose of study. There were also allegations that the tattooed skin of death camp inmates was carefully removed from victims and then made into gruesome trophies such as lampshades. This was later discovered to be untrue and examination of these specimens confirmed them to be goat skin, not human. The subject of the Nazi camps is an exhaustive study in its own right, but below is a list of the camps with fixed extermination facilities, where human beings were murdered during the Nazi Holocaust.

Belarus
Majdanek
Maly Trostenets

Croatia
Jasenovac

Poland
Auschwitz-Birkenau
Belzec
Chelmno
Sobibor
Treblinka
Warsaw

Ukraine
Janowska

Serbia
Sajmiste

There are possibly many more victims of the Nazi Holocaust unaccounted for; yet to be discovered hidden somewhere in a mass grave. One also must be reminded that the Soviets in the east carried out massacres of their own people, for which the Germans would later be blamed. Throughout the Second World War, Germany and Russia in particular were embroiled in one of the most ferocious, brutal and uncompromising struggles in their respective nation's histories. Both began fine tuning a machine tasked with the annihilation of huge numbers of people; one to rid itself of an ideological enemy, the other to protect itself and in revenge for its own sufferings.

Chapter Fourteen

Death in Sub-Humania

Operation Barbarossa, the German invasion of Russia, was Hitler's biggest gamble of the Second World War. Hitler had committed over three million soldiers and 3,500 tanks to the Russian campaign. The German invasion force advanced into Soviet territory in three groups: Army Group North headed for Leningrad; Army Group Centre for Moscow; and Army Group South to the Ukraine. Hitler also had the might of the Luftwaffe at his disposal. The Russians had not anticipated the German attack, having signed a peace treaty with the Germans in 1939. Although the Russians fought tenaciously, they were soon overwhelmed and forced to retreat from the German onslaught. This was, however, only a temporary military setback for the Russians. Hitler had greatly underestimated the resilience of his Russian foe and hoped for a quick victory. He had been over confident, anticipating a short campaign that would be over by the winter. Although the execution of Operation Barbarossa appeared meticulous, the plan was fatally flawed in many respects.

History, particularly in attempted invasions of the Soviet Union that have often ended disastrously for the invading army, should have served as a lesson to Hitler and the Nazi high command. Did they not take into account any delays or setbacks, which would leave them at the mercy of having to fight in the deadly Russian winter conditions? The quick victory over Russia that Hitler had committed himself to did not materialize. With the onset of winter, the German forces soon realised that they were badly equipped. Some of the winter clothing that did arrive in theatre was soon found to be inadequate and in too short supply. Magda Frueller aptly recalled the horrific effects of the Russian winter:

I used to see the German soldiers disembark trains at a station in Warsaw. They were soldiers who had mostly been invalided by the weather conditions in the east. The winter had turned out to be one of the coldest ever. Most of the soldiers were incapable of even talking to you. They shuffled along, barely able to walk, and had to be helped along. Many had fingers missing from their hands and ears missing from their heads. Some also had no eyelids, which horrified me. I thought, had these been sliced off in combat by the enemy? So I asked one of the soldiers, 'Soldier, what has happened to your eyes?' He didn't answer, but one of his comrades tells me, 'The cold there freezes everything, even your eyelids freeze; they turn black and fall off.' I swallowed hard and thought 'my God'. I went and sat back down on the platform and just watched the others coming off the train. The faces of the soldiers were grim and there were no smiles or conversation. Some young girls arrived and they were soon crying with their hands over their faces. I guessed some of the soldiers were their boyfriends or even husbands. Here they were coming back from the east as crippled men.

Quite apart from the freezing winter conditions, which stalled the German assault, the fighting itself had become increasingly brutal. The Russians were well adapted to the weather conditions in their vast country. The weather was a weapon in itself that had served them well against invaders for centuries. It was during that deadly winter that the Russians began to counter-attack. The savagery of the fighting in the east is often incomprehensible to those who didn't witness it. Rudolf Kafker, who fought in Minsk, recalled his experiences:

I was a soldier. I was used to fighting, but not fighting like that. The ground all around us was a carpet of corpses, theirs and ours. The dead just lay everywhere all around us. We fought constantly from dawn till dusk. Every metre of ground was desperately contested. I once killed an enemy with my trench shovel. I was in a ruined building and the enemy soldier turned the corner, surprising me. He lashed out at me with his rifle and I dropped my weapon as we ended up struggling on the ground. At that moment, my whole life was flashing before my eyes. I could be killed right now, but I don't want to die. I want to go home to my parents. All these things flashed before my eyes, all in an instant, just seconds. I reached and grabbed my shovel, forced the handle into his throat, and pushed with all my strength. I looked into the eyes of the enemy. He had the look of desperation in his eyes. He did not want to die either, but one of us was going to have to. I pushed the handle hard against his throat and, after some seconds, I felt his resistance weakening. I pulled the shovel away, raised it above my head, and drove it into his face. I repeated this over and over again, slamming it into his face with all my strength, until his face was no longer recognisable and he was dead. I was covered in blood and rolled off him, exhausted. From that moment on, I was more alert and careful than I had ever previously been. We captured the town after bitter, hard fighting and losing many of our men. The Russians were very good fighters with shovels, pistols, rifles, knives and grenades. I saw many German corpses with their throats sliced open. It seemed this was a ritual with some Russian soldiers; cutting the throats of their enemy. We also found corpses with genitals and eyes removed. Yet, I know our soldiers had done the same, if not worse, to theirs.

Russian dictator Josef Stalin issued orders making it clear to his commanders that surrender or retreat would incur the death penalty. Stalin had previously ordered the execution of any military commander or officer he felt had undermined the Red Army. Such was the fear instilled by Stalin that many Russian soldiers would refuse to give up ground, choosing to fight to the death. Even the Soviet people were urged to fight to the death after hearing of the massacres of civilians by the German forces. Rudolf Kafker recalls:

It had become a war of annihilation. We would capture large groups of Russian civilians. Some had been involved in the defence against us. There was nowhere we could hold these people anyway, so they were often eliminated there and then. We could not leave people behind us and have the risk of them taking up arms against us from the rear areas. We also did not have the logistics in place to deal with these people. So yes, we shot them there and then. The older soldiers within our ranks found this task difficult I think. Those of us young, fresh from the Hitler Youth, had no such troubles of conscience. This was an ideological war; a war of races that had to be fought and won at any cost. When you have been in battle for months on end, and you have seen your friends killed in the fighting, you feel no remorse or no pity about killing people, even civilians. When we saw the bodies of German soldiers we had only been talking to a day or so ago and shared our cigarettes with them, then find them hanging from wire in a building with their throats cut, their penises severed and thrust into their mouths, that made me hate everything in this land and I wanted to kill all of them. It mattered to me not who was a soldier or a civilian. To me, I could not distinguish, and I killed without hesitation, without pity, without remorse.

The Battle of Stalingrad took place between 23 August 1942 and 2 February 1943 and proved to be one of the pivotal battles in the east. The loss of life was astronomical among both combatants and civilians, with the Germans losing 728,000 men and the Soviet casualties numbering 1,129,619. In the wake of sustained bombing of the civilian population by the Luftwaffe, the city was reduced to a vast labyrinth of rubble and ruined buildings. Every square metre was bitterly fought over at very close quarters. In the end, the German army became trapped after the Russian forces launched a two-pronged attack under the name 'Operation Uranus'. Hitler issued an order to the German forces not to attempt to break out from the besieged city, but whether or not an escape would have been successful is still open to debate. Luftwaffe Chief Hermann Goering had given Hitler the boastful assurance that the Luftwaffe could supply the besieged German troops from the air, but supplies that were delivered were too few and too far between. By the beginning of February

1943, the German forces in Stalingrad were out of ammunition and food supplies. Surrender was the only feasible option under the circumstances. Hitler was furious upon receiving the news of the German surrender, yet it was down to his poor tactical decision making that the German 6th Army was sacrificed. Of the 107,000 Axis forces captured at the end of the Stalingrad battle, only 6,000 would survive Soviet captivity, returning home in 1955. Rudolf Kafker later wrote:

> The news makes me nauseous. All those fine German lives lost is just too much and what of Paulus? [General Friedrich Paulus, commander of the German 6th Army.] He is now squeaking that he is against Hitler! The man is obviously a coward, out to save his own skin, while those who served under him gave their lives with honour. It makes me sick to the stomach and I would shoot that dog Paulus myself if I ever had the chance.

The Stalingrad defeat severely dented German confidence on the Eastern Front. Many soldiers began to question whether they would see home again. They had been betrayed by the over confidence and poor decision making of their leaders. The twenty-year-old Max Diemer had joined the fighting on the Russian front in the summer of 1943. He had served with the 3rd SS Panzer Division Totenkopf as a loader in a Tiger 1 tank crew. He recalls:

> My task was simply to work with the gunner. I had the job of loading the 8.8cm ammunition into the gun. I was brought in to replace a guy who became badly injured through his own fault. He had somehow trapped his hand in the gun breech of the 8.8cm cannon. He got his ticket home and some felt he had done this on purpose because he was pining for his woman back home in Germany. I did not know him, so I cannot make any judgement. In battle, I was instructed on whether to load high-explosive or armour-piercing ammunition into the gun. The type of ammunition used depended on whether you were fighting tanks or just shooting targets such as buildings or enemy troop emplacements. High explosive worked against

troops very well. Usually we fired just one shot into troop emplacements and this was often enough to kill or cause significant casualties. When we fired shells into their positions, some would try and break away. We would use our machine guns to shoot them down. Often, if civilian dwellings got in our way, we drove the Tiger through them. I recall on two occasions we came upon civilian dwellings on the Kharkov advance. We knew there were people inside, probably hiding, so we drove through the building. We just went through it like a knife would cut through butter. It mattered not that we had killed people who were hiding inside. We never gave that a second thought. We pulled up during the advance, shortly before night fell the one evening. We checked the tracks of our Tiger and found human remains caught in the track links along with pieces of clothing. We would take a bayonet and use it to get rid of any body parts caught up in the machinery. One occasion was particularly sobering as one of the crew found a small child's teddy bear trapped between the track links. For a moment it hit you, a short pang of remorse or something. You had to pull back your emotions, as we could not permit these emotions. Emotions were, in this context, only for the weak. The race we were engaged in fighting was not human in my eyes. We spoke of them as one might speak of a cockroach in a food shop. We destroyed them without pity in many cases. We did encounter a heavy psychological burden, yet we swore an oath that this was our duty to our Führer. I did my duty, I can say that much. People argue today that we were criminals, yet our enemy were criminals, too, at times. We came across small cemeteries where we had buried our dead of previous battles. Partisans had been there and tore down the wooden crosses and defecated upon the graves. Some of the remains had been exhumed from their resting places. After that we checked our own dead and removed anything of value, such as wedding rings and things. If we could, we returned them to the families ourselves. The practice of vandalising the graves of the dead continued on until well after the war though.

From the moment the Germans began the invasion of Russia, there had been fears of counter-attack from the rear areas. Soviet resistance did spring up in the German rear areas, causing casualties and disrupting supply lines. To combat this problem, the Germans deployed their security divisions. The security divisions performed a policing role in the German-occupied areas. Operating under the control of the Wehrmacht, the security divisions were not linked to the SS, as is sometimes thought. A typical security division enjoyed all the assets of a regular army division. They were equipped with light artillery, anti-tank guns, medical, transport, butchery, bakery and ambulance platoons. The security divisions were never intended to have been combat units, yet many of its members were seeing as much combat as the frontline troops. Many of the SD members were older former soldiers or men capable of serving, but not in a frontline capacity. Thirty-one-year-old *Feldwebel* [Sergeant] Joachim Hans Ernst Pluschka was a member of the 403rd *Sicherungs* [Security] Division, which was originally formed on 15 March 1941 in Neusalz. Joachim Pluschka saw extensive combat action against partisans, saboteurs and other enemy groups in Bialystock, in central and southern Russia, in the Wehrmacht rear areas. He was also involved in extensive action at the battlefront, at Welikijie-Luki and Witebsk. Joachim received the coveted Iron Cross 2nd Class on 7 November 1943. It is a sad fact that many of the security divisions were later found guilty of war crimes. There was the persistent threat of partisan activity in the Wehrmacht rear areas and many people were rounded up and wrongly accused of being partisans, before being taken off for execution. Usually the victims were gathered together and forced to dig their own graves, before being machine gunned. There were many witnesses to the work of the security divisions operating in the rear areas. Sylwia Wczeniek, who, as a young girl at the time, witnessed an execution carried out by the SD. She was very reluctant to talk about the incident, but told me the following:

> It happened in the wintertime of 1943. A large group of Germans had arrived and they came along all of our houses, kicking open the doors and ordering everyone outside. It was

snowing heavily and freezing cold outside. There was a lot of shouting going on, much of which I couldn't understand. One of the Germans began shouting in Russian that we were hiding saboteurs in the village. To my knowledge, this was not true. They searched all the houses and the outbuildings where hay and grain was being stored. They looked in the hay storage barns and found nothing in there. They then set these on fire. A few of our men began protesting, so one of the Germans drew his pistol and shot both through their heads. My mother pulled me close and covered my eyes as they demanded to know where the saboteurs were. They told us that if no one spoke up and told them what they needed to know, that they would shoot us all. The people begged them, telling them they knew nothing and they had been hiding no one. After more shouting, and one poor man being beaten up with a rifle butt, they took all the men a few hundred yards away and told them to line up. One of them then stepped forward with a sub-machine pistol and began firing. When he finished, all the men were on the ground, dead. Their women and children saw this happen and wanted to run to them. The Germans with us pointed their weapons at them and shouted at them to stay where they were. The Germans began to search the clothing of the dead men. On one, they found a German cigarette case, still full of German cigarettes. In their eyes, this must have been construed as evidence of our guilt. The German who found the cigarette case came along each of us, demanding to know how the man got the cigarette case. 'Did he take it from one of our men after killing him? Surely, one of you must know, as you all live here. It's a small community?' We told the German we did not know where he got the cigarette case. The Germans then demanded that we women all remove our clothing. We did as we were told and the clothing was searched and nothing was found. We wanted to put our clothes back on but they would not let us. One of the Germans kicked the clothing away from us. We were forced to stand naked, shivering in the freezing cold. An elderly woman begged them that she needed her clothing or she would die. One of the Germans just said to her, 'Well, please continue to your death then!' The Germans just looked at us, but then began touching us. I had my breasts touched by one of the Germans and he made rude comments about how small my breasts were. Another made remarks about our nipples. It was disgusting and shameful. It soon became evident these men were not Wehrmacht soldiers but something else. They were older than most of the Germans we had encountered, and they behaved very differently. One girl was taken into one of the houses by one of the Germans. She later told us he demanded sex with her. She told him, 'No, please, no.' He forced her to kneel down on the floor put a pistol against her head and told her, 'If you bite my dick, I will blow your fucking brains out!' He forced her to perform a sexual act upon him and when he finished with her he left her alone. After nearly an hour, they left us alone, and when they left we picked up our clothes and ran inside our homes. My mother was frantic with worry, as my father was away at the time. She thought that maybe they had found him and killed him too. Father had been away hunting with traps with a neighbour. When he returned, two days later, he learned of what had happened. He never left us alone again. The thing was, this kind of action was commonplace. We later found out that these men were the rear guards; a kind of police unit. Others came afterwards, but these were different men, not the ones who had previously came to us and killed the men in our village. The murdered men were later buried. When our area was liberated by the Russians, we told them of what happened. I don't think those responsible were ever caught. We would not have remembered what they looked like anyway.

Joachim Pluschka was later badly wounded in the fighting in Witebsk. He was evacuated from the fighting to a German military hospital in Borisov, in Belarus. There he languished, falling in and out of consciousness. On 6 February 1944, he died in his hospital bed from complications resulting from his wounds. The few possessions he had on his person were put in an envelope and later returned to his next of kin. Joachim Pluschka's family later parted company with his *Wehrpass* and the Iron Cross 2nd Class that he was awarded for his service in the east. It is difficult to know whether he had any involvement in any of the executions. One can't assume that he had. What is known is that the security divisions were relentless in pursuit of their duties and carried them out with ruthless efficiency until the end. To the population of the east, the German invaders had arrived as a legion from Hades. Nazi indoctrination had dehumanised these people in the minds of the invaders, so they were not classed as human beings. The people of the east were classified as a sub-human species and, to the Nazis, ridding them from the earth was a valid course of action.

Members of the security divisions often gave special attention to any Russian thought to be in possession of important information. One young Russian soldier, who gave his name as Yaroslav Kuznetsov, had been a Red Army officer. Sworn to die rather than divulge information to the Germans, he was handed over to the security division prior to the battle of Kursk in 1943. He recalled:

> I was just twenty-two years of age at the time. The Germans captured me and, being an officer, they, of course, expected me to have been in possession of knowledge that might be of use to them. I told them I did not know anything and I could give them no useful information. They then began to use medieval torture methods. They were cruel and totally ruthless people. They placed a sharp, pointed knife in a fire and left it there until the blade was glowing red hot. The red hot point of the blade was inserted under my toenails. The pain was excruciating quite beyond description. If I screamed out I was punched in the face. They did this to all of my toes and the pain was so bad I lost consciousness. After they had finished with me, I was sent into custody with other prisoners from our army. They crippled me, and afterwards I could not walk properly, and even after fifty years I can still only shuffle around.

Max Diemer reflected on the war in the east:

> I soon learned to not only fear the eastern territories but to hate it too. During the last summer there I sat with my back

against the Tiger, thinking of home. I looked at the scars on our tank, all the grazes and scratches made by rounds that had impacted our tank but not penetrated it. I remember thinking, 'when is our luck going to run out in this place?' At that moment, I watched as a butterfly fluttered around on the warm breeze. It settled upon the gun barrel. I just watched it and thought how nice would it be to be that insect. I could just fly away out of here of my own free will. The next day we were in the thick of the fighting again. We encountered many of the Russian T-34 tanks. We knew by this stage in the war we were by no means superior to them. They could kill us, as I had seen our tanks hit by fire from T-34s. The problem is, when you get hit, if you survive the strike of the round, you then only have seconds to get out. If you are badly hurt, or trapped by debris, it is often impossible to get out. On countless times, I have heard crews inside our tanks burning to death. You can't see them, but you hear their screams; agonising screams. I watched one tank that was hit. The crew hatch lifted and two rolled out, falling onto the ground with their clothing on fire. They writhed in agony on the ground, desperately trying to put the flames out. A third crew member exits the hatch, falls from the Tiger, and flames now appear through the crew hatch. They are just trying to drag each other away from the burning Tiger, when bang! The whole thing just explodes and the escaping crew are blown to oblivion in the blast. There is nothing left of them, just bits of charred flesh and bones. The turret sails high into the air before falling back to earth. The mere thought of dying in that horrible manner is enough to make me consider renouncing the oath I had taken on becoming a soldier. I question my own discipline and tell myself, 'you are a fool!'

Max Diemer's luck did run out when, three weeks later, his tank received a hit from a Soviet anti-tank gun at close range. He recalls of this incident:

I only remember the sound of the shell hitting our tank. It was the loudest, most concussive force I can remember. We had been hit from the rear by a weapon we had not seen behind us. As we drove past they nailed us good. I don't remember much about it, as I was rendered unconscious in the initial impact of the shell. I remember it going black inside, and it was difficult to breathe for the smoke. I felt like my body was on fire. I woke up at an aid post, was transported to the rear, and flown out of the place on a Ju 52 transport. When I arrived in Germany, I was then sent to a hospital. My whole body hurt, yet I seemed to have everything still. I checked they had not blown my balls and dick off [he laughs]. Then I noticed my right arm, and all that remained was a stump; the rest was missing. They had to cut it off as it was no good, they told me. Other than the arm, I had suffered some deep cuts to my face and head, and lots of bruising. I asked after the others [his crew] and they told me they were all dead. I had been pulled from the Tiger by a nearby crew, who spotted the Russian gun shooting us. They fired a high explosive into the Russians and then came to our aid. That was very brave of them, as tanks nearly always blew up after being hit. I owe my life to that crew, but never learned who they were. They pulled me out of the Tiger, made sure I was in good company, and then pushed on. The unit I had been with literally fought itself to annihilation. It ceased to be a division by the end of the war. Of course, I was questioned after the war about it all. I was treated as a common criminal by the Allied authorities, who were actively seeking SS personnel. They tried to convince me I had been a war criminal. Only God can judge me on that. I think in war we are all criminals. Men behave differently in war to what they do in peace and that is always the way.

Although the Waffen SS have always been regarded as amongst the most ferocious in battle, many ordinary Wehrmacht soldiers found themselves thrown into the most brutal fighting. Panzer Grenadier *Gefreiter* Hans Wunsch recorded in his journals at the end of the Second World War:

The Eastern Front was the birth of brutality. If you were not totally ruthless, you could have no hope of survival. In combat with the Soviets, we used everything to kill them. I once found myself in a trench among the enemy. I was confronted by a Soviet. The small pistol I had in my hand refused to fire. It had been that cold, the trigger had frozen solid, even though I had kept it on the inside of my jacket in a pocket. I took off my helmet and struck him a blow as hard as I could with it. I felled him and he dropped his rifle. I pounced on him like a cat might a mouse. I sat astride him, withdrew my bayonet, and I stabbed him repeatedly through the chest with the bayonet. I held it with both hands and plunged it into him with every ounce of my strength. I put such force behind the bayonet that the blade actually went right through his back. His eyes were wide open as he died; blood oozed from his mouth. I dropped the bayonet down and took the enemy soldier's weapon. When comrades of my platoon found me, I had killed two more enemy soldiers: one by using the captured weapon, the other with my bare hands. I strangled the life from him. My comrades told me I should get an Iron Cross for this! I had managed to capture some paperwork and this was found to be quite valuable to our intelligence. In the event, they didn't give me an Iron Cross; they gave me the War Merit Cross 2nd Class with swords. My comrades just said, 'Never mind, Hans, maybe next time you will get your Iron Cross!' When I thought on it later, I did say to myself, 'Hans, if you carry on like this, you will not only feel less of a human when you return home, but you may not return home at all!' I don't know, but I think all soldiers who have experienced combat like that feel the same way and think the same things. I don't read books on the war, and many people do not understand this. My grandson used to ask me, 'Grandpapa, why do you not have any books on the war?' I used to try and explain to him that I fought in war, and yes, I killed men, so what can a book tell me that I don't already know about that. The mind of a child, eh! [He smiles]. I knew of one soldier who killed an enemy with a broken bottle. He used the broken end and killed the enemy by forcing the sharp jagged end into his throat. He held it there until the enemy stopped struggling. Another soldier I served with told me how he held a Russian soldier's head in a fire to kill him. There are so many horrors I could tell you. Killing an enemy with bayonets became a frequent course of action. It is one of the worst possible ways to have to kill. There is physical contact and blows are exchanged between you. Your enemy falls and you thrust the blade into him. He grabs the blade in a vain attempt to prevent it going into him. All the time, you are staring him in the face and you see his terror and horror. He knows he is going to die soon, and when you withdraw your blade, you see his entrails spill out of the hole. The blood runs down the blade onto your rifle. It runs down your rifle onto your hands and it feels like warm motor oil. You know you are going to have to do this time and again, and it never gets any easier. The law of war is that a soldier has to kill the way he was trained to kill. Stabbing straw-filled dummies in my training was nothing like stabbing a live human being in combat. It is dreadful, that's all I can tell you.

Vyacheslav Lebedev had been a farmer prior to the German invasion of 1941. He lived alone, clawing out an existence from the wilderness around him. He hunted game, fished and enjoyed the solitary lifestyle. His life changed when the war arrived on his doorstep. He was forced to flee his home and, from a distance, he watched as his animals were killed and his home burned to the ground. He recalled that, during his escape to find his own people, he came across what had been just a small village a few miles from where he lived. Vyacheslav recalled:

At the village where the Germans had been in occupation I found not a living soul remaining, apart from a small boy. The boy was close to death and, driven to the point of insanity by hunger, he had taken to eating his own excrement. I picked up the boy and carried him on my back with me. It was sad as he did not survive the journey and died the following night. There was nothing I could have done to save his life at that point. When I reached our soldiers, joining in the fight against the

Germans was easy for me. The knowledge of the land, and my skills at tracking, hunting and basic survival in the wilderness, meant I would make an excellent sniper. They gave me special, all-white thick clothing to wear, issued me with a scoped rifle, and off I went. I did not need to be taught how to use the rifle, as it's the way I survived all of my life. I went out on my own and hunting the enemy was not one bit different from hunting hares out on the tundra. I would track the Germans and pick them off at range with the rifle. When a high-velocity 7.62mm bullet strikes a human in the head it is deadly. I would watch, fascinated, through the scope of the rifle with a heart full of hate and thoughts for that little boy. The Germans said we were sub-human and devils. I was no devil before they brought war to my homeland, but I became a devil when they did. How many did I kill? I am not sure, as I never kept a personal score; maybe twenty or thirty, I don't know. Sometimes, I had to shoot twice to finish an enemy off, but that was not very often. One of their tanks once passed within five feet of me, as I lay hidden from their view. I had to lie perfectly still for hours, sometimes going without food for days, but we are tough people and we are used to such hardships. That is why we won our battle in the end, through determination, blood, fire and sacrifice. I am no sub-human. I would have welcomed anyone into my simple home, or helped them had they been in distress. I could not understand why the Germans hated us so much.

Anti-tank gunner Fritz Umberr recalled of his last engagement with Russian forces one winter morning in 1944:

I looked out across the snow-covered plain as I heard engines and a kind of rumbling noise in the distance. What I saw filled me instantly with fear; an endless horizon of Russian tanks and infantry advancing towards us. They had artillery trained on us, and this made it difficult for us as we tried to engage their T-34s with our 7.5cm Pak gun. Yes, we destroyed tank after tank, but they did not stop coming. Retreat was out of the question, as it was soon discovered that our enemy were behind us also. We had artillery firing on us now from all sides and we were forced to take flight to our trenches. I saw Russian shells explode on our trenches, throwing bodies and body parts in all directions. The screams and cries of the wounded filled my head. The Russians were forcing us to take cover, allowing their T-34s to bear down upon us. I knew grenades were hopeless, and we had only a very limited supply of Panzerschrek and Panzerfaust weapons. Herman Goering had boasted how his Luftwaffe would maintain our supplies. We did not receive any resupply from the air. Subsequently this was to be our last battle; a last desperate fight to the death. I watched helplessly as one T-34 drove over a hole my comrades were hiding in. They fired their rifles at the T-34, but the bullets just flattened on impact. The T-34 drove forwards and then it reversed, repeating this several times over. Then it turned on its tracks in a kind of circle, causing the trench my comrades were hiding in to cave in. After the T-34 had done its work, my comrades were crushed to death or buried alive. I imagined the agony of their last moments; being buried alive in that manner. There was no choice but to surrender, and our whole line broke. The war was over for us now, yet the thought of shooting myself crossed my mind momentarily. The only thing that prevented me from doing so was the thought of my mother and father back home. I did not want to face the prospect of being captured by these people, but had to face the fact we were all prisoners of the Soviets now. They turned out to be a brutal, unforgiving enemy, and I would not see my home again for almost six years. We were sent to camps deep in Russia. No one would ever know what happened to us and that was very frightening.

The German campaign in the east achieved little in the end. There were military opportunities along the way that, if exploited soon enough, may have changed the outcome for the German forces. With Hitler as supreme commander, they were doomed to failure. His decision making in military matters was childlike and inept. He argued with seasoned generals who knew better. He refused to give ground where his forces might have lived to fight another day, and insisted on pursuing unrealistic military goals. With hindsight, the German forces went to war far too soon. They were neither ready for a war on two fronts, nor to take on the might of Soviet Russia. Most military commanders would have understood that invading Russia was a huge gamble that would probably end in disaster. In order to have succeeded, the Germans would have needed millions more men, tanks and aircraft. Overwhelming force would have been the only means of securing victory over such a vast nation of hardy people. The Germans also failed from a logistical point of view when the Russian winter came. They failed to understand both the limits of their equipment in such conditions and the fact that the Russian winter would prove far more deadly than any enemy soldier. The Nazis had failed to learn from history that the four major historical attempts at invading Russia had all failed miserably.

Russia has been invaded over the centuries, and enemy forces have been in occupation of her territory for many years afterwards, but most of her enemies have been driven out. Mother Russia is like a bear. Sometimes the bear sleeps when its enemy attacks, but when the bear awakes, and angrily shows its teeth, only the foolhardy will not turn and run. Throughout the Second World War, Russia proved it was far from a nation of sub-humans. When Russian T-34 tanks ran out of fuel, the Russians mixed Vodka with diesel oil, which proved a useful substitute for keeping the tanks moving. As the German forces retreated, they attempted to destroy as much of the remaining infrastructure as possible. Railway lines, buildings; everything was destroyed in a vain attempt to slow down the Red Army advance. A German officer wrote a chilling letter home to his wife telling her, 'At this rate, the Soviets will have overtaken us here and will be on your doorstep in Germany!' Nazi Germany came to its end in the wastelands and winters of Soviet Russia. The Germans would never recover from the disaster in the east. Now the bear was awakened and its body racked with pain. Yet it drew strength from its pain. It was angry and now looking westwards towards Germany itself.

Chapter Fifteen

Revenge is Sweet

With the western Allies fast approaching from the west and the Russians from the east, there was a noticeable shift in the behaviour of German Third Reich society. It was a doomed society that now began to prey upon itself. Alexander Kohlman had recovered sufficiently from the wounds received in action on the Eastern Front. He was eager to return to the battlefront with his comrades, but was turned down on the grounds of fitness. It was suggested he apply for a role within the Reich security services. He was offered a position with the dreaded Gestapo [*Geheime Staatspolizei*], the Secret State Police. His association with the Waffen SS meant that he was an ideal candidate, and the role also appeared to fit his personality. He had become angry, resentful and frustrated by Germany's lack of progress in the war. Alexander was not stupid. He had experienced fighting on the Eastern Front and understood that Germany was losing territory in the east and west and, worse still, was losing the war. In his position with the Gestapo, Alexander was keen to settle a few old scores. The Boersch family, for whom his mother had worked, were an obvious target. Alexander blamed the Boerschs for many of his mother's troubles when he was a small child, growing up without a father. In mid-1944, he paid them a visit in his official capacity. He later wrote down in his personal journal what had happened:

In my eyes, the Boersch family were traitors. They treated my mother like a dog. So much so, that when my father died, my mother turned to other sources to support herself and, of course, me. I had been waiting for the moment when I might settle the debt with those people. When I called at their home they were blissfully unaware of who I was. This gave me immense pleasure. As I walked into their opulent home,

I invited them to a little game of trivia. It was a case of guess who your guest is, my good friends. They had not a clue who I was, other than that I was from the State Secret Police. I could tell they were frightened by my presence. The room took on a sweaty odour, strongly resembling that of warm butter. It permeated the stuffy air around these frightened people. 'I am Alexander Kohlman. Do you remember me now?' They turned a shade of pale and were obviously very nervous of my intentions here. I told them we could do business or I could do them much damage by having them arrested for being traitors. The man of the house argued, 'On what charges are we traitors, sir?' I told him I could think of something and my colleague waiting outside in the car would be my witness. All I wanted was a gesture of apology to my mother, not me, of course. I dictated my terms to them and left their home with a number of valuables. I understood that once this war was over, it may not be favourable to Germany. Our currency might end up worthless yet again. I took the valuables and hid them away safe, where no one would find them. I warned them in no uncertain terms never to cross me or try to report me to my superiors. I reminded them that it would be their word against mine. The Boerschs were not well liked in our area, and most people hated them, yet tolerated them. I just wanted compensation from them. I left with thousands of pounds worth of gold, silver and diamonds in my pocket. They were still the wealthy pigs they would always be. It was just that, in my current capacity, I had more power than them.

When Alexander's great-granddaughter began reading though his journal she became somewhat troubled. She knew that Alexander had a reputation for being violent; many who knew him would vouch for that. But here he was, admitting to being involved in corruption. There was plenty of corruption within the Third Reich, but this information came as a shock. Alexander met a young girl named Ursula Himmelbruck. She was eighteen years of age and had not long finished a work placement, which is how she came to be in Hamburg. The age difference didn't matter to them and they began to see one another regularly. Ursula's father was concerned at his daughter's choice of partner, but he said nothing. Alexander was often described as an intimidating personality, even when he was in a good mood. The couple had not been dating a year when Ursula discovered she was pregnant. Her family, particularly her mother, was horrified, insisting the couple marry as soon as possible to avoid a family scandal. Ursula came from a good background. She was described as being a pretty, kind, but very timid girl. The wedding was arranged very quickly and took place in a small church in a village outside the city. In fact, the wedding service was momentarily interrupted by an air raid, but the families insisted the service continue as the bombers were heading to the city and unlikely to drop bombs on them. The couple enjoyed a few days' honeymoon in Lubeck before returning home. At this time, they still had nowhere of their own to live. Again, Alexander paid a visit to the Boersch family. It is not known if threats were made towards the Boerschs on this occasion, as nothing was written about this second visit in Alexander's journal. It would, however, appear odd that, after just a few weeks, he had managed to secure a four-bedroom apartment on the outskirts of Hamburg rent free. When people enquired as to how he got the apartment, he would say, 'It was just a favour owed to me!' Someone once remarked, 'That place is owned by the Boersch family and those cunts wouldn't give anything for free!' Alexander smiled at them, yet said nothing. He performed his duties in an exemplary manner. He followed tip-offs in a meticulous fashion and made a few arrests of people who had been termed as, 'bad mouthing the regime.'

Alexander was not afraid of anyone, and he certainly was not afraid of violence. He was once in a bar in Hamburg with his pretty young wife, Ursula, when he caught a man staring at her as she walked to the ladies room. He challenged the man, asking him not to look at his wife in that manner. The man replied, 'Who are you? Her dad or something?' He then summoned one of his friends to help confront Alexander. Not wishing to fight inside the establishment, he coolly removed his jacket, handed it to Ursula and told her he would be back in a moment. He walked outside, followed by the two men. A few minutes later, he calmly walked back inside without a mark on him. Ursula, not believing her husband had been up to no good, went to take a look outside and saw two men sprawled on the ground with bloody noses. Other people were in the process of helping them to their feet. When Ursula returned, Alexander had almost finished his drink. He just smiled at her and it seemed all was forgotten.

Alexander's mother Hilde doted on Ursula; she absolutely adored the girl. Alexander bought his mother a small single-bed apartment in the city. When she enquired as to how he got it, he simply told her, 'It was just a favour owed to me!' This became a private joke within the family after a while. Ursula's father even noticed, and was compelled to comment, 'Everybody in Germany must owe this man favours!' It was all too easy. Anyone accused of non-conformism could buy Alexander's silence, if they had the money, and they preferred a financial penalty to a more violent one. Alexander also sought out those who had bullied him as a youth. He found that many of those boys, who were now young men, had joined the German army and were subsequently away from home fighting at the front. He did speak to the father of one of them, who told Alexander that his son was in Russia. Alexander explained that Russia was where he got wounded: 'Probably the worst place on earth for any soldier to be sent,' he told the father. Alexander, for once, appeared sympathetic, which was unusual. There were no threats and no offers of a deal. He shook the father's hand and went on his way.

It was to Alexander's great consternation that he learned one morning that bombs had fallen on the periphery of Hamburg. This was nothing out of the ordinary. The city had been a priority target for some years and was bombed frequently. On this occasion, bombs fell directly onto the Boerschs' house, killing all of the family. The fact that they were not popular was reflected in the looting that took place almost instantly. One of those sent to prevent any further looting of the property was Alexander himself. He surveyed the scene and discussed the situation with other local police. He spent some time at the property. A few days later, a bag of jewellery was mysteriously deposited at Alexander's home. Again, when questioned about it, he replied, 'Someone owed me a favour, that is all!'

When Ursula gave birth to a little girl, named Anna, Alexander was overjoyed. The arrival of the baby girl appeared to mellow him and he seemed to quickly lose interest in his Gestapo activities, preferring to spend as much time as he could at home with Ursula and their new baby.

He began to complain to his doctor of pain in his legs, though it is believed he did this in order to be relieved of his duties with the Gestapo. He even got himself a stick to increase the authenticity of the charade. He took a desk job as clerk for a local Hamburg firm and settled into life away from the war. His nefarious activities had secured enough money to keep his family going for some years. He often bought goods on the black market that were too expensive for many Germans. The authorities briefly investigated, but Alexander had friends in high places and any unwanted attention was soon diverted elsewhere. By late 1944–early 1945, it was clear that Germany was on the verge of defeat. Alexander relocated his family further away from the city and into the countryside. This is where they would live out their lives and raise their baby daughter. Another two children would follow; a second daughter, named Trudi, and a son named Frank, in honour of Alexander's uncle. Alexander's move from the city proved to be a wise decision.

As the Western Allies approached Hamburg, they passed through the village that Alexander and his family were living in, leaving it more or less intact but under British occupation. The war was now over for Alexander and his family, though the battle for control of Hamburg raged on. When the British arrived they searched everyone's house. Alexander had gone to great trouble to burn any incriminating evidence of his past before leaving the city, and to the invading Allied force, he was just another wounded ex-soldier who had been retired. He limped around on his stick and convinced them he had once been a regular Wehrmacht corporal until a sniper's bullet ended his career. The British believed his story and so his past remained a closely guarded secret. A Hamburg doctor, who Alexander knew, had cleverly removed the blood group tattoo that would have incriminated him. The flesh was burned around the tattooed area and several incisions made, then stitched, to simulate a battlefield injury. Afterwards, there was no trace of the tattoo and no evidence to link him with the SS. Even his family knew little of his past.

During the 1960s, Alexander would often be seen sitting at his desk, writing. No one, not even Ursula, was permitted to read any of his words. The papers were always locked in a metal box and then hidden away in a cupboard. Alexander's children always referred to the cupboard as 'Papa's secret cupboard'. Alexander's mother, Hilde, died from illness in the early 1950s. Her death had a profound effect upon him. He began to attend the local Sunday church services, something he had never done before. Later in life, it became noticeable to his children that something was troubling him. As an old man, he would often burst into tears, telling them, 'If I told you the truth, you would probably hate me and never wish to speak to me or call me your papa again. I could not live with that.' The children, in particular, had their suspicions from little things they had heard. Alexander was resolute that his past would only be revealed upon his death. Anna was entrusted with the two keys to the secret cupboard and the locked metal box inside.

Upon Alexander's death in the 1990s, Anna waited until her father's funeral had taken place before opening the secret cupboard. This was not something she relished, as she was afraid of what she might learn. She unlocked the cupboard and inside was a grey metal box. The padlock on the metal box was opened and inside was the Iron Cross 2nd Class, a War Merit Cross 2nd Class with swords, a Wound Badge, Nazi Party armband, a Walther Pistol with a loaded magazine, a wad of papers and a bundle of large notebooks. Several of the notebooks belonged to Werner and Hilde Kohlman and were written like diaries. On the cover of Alexander's notebook were the words 'Revenge is Sweet'. Anna recalled that her father often took the small Walther pistol down to the bottom of their garden. There he would set up empty food tins and shoot them off a wall. She would often join her father, who taught her how to use the pistol. She recalled, 'It was not big or heavy, and fitted my hands well. When it fired, it did not have a big kick, as it was only 6.35mm. It would have been perfectly lethal against someone, providing you were at relatively close range. My father carried this with him during his war service. Presumably, this was the same weapon he shot the prisoner with.' The ammunition that was inside the box was handed in to the police in Germany. The pistol was later decommissioned in the UK. Anna spent many months reading through all the paperwork. Although shocked at discovering certain aspects of her father's past, she forgave him. Anna told her siblings the story and they, too, were happy to let sleeping dogs lie. Alexander's children, grandchildren and great-grandchildren had no connections with what had occurred during the Second World War. Although they were not happy with many of the things they learned about their family's past, they did not feel an obligation to hate. As Anna said, 'There had been enough misery, suffering and hate because of the war. We, as a family, refused to let the war destroy us or tear us apart. We closed that Pandora's box, put it back in the cupboard, and then replaced the padlock. That's where it will stay now.' It seems that Alexander Kohlman had been a complex and contradictory character. The problems of his youth had, to some degree, shaped his adult persona. He could be very kind, but also prone to outbursts of violence. He was a man who never backed away from a confrontation and was reluctant to let things pass. Yet, ultimately, in later years, he began to question his own actions during his involvement in the war.

Chapter Sixteen

A Reciprocal Genocide

What I describe as the reciprocal genocide of Germans during the Second World War began the moment German forces began to lose ground in the east, and it was not confined to the eastern territories retaken by the Red Army. It appears that the murder of both German military personnel and civilians occurred all across Germany. Many would argue about what actually defines an act of genocide in war. The Jewish Holocaust is the clearest example of an act of genocide perpetrated on a mass scale, but is it any less a criminal act if perpetrated on a lesser scale? The Dresden bombings are perhaps a good example. The bombings took place between 13 and 15 February 1945, and have been a subject of much controversy and debate among historians. Fury raged over the Dresden bombings even before the fires of the city were extinguished. When the smoke finally cleared, many horrors were unveiled to those who entered the ruins. Some 3,900 tons of high explosive and incendiary bombs were dropped during the raids on a city that had been packed with refugees. It is estimated that between 22,700 and 25,000 people perished in the Dresden bombings. After the war, many questioned the justification of bombing Dresden, arguing that the blanket bombing of the historic city was not proportionate to the military gains. The counter-argument was that the raids were justified in order to eliminate the threat of German counter-attack against Marshall Konev's extended line. The city also possessed one of the few remaining rail and communications centres, and it was also thought that ammunition for the German war effort was being produced there. Furthermore, the Battle of the Bulge, fought in the Ardennes, was the last major German offensive on the Western Front and a salutary lesson against the Allies being complacent towards Germany's ability to strike back.

French-born Tilly Mateisse was eight years old and had arrived in Dresden a month prior to the bombing of the city. She recalls:

Whole families moved into the city, as many felt they would be safe there. People, particularly refugees like us, stayed in churches where we were made welcome. We were in a church the night the RAF bombers came on the thirteenth. We were a superstitious family and the thirteenth didn't bode well with us at all. My father had a bad feeling about the whole day. I remember during the night, hearing the sound of the bombers approaching. We never thought too much about it, as the city had been relatively unscathed, and we didn't think it would be attacked in the way it was. When the bombs began to fall, it was just terror everywhere. Such was the violence of the raid, my father took us out of the church and we ran as fast as we could away from the centre of the city. The church was hit shortly after, and all those who stayed behind were killed and buried under tons of rubble. We did not return to the city but stayed in a small camp a few miles from the city suburbs. The next night, the bombers came again, and again the night after that. One could tell it was bad as the sky above the city glowed deep red, and you could feel the heat all the way to where we were, and we were miles away. When the bombers finally left the city alone, it was full of cremated bodies. I saw whole families huddled together in basements that had perished from burning to death. Some had suffocated in the heat or smoke; men, women, children and babies, all of them perished. You could not go up a single street in that city without seeing a group of people huddled together, dead. All the skin was burnt from their bodies; all that was left was skulls and bones. The mouths of the skulls wide open, as if screaming, before death took their lives. I was French by birth and I didn't agree with the way the Germans had executed their war in Europe, but this was not waging war. The RAF was dropping bombs and incendiaries onto civilians. Yes, they may have scored some tactical victories in hitting the rail yards and few factories there, but a hell of a lot of innocent people died. Why is this not an act of crime or genocide like the Holocaust? Are 25,000 dead not enough to be considered victims of a criminal act in war; genocide even?

Allied fighter aircraft flying over German territory, often after bomber escort missions, should also receive some brief examination here. Though hardly on a genocidal level, there were murders committed against German civilians by late 1944, particularly in the absence of the Luftwaffe. The following is typical of a few cases that were reported, yet nothing was done about them. Ada Bohm was twenty-three years old and her family ran a farm near a village outside the city of Essen. Ada had woken early one morning, in September 1944. She had filled a hay cart with animal feed with the intention of feeding some of the remaining cattle left out in the fields. Her parents were not even aware that she had left the farmhouse that morning. They had warned their daughter about going out, even along the relatively quiet lanes in daylight. The first her parents knew that something terrible had happened to their daughter were the frantic cries and screams, as locals ran to the farm to alert them. Ada's blood-soaked body , riddled with machine-gun bullets, was carried back to the farm by two young men and placed carefully in the farmhouse while people tried desperately to call for the authorities. A local, who was in the fields walking his small dog that morning, gave the following report of the incident:

> I was out early walking my dog and I stayed close to the tree line out of habit. I saw the girl on a cart coming along the road and I tried to wave her over and tell her it was not safe to be out like that, even with horses pulling a cart. Either she didn't see me or she didn't care, I'm not sure which. I carried on walking straight ahead. I had just crossed the lane where the girl and cart had driven along, and was going into the small wood across the road, when I heard aircraft approaching. I knew from their engine sound they were not our aircraft. I turned and stooped down instinctively as they passed overhead. They were very low indeed and I estimated their speed to be 300 or

400mph at a guess. The windblast made by the planes as they passed overhead almost threw me over. I heard them open fire on something. Two of them then climbed high into the sky, rolled over, and came in again, very low. I heard machine-gun fire again, but nothing else. I was very concerned for the girl I had seen going past on the cart. I tied my dog to a tree and ran several hundred yards up the lane. I could see the upturned remains of a hay cart. The horses lay dead in their traces and the girl was covered in blood. She had been thrown several yards away, either when the planes machine-gunned her or as the cart lost control before rolling into a ditch. I checked the young woman's pulse and there was none. Her body had bullet wounds all over, including in her heart. By this time, people were running along the lane to see what the planes had been firing at. Two young men knew the young woman and between them they said they would carry her body back home. I went back, untied my dog, and walked up to the farmhouse. The military authorities were there and I told them what I had witnessed. They wrote it all down. I then saw the girl's father and talked with him for some minutes. He was in deep shock and the poor fellow just kept saying, 'I warned her not to go out in the cart alone without me or her mother, especially in daylight. "Never do this", I told her repeatedly. They don't listen, though, do they? What am I going to do now? What did they kill her for?' The poor man continued to question, but we had no answers to give him. We were as shocked, upset and disgusted as he was about it. I never saw anything like that again, and it made me afraid of going outside. I do know the planes were Americans, as I could clearly see the white stars on them. They had probably been on a sweep, or had been involved in bombing escorts or something. I don't know.

Finding official records on incidents such as this at the end of the war are virtually impossible. Many such stories only remain in the memories of those who witnessed them, or were told about them. American Second World War gun camera footage, released after the war, does show that these incidents occurred frequently. Anything that moved on the roads by day was fair game for Allied aircraft. Figures for civilians killed by Allied aircraft in this manner are difficult to ascertain, but must be in the hundreds, at least.

There could be no notions of chivalry by the last months of a brutal war, as exemplified by events that unfolded in the east. By mid-1944-early 1945 the Nazi government had begun the first phase of an organised evacuation of men, women and children from the German occupied territories in the east which were now under threat from the advancing Red Army. Initially, the first phase of this operation was successful in transporting many German settlers who had arrived in the wake of Operation Barbarossa. Many were rightfully fearful of Soviet reprisals, as news of atrocities slowly trickled back from the battlefront. Such atrocities were not restricted to German soldiers; German civilians also suffered rape, beatings and summary execution. As the Wehrmacht collapsed to defeat, it was unable to offer any protection to German citizens in the eastern territories. Panic soon began to spread throughout the populace and the attempted organised evacuation through the second phase of the operation deteriorated into chaos. German families grabbed what personal possessions they could carry and set off for Germany on foot, spurred on by horror stories from witnesses to Soviet reprisals. Margaret Schummer recalls her father gathering the family together in a panic. He threw as many essential items as he could into the back of a stolen vehicle and screamed at them, 'Get in the vehicle quickly! We have to go now, right away!' Margaret recalls:

> I had never seen him like that before. My father had been a soldier, a hardened combat veteran, yet his eyes were wide with fear and he looked pale. He screamed at other Germans on the way, 'Get out of my fucking way!' He almost ran people over in his haste to get us out. I understood we had to leave, as the Russians were not far away. I asked father what was going on and he didn't answer; he just kept driving as fast as he could, swerving around carts and long lines of people. The car we were in soon became damaged and we had to abandon it and walk the rest of the way. Soviet ground attack aircraft harassed

us on the way. They fired on us indiscriminately; cannon shells tearing into men, women and small children, it was horrible. By the time we began to meet our own soldiers again, we were almost near Berlin.

The fate of those who were not quick enough to make their escape was varied. Any SS personnel captured by the Russians were beaten and tortured, or subject to summary execution. One eye witness recalled: 'The Russian soldiers boiled water then forced the German soldier's head back and one of them put a knife against his tongue to make sure he didn't close his mouth. The boiling hot water was then poured down the soldier's throat. Then they sliced his tongue out of his mouth.'

The evacuation of East Prussia is a good example of how German civilians, surprised by the speed of the Soviet advance, became trapped in the middle of the fighting. Young children soon died due to the bitter winter conditions. Nemmersdorf became a name synonymous with the Red Army terror. The Red Army soldiers did not believe in individual sexual liaisons with German girls or women. When caught, they were raped collectively by up to twelve men at a time, sometimes more. One Soviet Red Army Officer named Liev Kopelev tried to prevent his men from committing atrocities. He was accused of showing pity for the enemy and was consequently sent to the Gulag. Former Red Army veteran Mikhael Petyushkin talked openly and honestly to me during an interview on the subject many years ago. He recalled:

I had a heart totally devoid of any pity. My individual experiences had hardened my urge for vengeance. There were thousands of Russians who felt the same way; to not only defeat the Germans who had invaded our soil, but wipe them out too. We were so full of the urge to get revenge we killed men, women, girls and boys. We killed any Germans we came across and I felt nothing for them. This is because of what they had done to us. An eye for an eye, a tooth for a tooth, is the way it was. Did we take German girls and women? Yes, we did take them, if we saw ones we wanted specifically for sex. We took them from their families, somewhere quiet,

and forced them to have sex with us. If they did not comply
with our wishes, it would just make it more painful for them,
wouldn't it? That's what we tried to tell them. Just shut up,
lie down, open your legs and it won't hurt too much. If you
resist, I will restrain you and still have sex with you. Three of
us took one girl. She was typical of the German propaganda
images: tall, blonde-haired, pretty, with blue eyes. She knew
what we were going to do with her and she came along quietly
and very bravely. We took her into a house and pushed her
upstairs. A filthy mattress lay on the floor in the room. She
didn't need to be told; she just undressed and lay down. After
so long of not having had sex with a woman, this was heaven.
Each one of us had sex with her, one after the other. It was
really nice; as I have said, we had not had sex for a long time.
Even soldiers grow tired of masturbating themselves. After
we had done what we wanted with her, we took her back to her
family. As we were leaving, more of our soldiers were entering
the house. One of them had hold of the girl's wrist we had just
fucked and was in the process of taking her away. He was ugly
and fat with a beard, and probably thirty or more years older
than the girl. I could not allow this, as much as I hated the
Germans. I told him to let her go or I would shoot him here
and now. He let her go and left the house after I told him she
was mine. Why did I do that? I don't know. After all, I hated
all Germans the same. It has taken a great many years for me
to feel any pity. At the time I felt none towards the Germans,
purely because of what they did to our people. They didn't
rape tens of thousands of our women, but they murdered
tens of thousands, didn't they? They starved and worked
our people to death, too. Now can you see why I once felt the
way I did? Thousands of Russian soldiers felt that same way;
that somehow we had to avenge the death of our people. We
felt that genocide had to be returned with genocide. It was
our duty. It was done and that is that. Would I act differently
if it were now? I can't answer that question. I don't know. I
was a young man back then. I am older now and I rationalize

differently to how I did as a young man. I feel pity for the
girl we raped only now, all these years after. She was lucky,
though, as we could have easily killed her.

Captured Wehrmacht soldiers fared no better. They were often subjected
to terrible beatings, or were murdered on the spot. Millions were
transported to labour camps deep in the Soviet Union, where they would
be worked to death in atrocious conditions. Civilian men, women and
children were also rounded up and transported east to the forced-labour
camps. During their internment, many German prisoners of war were set
to work on construction projects. Others were less fortunate, and forced
to work in the copper mines of southern Kazakhstan, or in the coal mines
of Vorkuta, in the far north. The coal mines were dangerous, dismal
places to work. The sub-arctic climate is harsh in the extreme; even in
summer the temperature rarely exceeds thirteen degrees. In winter, the
temperature plummets to a bone-chilling minus twenty, or even lower,
with freezing winds. Many German prisoners perished in the mines,
through accidents, malnutrition, illness or ill treatment.

Josef Stalin proposed the use of German labour as a war reparation
in 1943, when the issue was raised at the Yalta Conference, and the
Russians began deporting ethnic Germans from the Balkans in late 1944.
Information on the subject of German forced labour in the Soviet Union
was suppressed in the Eastern Bloc until the dissolution of the Soviet
Union. Most of the German POW survivors of the Soviet labour camps
were not released until 1953, with the last major repatriation of Germans
from the Soviet Union taking place in 1956. When they returned home
from the labour camps, they did so to a divided Germany where no one
was interested in hearing their stories. There are still around 1,300,000
Germans taken into Allied custody as prisoners of war who, to this day,
are still officially listed as missing.

As the Red Army approached the German capital, Berlin, bands of
Hitler Youth Police, known as the SRD [*Streifendienst*], sought out anyone
unwilling to fight in the defence of the city. These bands of youths wielded
considerable power and were able to execute citizens who disagreed with
them or what they were doing. Ursula Kerkhof remembers seeing the
Hitler Youth SRD at work in the city:

They had total self-determination to enforce the law as they interpreted it. I remember an old man arguing with them. All he was saying to them was, 'Why don't you just go home to your families. The war is over. We have lost!' They argued for a few minutes and, when the old man turned to walk away, a shot rang out. One of the boys shot him in the back with a pistol. The SRD were all over the city ordering families out of basements and ruins and telling them they must fight or be considered traitors to the Führer. These boys were crazy with the power they had. Nazi lynch mobs also sought out people they viewed as cowards or deserters. In some areas, trees and lampposts were decorated with corpses. Whole families were strung up as traitors. It was like Germans began to prey upon other Germans in the last days of the war. Most people had had enough and just wanted to hide, let the Soviets take the city, and end the fighting. Yes, we knew what was coming, and that they were not going to be kind to us after all our forces had done to them over the years of war. Yes, we knew that, and we understood it all and why the Russians were going to do what they did to us. There was a huge debt owed for what we had done to the people in the east.

Many young men's lives were pointlessly sacrificed in the closing stages of the Second World War. My daughter, Tina, while working at a care home in Plymouth in 2017, discovered an example of this. One of the elderly women she was caring for was Hannelore Rees [born Kaufholz] in Spandau, Berlin, Germany on 12 December 1930. It was inevitable that a conversation about the Second World War would take place. Tina possesses the same natural curiosity as her father and mentioned that I was involved in Second World War research work, particularly about the Third Reich. Hannalore later asked Tina if she could ask me to help her solve a mystery which had troubled her greatly, ever since she had been a young girl of fifteen back in Berlin in 1945. Although in her late-eighties, and having suffered from cancer, Hannelore sat down with Tina and began to tell her story:

My father, Ludwig George Kaufholz, was a scientist who was summoned to work for the German Air Ministry, yet I learned very little about what he was involved with during the war years. I had a friend named Siegfried Strelow, and he was older than me, born on 27 April 1927, also in Spandau. Siegfried's mother was my mother's best friend, so, although there was a few years age gap between the two of us, we more or less grew up together and became inseparable right from small children. My mother said she had showed me to Siegfried not long after I had been born and from that point onwards we never really left each other's side. Siegfried was a lovely young man and was just like a brother to me. We went everywhere together, and wherever he went, I went with him. He used to take me to play football with the boys, and he would always say, 'Hanna, you go in goal.' I think he used to do that so he could keep an eye on me and so I couldn't wander off [she laughs]. He was very protective of me and if his friends asked, 'Why is she coming out to play, too?' he would reply to them, 'If Hanna can't play, then I'm not playing!'

I remember we used to go down to the butcher's shop with our pocket money. We would put some of our money in the donations box and would be given a great big bag of scraps. The scraps would be all of the cuttings from sausages, and there were many different types. I remember we went out with Siegfried's friend, Heinz, once. We took a big wash basket with us and headed for a nearby army barracks. Our soldiers had not long left the camp at that time. We climbed over the fence. The basket would then be passed over and we would go searching for food as, at the time, we had very little. The soldiers ate very well and we found lots of fruits, sweet treats and other sugary things. I found a big bag of potatoes that fed us for a very long time. I remember Siegfried taking me out sledging one winter, in the big park in Spandau where we first lived. I would sit on the sledge and Siegfried would push me. One day, while we were sledging, we stumbled upon a large unexploded bomb.

I knew that Siegfried had been called for training in the German army. He was studying at the time, and his mother really didn't want him to become involved in the war. The last time I ever saw Siegfried was the day he left to join the army in the fighting in the east. He did not say much. I couldn't stop crying as we had been together every day of our lives up until that point. I was fifteen years old and Siegfried was eighteen years old at the time, in 1945. All he said to me before he left was, 'Don't worry, I will come back, and when I do, I will come and find you, Hanna.' I watched him leave and that was the last time I ever saw or heard from him again. The war ended and the days turned to weeks, the weeks to months, and still nothing from Siegfried. I started going to the Bahnhof Zoo train station, which was used a lot during the war by the soldiers. I would spend the whole day there, sitting on the wooden bench on the platform, watching all of the soldiers coming off the train and hoping that Siegfried would be among them. The soldiers all looked so sad and miserable; they must have seen some horrible things. I never found out what happened to Siegfried. His mother was just told he was missing and presumed dead. His identity discs were never returned, and because of this, I thought he might still be alive somewhere. Siegfried's mother was very unhappy about him going to the war to fight. Siegfried was all she had, as Siegfried's father died quite young, shortly after the end of the First World War. Siegfried's mother was grief-stricken when Siegfried failed to return home. She died shortly afterwards and I'm sure she died from a broken heart.

Tina asked Hanna whether she had any other recollections from the war years and she recalled:

We lived in a three-storey block and six families were in residence there. My aunt lived opposite and I can remember we used to wave to them to let them know we were okay. My parents took in a German boy named Paul. His parents had been killed in the bombing. As mentioned, my father had been called to work for the Air Ministry, as he was a talented scientist. We never learned much about what he did as the information was classified. I remember we were sat having lunch one day and my father said to me, 'Daughter [he always called me daughter, never Hanna], I think it's about time I showed you where I work!' We took a journey on the bus to the Green Forest area of Grunewald. When the bus dropped us off, we still had a long way to walk. Well, it seemed a long walk to me back then, but I was young. I was so impressed by the site when we arrived. It was so big and all enclosed. Everyone in there was on first name terms with each other. I felt I shouldn't have been there. All the girls wanted to be friends with my father as he was so good looking. I believe my father was involved in some way with nuclear weapons research.

As the war progressed, the bombing became very intense. Playing outside became too dangerous and soon stopped. We had to live in the cellar, where it was safer. I remember Hitler visiting our street once. All the kids ran down our street, knocking on the doors of the houses, shouting, 'Hitler is coming!' Everyone went out into the street. My parents were against me joining the *Bund Deutscher Madel* [League of German Maidens]; they never let me join. People often ask if Hitler was scary. Good God, no. He was not scary to me and at the time, I never realised just how bad Hitler was. I thought he was rather funny looking and comical. Only afterwards did we discover everything that had gone on during the war. I can also remember the constant propaganda broadcasts on the radio. After the war the Russians captured my father and made him work for them. My father died around 1955, aged forty-two, so was quite young. I was later told that his death was caused partly due to exposure to radiation. I later moved to England, married, and had children myself.

I promised Hanna I would try and find out what happened to Siegfried and immediately began making enquiries with my contacts in Germany.

After a few days, I received an email from the German War Graves Commission in Kassel. The information attached stated the following information: Siegfried Strelow, born on 10 April 1927 in Spandau, Berlin, Germany. Joined the Wehrmacht aged 18 in 1945. It was recorded that he went missing in action on 1 March 1945, during the fighting in Silesia in south-west Poland. Siegfried's body was never recovered and he is remembered on the memorial at the German Military Cemetery at Gross Nadlitz–Nadolice Wielkie, which is in modern-day Poland.

Many young men were thrown into the pointless fighting in Upper and Lower Silesia, in a desperate last attempt to stop the Red Army entering Berlin. Siegfried Strelow was one of the young men sacrificed in the madness at the twilight of the Third Reich. I gave the information to my daughter, Tina, and she went to visit Hanna to break the news to her. She was visibly upset and said, 'All these years, I have waited for an answer and now I know finally. My family have been trying for years to find out what happened to Siegfried with no luck, but we know what happened to him now.' As I was in the process of researching this book, I felt it was only right to include Hanna's story here. Hanna gave me a photograph of Siegfried, taken back in 1944, when he was seventeen years old. Tina asked her what Siegfried would have made of his story being included in a book. Hanna replied, 'Oh, he would have thought that was wonderful. He would have felt like a king. That is how he would have reacted. He really was a lovely boy and I have missed him so much over the years.'

By March 1945, it was perfectly clear to the Nazi hierarchy that their war was lost. It was an unrecoverable disaster, for which they only had themselves to blame. The fact that they continued to throw young men into futile battles was typical of the Third Reich's ruthless policies. It was almost like an act of genocide against its own youth. The fighting in Silesia would have come as a huge shock to uninitiated young men such as Siegfried Strelow who were not really interested in becoming soldiers. Siegfried was killed in the fighting in Upper Silesia during the strategically important Soviet offensive. The primary objective of the Soviet offensive in the region was the capturing of industrial and natural resources. The 1st Ukrainian Front, under Marshall Ivan Konev, was set the task of carrying it out. The Germans deployed considerable resources to Army Group Centre, who had the task of defending the region. The exact strength of the German forces deployed remains unknown. What is known is that many German males, well below the accepted fighting age, were rushed to the battlefront. The LVI Panzer Corps and XXXIX Panzer Corps were combined under the command of General Nehring. A two-pronged attack began on 1 March, with the 17 Panzer and Führer Grenadier Divisions attacking in the north and the 8th Panzer Division in the south. The hand-to-hand fighting which ensued, even as the German forces were slowly driven back to the Czech border, was horrifying. One Russian veteran described it as 'collapsing into an unimaginable barbarity'. Such was the proximity of the fighting, men often used pistols, sub-machine guns, knives, entrenching shovels and even their steel helmets to kill the enemy. Gregor Sokolov, a veteran of the Soviet 3rd Guards Tank Army, testified to the horrors that prevailed:

Wiping the Germans out by any means is how it was, it was how we fought. Stabbing with knives and throat cutting was common at close quarters. So was strangling your enemy to death. There were times when you were so close, physical brawling took place. I once strangled an enemy to death with my bare hands. It was either him or me; that was the way it was. A pistol was the best weapon for close quarters, or a PPSh [Russian-made 7.62mm sub-machine gun]. The PPSh was a very good weapon. I surprised one German, who swung around to fire on me. In fact, he was the quicker of the two of us. His weapon jammed, and I heard it click as he squeezed the trigger to fire it into me. Had it functioned, I would not be here talking to you now. The look upon his face was that look that any man would have when his luck had all but run out; facing death, and knowing that he wasn't returning home to Germany and family. In that instant between us, I fired and he dropped to the ground. There was no time to stand around thinking; we had to keep going, keep pushing on forwards. Killing became instinctive; blood stained the ground everywhere. It was also littered with body parts and entrails from bodies. I recall one afternoon, as we pushed on through German lines our forces had destroyed. I recall seeing a group of squashed German corpses. One of our tanks had driven over them and they were squashed on the spot as they huddled together. They had probably been killed the night before and may not have seen the tank until it was too late.

On summing things up, both my daughter and I felt it was better to spare Hanna any of the above narratives. In all probability, Hanna's friend Siegfried Strelow, a young man so dear to her and one she has never forgotten, was killed during the ill-fated counter-attacks against the 3rd Guards Tank Army.

One cannot seek to blame the Soviets for the death of Siegfried, or the thousands of other young German men, women and children ordered into the fighting at the end of the Second World War. The blame lies purely with the Nazi state, which, together with the Soviet liberators, inflicted a form of reciprocal genocide upon the people of Germany. As the Soviets arrived in Berlin, the charity institution known as the Haus Dehlem was attacked. The Haus Dehlem was an orphanage, maternity hospital and foundling home. It was full of children, pregnant women and women in labour. The Red Army's desire for revenge had taken on an unsurpassed brutality. Helpless women who had just given birth were then raped on their beds. Nurses were assaulted and dragged away into side rooms, where their uniforms were torn from their bodies, and raped. One young woman in the throes of labour was assaulted where she lay. Infants were tossed from their cribs onto the floor. Screams and gunfire filled the air. Drug cabinets were broken open and bottles of surgical alcohol were removed. One brute was seen to take a swig from one of these bottles, his face momentarily contorting as the alcohol burned his mouth and throat. The bottle was then smashed to the floor. Murder and mayhem had arrived in a place that should have remained neutral to the fighting outside. In the aftermath, the surviving children wandered the corridors, naked and splashed with blood. In one room a young girl lay dead, her body and the once-white sheets soaked red with her blood. Her dead infant lay in one corner of the room where the soldiers had thrown it, a large impact bloodstain on the wall above the corpse. The placenta had been forced into the dead girl's mouth. There were the corpses of newborn babies that had been stamped into the floor. It was a scene that anyone who had witnessed it would never forget.

Nurse Gerda Olsen, who survived the horrors of the Haus Dehlem, told me back in 1997:

> I was nineteen years of age. We knew the Haus would be overrun, but we could not leave women and girls who had just given birth, and the children and babies in there. I could have run away, but I chose not to. When they came, there was shooting everywhere. They shot at everything and anything that moved or didn't move. I was grabbed so violently around my throat I could barely breathe. It felt like he was going to crush my throat within his grip. I knew what he was going to do with me. The Red Cross meant nothing to him. It would not mean I would be spared any less than the other women here. I was thrown to the floor. He sat astride me, ripping my uniform top away from me. I tried to stop him removing my top. For a moment, I was just trying to stop the material from tearing away. I must have angered him, as the next thing, he drew his fist back and hit me in the jaw. I don't remember anything much after that, other than him on top of me, raping me. I don't know how long I had lain on the ground, dazed. I remember at one point vaguely being dragged along the floor to some other room. When I recovered, my body hurt all over. There were bruises everywhere. I had to grab hold of a door to pull myself up. I knew I had been raped, as I could feel the fluids running out of me, and I knew it couldn't be anything else. I staggered around trying to cover my chest with my arms. There was blood and dead bodies everywhere. I was found by a colleague. When she saw me, she burst into tears. She kept saying, 'Oh, no, Gerda. What have they done with you?' It seems none of us were spared. We were their revenge for all our government had done to them.
>
> When I look back on it now, I understand their hate; their need for vengeance. Yet I had never endorsed hatred, and I was not a Nazi. I was a nurse, and had been ever since I had graduated. I had never harmed or spoken ill of anyone in my life. I had a very strict Christian upbringing. My family were

very religious people. Do I forgive them for what they did? That is a question I know you may ask. To this day I don't know how I feel, as it left me numb to everything in the world. I did not marry. I had no children, and I lived my life alone, with just my dogs. I could not go back to nursing after what had happened. When I had to go into a hospital for an operation once, I became hysterical and had to be sedated. It was only afterwards, whilst recuperating, that I told the doctors what had happened to me at the Haus Dehlem. One of the doctors cried and they didn't know what to say to me. What could they have said? I just wanted to get out of there and go home. Home was the only place I felt safe. I didn't want to leave the house. My sister used to come and help me with things, and some of my friends used to come and take me out. I am better than I was, and I can do more now, but the memories are still there.

With hindsight the end was inevitable, yet nothing could have prevented it, it would seem. Had Britain, America and Europe acted early enough in the turbulent years that followed the First World War, a Second World War may have been avoided. The disease of political complacency, coupled with the policy of appeasement and the attitude that it was someone else's problem, these were all to blame. The German journey to genocide was much like a roller coaster, which, once moving, could not be stopped. When the end came, it was not a quick death for Germany. Many believe to this day that she deserved all she got in the wake of the Second World War. Yet the rise of communism in Europe after 1945 soon distracted the world's attention. Germany was divided amongst the victors, as a cake might be at a wedding. With the perceived threat posed by communist Russia, West Germany would be swiftly embraced by NATO as a bulkhead against possible Russian aggression. The Third World War that many believed would follow failed to materialise, but only just. The world came close to nuclear war on countless occasions, and it was only the skilful, though sometimes aggressive, US diplomacy that prevented it from happening. The end of the war brought about mixed feelings in many. Melitta Jorge's last entry in her wartime diary recalls:

Everything has to end; even war has to end. There are winners and losers but everyone loses something or, even worse, someone. I consider myself extremely lucky. Before the war started we had visited England and the USA many times. My English was as good as many a Londoner, even though I was born a 'pure' German. Hitler denied me the right to live in my rightful country, my place of birth, because of our Jewish ancestry. Has Jewish blood poisoned me or made me a lesser person? Course it hasn't. I am as much a person, a human being, as many of those poor souls who perished in those dreadful extermination camps we are now hearing about. Father intends going to Germany when it is feasible to do so. He fears that there are dear relatives of ours that may not have survived. Until he can go there and consult with the authorities, we will not know. It may be months, even years, before we know what has become of the people we once lived among as a community. As for Hitler, he was nothing more than a coward, along with those responsible for carrying out his orders. I have heard many within his inner circle killed themselves. It is the ordinary German people I feel for. I can't help but feel empathy for them, despite everything that has happened. I feel guilty in many ways of my own privileged lifestyle. I can't change who I am, or what I am like. It's too late for that.

Melitta Jorg and her family did not return to Germany. Melitta eventually settled down in the USA and, much to her family's surprise, became engaged to be married. She went on to marry and had a child, a daughter named Phoebe.

Afterword

Germany was without doubt one of the twentieth century's greatest tragedies. Yet, even today, many are of the opinion that she was the executor of her own misfortune. From the year 1914 she was effectively an instrument out of tune with the rest of the world orchestra around her. The three decades which followed witnessed her rise as a conventional military superpower, and her descent into social and political chaos, and mass murder. One can clearly see why there were few mourners at the funeral pyre of the German Third Reich in 1945. Subject to a dichotomic autopsy which saw her carved up amongst the victorious powers, all were anxious that she would never again be permitted to become a threat to world peace. Yet the darker aspects of Germany's twentieth-century history have continued to fascinate historians and scholars ever since, and thousands of books have been written on the subject.

Today, a new generation of Germans are rightfully severing the links to that of their grandparents and great-grandparents. There is little desire to open the wounds of the past in order to explore the pain, infatuation, death and suffering that their ancestors may have been party to. Yet, at the same time, the Swastika has become an indelible birthmark upon successive generations of Germans. My philosophy when researching the two world wars has always been a relatively simple one; if you wish to understand how the two world wars were won then ask those who lost. It will always be the ordinary soldier, man, woman or child on the street who will give you the most honest accounts. Be warned, though; not all will want to talk of their experiences. With each passing year, there are fewer people left to tell their stories.

In my capacity as an author who specialises in the social history of Germany and the Third Reich, I feel duty bound to, wherever possible, remain impartial where political matters are concerned. Yet, at the present time, it is obvious to most that Germany, under the Merkel government, is facing perhaps its greatest social challenges to date. Politically obliged, due to her violent past, to embrace every humanitarian crisis that may erupt within Europe and beyond, she is slowly becoming a nation where whispers of social discontent can be heard yet again. While unemployment is generally low at this time, her highly developed social market economy remains one of the strongest in Europe.

Germany today provides the beating heart of a modern Europe. Yet Europe has changed beyond all recognition, particularly to those who fought to liberate her so long ago, and is retreating towards a dangerous and anarchic past. Europe seems like an unfulfilled courtesan, uncertain of who is going to pay her the going rate and guide her from the darkness that she has imposed upon herself. Many countries have permitted the evolution of what can only be described as democratic dictatorships, undermining the decisions made by their respective populations for their own political advantage. This is not the way that any government today should attempt to represent its people. Consequently, it comes as no surprise that, in many countries, we are seeing extreme political elements slowly emerging from the shadows of the political wastelands, with the mainstream political world seemingly unable to counter the threats they may pose.

The basic ideology of Nazism was not entirely destroyed with Adolf Hitler's Third Reich at the close of the Second World War. In the world today there is still much evidence of anti-Semitism, hatred, racism and intolerance. There are communities today who feel that they are experiencing a form of cultural ethnic cleansing. If this is so, then we have a very worrying problem that the world needs to address. If I am guilty of tearing the scab from an otherwise healing wound, then painting an unattractive picture of our future with the blood that oozes from it, then so be it. It is far easier to embrace the painful reality than have to adapt to the anaesthetised fantasy. The rise of Hitler's Nazis and the crimes perpetrated under the Third Reich are a classic case of why one should never leave the baby home alone. Human society is an emotionally complex beast requiring stability, morality, equality, strong leadership, honesty and justice if it is to thrive along the accepted principles of civilization. Can you recall your first steps into the playground as a child? Even within that relatively innocent community of childhood, did you not soon experience conflict with that inherent struggle for control? How some would revert to violence as a matter of course to impose their will upon others, while others would stand watching? I can recall vividly as a young child a crowd of baying children all jostling for a better view. Unable to see what was going on until one would emerge from the middle of the crowd nursing a bloody nose and split lip. It was a scene I would witness many times throughout my school life and each time it horrified me.

As I have said before, conflict is an endemic component of the human persona. Conflict appears to be just one of humankind's incurable diseases; a genetic anomaly present from the moment we are born into this world. Today, dictatorships, not unlike that which dominated Germany throughout the 1930s and 1940s, still flourish, and wars are still being fought. Human history, if written as a piece of literature in its entirety, would be all but a few pages in comparison to the wonders of the universe. Even by today's standards, it would appear that the human race is millions of years away from being truly civilised. Many fear it will destroy itself long before it ever reaches that ultimate goal.

Note on sources for this volume

Much of the material contained within this work was gained directly through my own collection of papers, letters and documents and, of course, my contributory sources. Therefore archives, museums or other institutions were not consulted for the preparation of this particular work.

Acknowledgments

I would like to acknowledge and offer heartfelt thanks to all those who have contributed to this work: the Kohlman family; the families of Theobald Ebner, Gunther Priestl and Kristensen Traumann; Otto Rische; Albert Friest; Ingrid Altmann; the family of Melitta Jorg; Pauline Rischner; Ursula and Rudolph Metschuldt; Bella Schonn; Helga Bassler; Paulina Grier; Gertrud Klumm; Heinz Mollenbrock [*Oberleutant*]; Karl Voght; Natasha Kizl; Mirka Lamorska Yarnold; Mariska Dickinson; Vyacheslav Lebedev; Fritz Umberr; Horst Vitalowski; Eric Child; Karl Lutz; Karl Retschild; Joyce Smith; Heinz Knoke [*Hauptman*-KC]; Herbert Schiller; Katrina Roth; Kurt Rischner; Martha Pohlmann; Stefanie Engeler; Gerhard Neuhoff; Lieniev Ivavanhovich; Michael Thornley; Magda Frueller; Rudolf Kafker; Max Diemer; Sylwia Wczeniek; Hans Wunsch; Tilly Mateisse; the Bohm family; Margaret Schummer; Liev Kopelev; Mikhael Petyvshkin; Ursula Kerkhof; Gregor Sokolov; and Hanna Rees [Kaufholz].

I would also like to extend heartfelt thanks to Claire Hopkins and all the staff at Pen & Sword Books for their support and encouragement throughout the writing of this work; Alan Murphy, for the unenviable task of copy-editing my raw manuscript; my daughter, Tina Hayward, for her contribution towards this work; Katherine H. Jorgensen for her contribution to the Norwegian section of this work; Chris Warren Photography in Evesham; Ian Tustin and Jenny Powell of The Vale Magazine in Evesham; Lenny Warren & The Militaria Collectors Network; Jody Warner, for not only indexing this volume but also assisting with the smooth production during the course of its development; and all of my family and friends for their support and encouragement. Special thanks to my partner, Paula, for her love and continued support with every aspect of the writing of my books. None of my books could have been written without you being at my side, or without your invaluable support. Love to each and every one of you as you have all played a part in the creation of this work.

Index